CurriculumBank

KEY STAGE ONE
SCOTTISH LEVELS A-B

RELIGIOUS EDUCATION

D1390178

LYNN GENT AND BILL GENT

Published by Scholastic Ltd,
Villiers House,
Clarendon Avenue,
Leamington Spa,
Warwickshire CV32 5PR
Text © Lynn Gent and Bill Gent
© 1997 Scholastic Ltd
234567890 7890123456

AUTHORS
LYNN GENT AND BILL GENT

EDITOR
CLARE GALLAHER

ASSISTANT EDITOR
KATE PEARCE

SERIES DESIGNER
LYNNE JOESBURY

DESIGNER
ANNA OLIWA

ILLUSTRATIONS
MAGGIE DOWNER

COVER ILLUSTRATION
GAY STURROCK

INFORMATION TECHNOLOGY CONSULTANT
MARTIN BLOWS

SCOTTISH 5–14 LINKS
MARGARET SCOTT AND SUSAN GOW

Designed using Aldus Pagemaker
Printed in Great Britain by Ebenezer Baylis & Son,
Worcester

British Library Cataloguing-in-Publication Data
A catalogue record for this book is available from the
British Library.

ISBN 0-590-53410-6

Contents

RELIGIOUS
EDUCATION

ACKNOWLEDGEMENTS

The publishers gratefully acknowledge permission to reproduce the following copyright material:

Ashton Scholastic (Australia) for the use of *Wilfrid Gordon McDonald Partridge* by Mem Fox © Mem Fox (Omnibus Books); Maurice Lynch for the adaptation of 'Forget-Me-Not' retitled 'The Girl Who Saved the People' from *Creation Stories* © Maurice Lynch.

The authors would like to thank Samuel Chaplain (ex-Jewish member, Redbridge SACRE), Indriyesha Das (ISKON Educational), Maureen Hart (Early Years Adviser, London Borough of Redbridge), Ngaire Moorhouse (The Clear Vision Trust), Gurinder Singh Sacha (ex-Sikh member, Redbridge SACRE), Canon Trevor Shannon (Shap Working Party).

Introduction

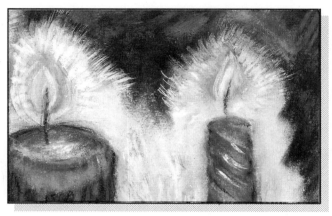

Scholastic Curriculum Bank is a series for all primary teachers, providing an essential planning tool for devising comprehensive schemes of work as well as an easily accessible and varied bank of practical, classroom-tested activities with photocopiable resources.

Designed to help planning for and implementation of progression, differentiation and assessment, *Scholastic Curriculum Bank RE* offers a structured range of stimulating activities with clearly stated learning objectives that should be compatible with local agreed syllabuses for religious education, and detailed lesson plans that allow busy teachers to put the ideas into practice with the minimum amount of preparation time. The photocopiable sheets that accompany many of the activities provide ways of integrating purposeful application of knowledge and skills, differentiation, assessment and record-keeping.

Opportunities for formative assessment are highlighted where appropriate within the activities. Ways of using information technology for different purposes and within different contexts, as a tool for communicating and handling information and as a method for investigating, are integrated into the activities where appropriate and more explicit guidance is provided at the end of the book.

The series covers all the primary curriculum subjects with separate books for Key Stages 1 and 2 or Scottish Levels A–B and C–E. It can be used as a flexible resource with any scheme, to fulfil National Curriculum and Scottish 5–14 requirements and to provide children with a variety of different learning experiences that will lead to effective acquisition of skills and knowledge.

RELIGIOUS EDUCATION

SCHOLASTIC CURRICULUM BANK RELIGIOUS EDUCATION

The *Scholastic Curriculum Bank Religious Education* books provide structured support for teachers when planning the primary religious education curriculum in the context of their locally agreed syllabus. They enable pupils to develop knowledge, understanding skills and attitudes appropriate to religious education.

Each book covers one key stage. The Key Stage 1 book includes activities for Early Years children in reception classes. Each book is divided into seven sections, each section covering an important aspect of religion and human experience.

Bank of activities

This book provides a bank of activities that can be used in many different ways: to supplement a scheme of work derived from the local agreed syllabus; to add breadth and variety to an existing scheme; and to supplement a particular topic. The activities are designed to address a number of key human experiences which raise questions about belief and value, while at the same time giving children increasing familiarity with material drawn mainly from Christianity but also from the other principal religions represented in Great Britain.

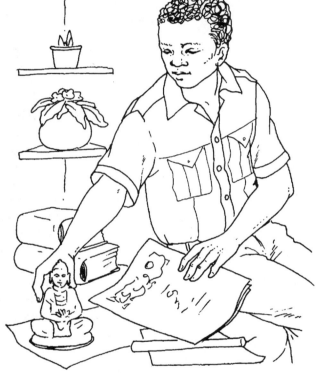

Lesson plans

Detailed lesson plans, under clear headings, are given for each activity and provide material for immediate implementation in the classroom. The structure for each activity is as follows.

Activity title box

The information contained in the box at the beginning of each activity outlines the following key aspects:

▲ *Activity title and learning objective.* The activity title is given in the form of a question which relates to the learning focus of the activity and can easily be referenced to locally agreed syllabuses and Scottish 5–14 requirements by using the overview grids on pages 9 to 12. For each activity, a clearly stated learning objective or objectives is given in bold italics

and will aid planning for progression.

▲ *Examples of concepts.* For each activity two important underlying concepts are given.

▲ *Class organisation/Likely duration.* Icons ✝✝ and 🕐 signpost the suggested group sizes for each activity and the approximate amount of time required to complete it.

Key background information

The information in this section provides guidance about how the activity contributes to religious education and also provides a context for religious material so that the teacher might feel confident in referring to it.

Preparation

Advice is given for those occasions where it is necessary for the teacher to prepare materials, or to set up a display or activity ahead of time.

Resources needed

All of the materials needed to carry out the activity are listed, so that the pupils or the teacher can gather them together easily before the beginning of the teaching session. There is also a main resource list, 'Useful books and resources', which is on pages 107 to 108.

What to do

Easy-to-follow, step-by-step instructions are given for carrying out the activity, including (where appropriate) suggested questions for the teacher to ask the pupils in order to help instigate discussion, stimulate exploration and encourage reflection.

Suggestion(s) for extension/support

Ideas are given for ways of providing easy differentiation where activities lend themselves to this purpose. Suggestions are provided as to how each activity can be modified for the less able (or younger children in reception classes) or extended for the more able.

Assessment opportunities

Where appropriate, opportunities for ongoing teacher assessment of the children's work during or after a specific activity are highlighted. The assessment of knowledge, understanding and skills can be carried out in religious education. The assessment of attitudes, however, is often inappropriate.

Opportunities for IT

Where opportunities for IT present themselves these are briefly outlined with reference to suitable types of program. The chart on page 158 presents specific areas of IT covered in the activities, together with more detailed support on how to apply particular types of program. Selected lesson plans serve as models for other activities by providing more comprehensive guidance on the application of IT, and these are indicated by the bold page numbers on the grid and the 🖳 icon at the start of an activity.

Display/assembly ideas

Where relevant, display ideas are incorporated into activity plans. In those cases where the material lends itself to inclusion in an assembly or act of collective worship, ideas about how this might be done are given and include suggestions for themes and a closing thought or reflection.

Reference to photocopiable sheets

Where activities include photocopiable activity sheets, small reproductions of these are included in the lesson plans together with notes on how they should be used.

Assessment

Each activity presents advice on what the teacher should look out for during the course of the activity. The notes made while observing the children can contribute to a descriptive profile of the child's performance, compiled and refined throughout the school year, which might also be supported by annotated samples of the work that the child produces. Assessment is integrated into everyday performance. The activities have been designed so that they can be used as individual tasks to provide the teacher with ongoing evaluation of children's progress (formative assessment). Alternatively, certain activities can be used for summative assessment at the end of Key Stage 1. Those activities most appropriate for summative assessment are highlighted by the ✍ icon.

Photocopiable activity sheets

Many of the activities are accompanied by photocopiable activity sheets. For some activities, there will be more than one version in order to provide differentiation by task. Some sheets are more open-ended to provide differentiation by outcome. Simplified versions of stories from religious and other traditions, which teachers may otherwise find difficult to obtain, are provided. The photocopiable activity sheets provide purposeful activities that are ideal for assessment and can be kept as records in pupils' portfolios of work.

Cross-curricular links

Cross-curricular links are identified on a simple grid which cross-references the particular areas of study in RE to the programmes of study for other subjects in the curriculum, and where appropriate provides suggestions for activities.

Glossary

To assist teachers in their understanding of key terms from Christianity and the other principal religions, a short glossary is provided on pages 105 to 107.

RELIGIOUS EDUCATION WITHIN THE CURRICULUM

Religious education and the law

Unless partially or wholly withdrawn by parents, all registered pupils (but not including pupils in nursery classes or schools) are required to have religious education as part of their curriculum. The 1988 Education Reform Act used the term 'basic curriculum' to describe the National Curriculum and religious education together.

Locally agreed syllabuses

One of the reasons why religious education was not included in the National Curriculum was because the religious education curriculum is a matter for each local education authority to decide. The principles upon which religious education stands, and the requirements which most schools must follow (apart from voluntary aided schools, that is) are made clear in the locally agreed syllabus for religious education. The local body which brings together the material for an agreed syllabus is called an Agreed Syllabus Conference. The 1988 Education Reform Act stipulated that all locally agreed syllabuses published thereafter should 'reflect the fact that the religious traditions in Great Britain are in the main Christian whilst taking account of the teaching and practices of the other principal religions represented in Great Britain'.

National guidelines in Scotland

In Scotland the Scottish Office Education Department has issued national guidelines for the 5–14 age group for the five curricular areas, one of which is Religious and Moral Education (RME). The RME programme includes aspects of Personal and Social Development (PSD) which explore moral values and relationships. PSD is not a curricular area, but it permeates all studies across the curriculum. National guidelines for PSD have been produced to ensure systematic planning. The RME guidelines are structured under the headings 'Christianity', 'Other world religions' and 'Personal search'.

The national model material

To assist Agreed Syllabus Conferences in following the requirements of the 1988 Act, the Schools Curriculum and Assessment Authority (SCAA) published a series of booklets in 1994. One contained advice from working parties representing Christianity and the other principal religious traditions (Buddhism, Hinduism, Islam, Judaism and Sikhism).

Another contained a glossary of terms for each religion. Further booklets suggested two attainment targets for religious education – 'learning about religion' and 'learning from religion' – and outlined how religious content might be structured in an agreed syllabus so as to further educational aims. These booklets have been consulted in the production of *Scholastic Curriculum Bank Religious Education*.

Religious education and collective worship

It is important that, in planning and thinking, religious education and collective worship are seen as distinct and separate aspects of school life. The legal requirements for each are different though, as with religious education, parents have the right to withdraw their children from daily collective worship (though not, technically speaking, from assembly). Most local education authorities have produced guidance on collective worship separate to that on religious education. Nevertheless, there can be a fruitful overlap between religious education and collective worship. For this reason, some of the activities in this book suggest ways in which material and insights from work in religious education might be used to support meaningful acts of collective worship.

RELIGIOUS EDUCATION AT KEY STAGE 1

At all key stages, there are two dimensions to religious education, though how particular agreed syllabuses express this might differ. One dimension involves the exploration of religion in its many forms and contexts. The other involves children investigating and reflecting upon their own lifestyles and experiences. The two dimensions are inextricably linked, however, and activities in religious education often involve both at one and the same time. In looking at 'pilgrimage' in religion, for example, teachers will usually encourage children to think about special journeys that they themselves have made. It was for this reason that the national model syllabuses (see above) spoke of two attainment targets: 'learning about religion' and 'learning from religion'.

The respective emphasis given to each of the two dimensions of religious education will differ as pupils progress through each key stage. At Key Stage 3 there is often a heavy emphasis on learning about religions. At Key Stage 1, by contrast, there is usually a heavy emphasis on children reflecting on their own experiences and the many things and people which stand out as 'special'. The concept of 'specialness' which is identified in many of the activities in this book carries with it the implication of worth and value. Religious education has often been described as that part of the curriculum which, *par excellence*, is concerned with worth and value. It is its role in encouraging children to reflect on their own experiences that also gives it its central place in the spiritual development of children, though of course this responsibility is not exclusive to religious education.

Because many of the activities at Key Stage 1 involve looking at and reflecting on special things – objects, people, places and events – it will be important for the teacher to think about context and atmosphere. Some teachers use a 'stilling exercise' to prepare for some work in religious education. Others will place a religious or other artefact into a 'mystery' or 'feely' bag, made of material such as velvet, to emphasise its worth and value.

Most schools now have their own collections of religious artefacts, and teachers are becoming increasingly competent in using them. There is no one 'correct' way of using an artefact, of course, though a three-fold process has often been identified: the 'puzzling' stage (in which the artefact is investigated and clues to its meaning and use sought), the 'supplementing' stage (in which additional information is supplied) and the 'personalising' stage (in which links with the lives of the children are explored).

Note on dating: The abbreviations used after some dates in this book follow the convention which is now universally used in literature dealing with a number of religions. Instead of the older BC, the abbreviation BCE (before the common era) is used and instead of AD, the abbreviation CE (common era) is used.

Learning objective	RE focus	Content	Type of activity	Page
Living with ourselves				
To reflect on personal feelings. To listen with empathy to others reflecting on their feelings.	Early Years; Rec/P1 *PSD: Self awareness* Human experience	Listening to a story and exploring feelings using masks.	Whole class, then paired/group work.	14
To identify physical objects which are of personal value. To understand what makes these physical objects special.	Early Years; Rec/P1 *As above.* Human experience	Listening to a story and talking about personal special objects.	Whole-class listening and discussion, followed by individual work.	15
To understand that some rooms are more special than others. To understand that some rooms require particular kinds of behaviour.	Early Years; Rec/P1 *As above.* Human experience	Drawing/painting pictures of homes, identifying special rooms and making a special area in the classroom.	Individual work, followed by whole class.	16
To understand that what people wear can affect the way they feel about themselves.	Year 1/P2 *As above.* Human experience	Sorting magazine pictures of clothes. Discussing appropriate clothes for different occasions.	Group sorting, followed by whole-class discussion, then individual drawing.	17
To understand that Christians believe that Jesus is special. To identify who is special for oneself.	Year 1/P2 *RME: Christianity – beliefs PSD: Interpersonal relationships* Christianity	Using an artefact and a story to explore why Jesus is special to Christians. Thinking about who is special to us.	Whole-class listening and discussion, followed by individual work.	19
To identify unique qualities in yourself and others. To increase a sense of personal worth.	Year 1/P2 *PSD: Self esteem* Human experience	Listening to a story and reflecting on what makes each person special.	Whole class listening to and discussing a story, followed by paired work.	20
To identify the range of feelings associated with friends arguing.	Year 2/P3 *PSD: Interpersonal relationships* Human experience	Writing a story about an argument with a friend. Listening and responding to a story. Role-play.	Individuals, then whole class listening to a story and discussing it.	21
To understand that life is made up of many changes. To identify feelings associated with these changes.	Year 2/P3 *PSD: Self awareness* Human experience	Discussing changes in our own lives and identifying the feelings associated with them.	Group work, followed by whole class, then paired work.	22
To understand that loss is a common human experience. To respond to personal experiences of loss.	Year 2/P3 *RME: Personal Search – ultimate questions* Human experience	Exploring personal feelings of loss after listening to a story.	Whole class listening to and discussing a story, followed by small-group discussion.	24
Living with others				
To identify some of the times when we meet together as a family. To know some of the things that a Jewish family does when sharing the Shabbat meal.	Early Years; Rec/P1 *RME: Other World Religions – moral values and attitudes* Judaism	Becoming familiar with the Friday night rituals of Jewish Shabbat. Reflecting on times when families meet together.	Whole class discussing significance of rituals, followed by individual work.	26
To know the Buddhist story of 'The monkey king'. To identify times when they have helped other people.	Early Years; Rec/P1 *RME: Other World Religions – sacred writings and stories* Buddhism	Thinking about times when people have been helpful. Hearing a Buddhist story with the same theme.	Whole class examining a Buddha statuette, followed by discussion.	27
To understand that feelings are associated with giving. To know that people called Muslims give because God wants them to.	Early Years; Rec/P1 *As above.* Islam	Discussing feelings associated with giving to street charity collections. Hearing a Muslim story about giving.	Whole-class discussion, followed by role-play.	28
To understand the role of rules within social groups.	Year 1/P2 *RME: Christianity, Other World Religions – moral values and attitudes* Human experience	Making and agreeing rules for the classroom. Inventing rules for a game. Hearing about religious rules.	Small groups, followed by whole-class discussion. Small groups completing photocopiable sheet.	29
To know how the Hindu festival of Raksha Bandhan is celebrated. To understand that brothers and sisters relate to each other in different ways.	Year 1/P2 *RME: Other World Religions – festivals...* Hinduism	Exploring the relationships between brothers and sisters. Using an artefact to learn about a Hindu festival.	Whole class for information giving and discussion. Small groups for activity.	31
To know why the five K's are important to Sikhs. To understand the function of uniform in developing group identity.	Year 1/P2 *RME: Other World Religions – festivals, ceremonies...* Sikhism	Thinking about the purposes of uniforms. Hearing the reasons why some Sikhs wear the five K's.	Whole class for discussion and story. Paired work for activities.	32
To know a well-known parable told by Jesus. To understand the concept of forgiveness.	Year 2/P3 *RME: Christianity – sacred writings* Christianity	Listening and responding to a Christian parable. Discussing forgiveness.	Whole class for parable and discussion. Small groups for activity.	33
To know a story familiar to Christians, Jews and Muslims. To relate aspects of the story to their own experience. (Session One)	Year 2/P3 *As above.* Christianity; Judaism; Islam	Hearing and discussing the first part of the story of Joseph. Talking about personal experiences of jealousy.	Paired work, then class discussion. Individual completion of photocopiable sheet.	35

RELIGIOUS EDUCATION

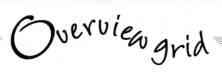

Learning objective	RE focus	Content	Type of activity	Page
(Session Two)	As above.	Hearing and discussing the second part of the story of Joseph. Role-play experiences of being wrongly blamed.	Class listening and discussion. Individual completion of photocopiable sheet. Small-group discussion.	35
(Session Three)	As above.	Hearing and discussing the last part of the story of Joseph. Talking about personal experiences of 'making up', focusing on feelings.	Friendship groups, class discussion. Individual completion of photocopiable sheet.	35

Living in the world

Learning objective	RE focus	Content	Type of activity	Page
To understand that, within the natural world, processes of transformation occur.	Early Years; Rec/P1 *RME: Personal Search – the natural world* Human experience	Observing and talking about the changes in growing things. Listening to and reflecting on a story.	Class observation and discussion. Whole class listening to and discussing a story.	38
To understand that snow transforms the appearance of the world and people's behaviour.	Early Years; Rec/P1 *As above.* Human experience	Watching and discussing a sequence from *The Snowman* video. Creating a dance. Modelling snowmen.	Whole class watching video. Individual movement activity.	39
To know a story associated with the life of St Francis. To identify an animal with which they have a special relationship.	Early Years; Rec/P1 *RME: Christianity – moral values and attitudes* Christianity	Listening to a story about St Francis. Identifying an animal which is important to us.	Whole class listening to a story. Individual drawing.	40
To understand that human beings have a relationship with the natural world.	Year 1/P2 *RME: Personal Search – the natural world* Human experience	Listening to and reflecting on a story. Discussing how people look after, and harm, the world.	Whole class listening to a story, followed by individual drawing.	41
To understand why harvest time has been important for many Christians.	Year 1/P2 *RME: Christianity – festivals and customs* Christianity	Exploration of a Christian Harvest festival.	Whole-class discussion, individual completion of photocopiable sheet.	42
To know that Muslims have beliefs about the relationship between humans and animals. To encourage a caring attitude towards animals.	Year 1/P2 *RME: Other World Religions – moral values and attitudes* Islam	Discussion of the needs of animals. Listening to a Muslim story.	Group work for discussion. Whole class for story. Individual for activity.	44
To demonstrate that the children themselves can have a personal impact on the environment. To encourage a responsible attitude to the physical world.	Year 2/P3 *RME: Personal Search – the natural world* Human experience	A walk around school identifying good and bad features of the environment. Listening to and discussing a story about the environment.	Whole-class outdoor observation. Listening to and discussing a story. Individual or paired design work.	45
To know a story from the Judaeo-Christian tradition. To relate this story to their own experience of creating.	Year 2/P3 *RME: Christianity – beliefs* Judaism; Christianity	Listening to a Judaeo-Christian story about creation. Creating a model.	Whole class listening to a story and discussing it. Individual model-making.	46
To encourage a reflective attitude towards living things.	Year 2/P3 *RME: Personal Search – the natural world* Human experience	Listening to a story about whales and drawing their feelings about it.	Whole class listening and discussing. Individual contributions.	47

Following guidance

Learning objective	RE focus	Content	Type of activity	Page
To understand that there can sometimes be consequences if guidance from elders is not followed.	Early Years; Rec/P1 *PSD: Interpersonal relationships* Human experience	Sequencing pictures of the story. Discussion about consequences when children don't do as they are told.	Class activity for sequencing and discussion. Individual painting and drawing.	50
To identify books which are special in our own lives and some of the reasons why. To understand that the way in which some books are treated indicates their special nature.	Early Years; Rec/P1 *PSD: Self awareness* Human experience	Making a class book about the children's special books.	Whole-class discussion. Individual drawing.	51
To know a story associated with the life of Jesus. To understand that Christians believe that knowing Jesus can change people's lives.	Year 1/P2 *RME: Christianity – sacred writings* Christianity	Hearing, discussing and dramatising the story.	Whole class for story. Large groups for dramatisation. Individual sequencing of sentences on the photocopiable sheet.	53
To understand how the festival of Simchat Torah shows how special the Torah is for Jews.	Year 1/P2 *RME: Other World Religions – festivals and customs* Judaism	Using an artefact to discover what happens at Jewish Simchat Torah.	Whole class learning about Simchat Torah. Individual completion of photocopiable sheet.	54
To know that the Bible is a special book for Christians. To know that the Bible is divided into two parts.	Year 1/P2 *RME: Christianity – sacred writings* Christianity	Looking at a variety of bibles and understanding why it is special for Christians.	Whole class.	56

RELIGIOUS EDUCATION

Learning objective	RE focus	Content	Type of activity	Page
To understand why Muslims believe that the Qur'an is special. To understand why the use of a Qur'an stand indicates the special status of the Qur'an for Muslims.	Year 2/P3 RME: Other World Religions – sacred writings Islam	Using an artefact and story to find out why the Qur'an is special to Muslims.	Whole class looking at artefact and listening to story. Individuals designing own Qur'an stand.	57
To know about the life of Joan of Arc. To understand that some people are prepared to die for their belief in God.	Year 2/P3 RME: Christianity – moral values and attitudes Christianity	Finding out why Joan of Arc is special to some Christians.	Whole class for story and discussion. Group work designing a frieze.	58
To understand that significant people can shape and influence the lives of others. To identify a person who has influenced your life.	Year 2/P3 RME: Personal Search – relationships and moral values Human experience	Reflecting on people who have had an effect on their lives.	Whole-class discussion. Individual for activity and paired work.	60
To understand that some people believe that God wants them to do certain things. To reflect on the experience of being told to do something without understanding why.	Year 2/P3 RME: Christianity – sacred writings Christianity	Role-play. Listening to the story of Noah's Ark.	Group work for role-play. Whole class listening to story, then return to role-play.	61

Encountering special times

Learning objective	RE focus	Content	Type of activity	Page
To understand what celebration means. To know that Christmas is celebrated in a range of ways, including the giving of presents.	Early Years; Rec/P1 RME: Christianity – celebrations... Human experience	Thinking about what makes Christmas a special time.	Whole-class discussion. Individual drawing of a present.	64
To understand the nature and purpose of group celebration.	Early Years; Rec/P1 As above. Human experience	Planning and giving a birthday party for a teddy.	Whole-class discussion. Group work completion of activities.	65
To understand the link between eggs, new life and Easter.	Early Years; Rec/P1 As above. Christianity	Using eggs and chicks to think about 'new life'.	Whole-class discussion. Individuals making pop-up Easter card.	67
To be aware of the variety of ways in which people prepare for Christmas. To know that the period leading up to Christmas is called Advent.	Year 1/P2 As above. Christianity	Understanding that Advent is a preparation for Christmas (for Christians).	Class discussion of Christmas celebrations. Individual completion of photocopiable sheet.	68
To know what happens at a traditional Christian christening.	Year 1/P2 As above. Christianity	Finding out what happens at some Christian christening services.	Whole class for information giving. Individuals writing about christenings.	70
To know in what ways Hindus celebrate Divali. To reflect upon good and evil in the world.	Year 1/P2 RME: Other World Religions – sacred writings, stories... Hinduism	Exploring stories with the theme of good and bad. Hearing the story of Rama and Sita. Finding out what (some) Hindus do to celebrate Divali.	Group/paired work for story writing and activities. Whole class listening to a story.	71
To know what happens at the Buddhist festival of Kathina. To identify times when others are thanked.	Year 1/P2 As above. Buddhism	Finding out what happens at the Buddhist festival of Kathina.	Group discussion, whole class listening to information, individual work.	74
To understand the nature and purpose of festival. To be able to use symbolism.	Year 2/P3 As above. Human experience	Inventing a festival to celebrate Elmer's day.	Whole class listening to a story. Group work carrying out various activities.	75
To know what Muslims do during Ramadan. To know that Ramadan is a special time for Muslims.	Year 2/P3 As above. Islam	Identifying personal special months. Finding out why Ramadan is a special month for Muslims.	Individual completion of photocopiable sheet. Whole class for information giving and discussion.	76
To know what foods are eaten at a Passover Seder meal. To understand that food can form a link with the past.	Year 2/P3 As above. Judaism	Hearing the Jewish story of the Exodus. Learning how Jews celebrate the festival of Passover.	Whole class for story and information giving, followed by individual work.	78
To know the outline of the Christian Easter story. To identify sad times and happy times in their own lives.	Year 2/P3 RME: Christianity – festivals Christianity	Investigating symbolism in Christian Easter story. Thinking about sad/happy times.	Whole class listening to the Easter story. Individual work.	80
To know the outline of the traditional nativity story. To understand some of the underlying ideas and beliefs which make it a special story for Christians.	Year 2/P3 As above. Christianity	Hearing the traditional Christmas story and understanding why it is special for Christians.	Whole class looking at an artefact and listening to a story. Individual completion of photocopiable sheet.	82
To know that Sikhs celebrate Divali. To know the story associated with Sikh Divali.	Year 2/P3 RME: Other World Religions – festivals Sikhism	Hearing Sikh story which is told at Divali. Thinking about 'helping'.	Paired work, followed by whole class listening to story, then pairs completing photocopiable sheet.	83

RELIGIOUS EDUCATION

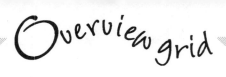

Learning objective	RE focus	Content	Type of activity	Page
Encountering special places				
To understand that some people have places which have special significance for them. To understand what makes these places special.	Early Years; Rec/P1 *PSD: Self awareness* Human experience	Listening to a story and thinking about a personal special place.	Whole class listening to story, individuals drawing a picture.	86
To understand that a journey is a significant human activity. To understand that feelings are associated with going on a journey.	Early Years; Rec/P1 *As above.* Human experience	Packing a suitcase and exploring feelings when going on a journey.	Whole-class discussion. Individual work.	87
To understand why a church building is special to Christians. To know some of the main features of a church building.	Year 1/P2 *RME: Christianity – sacred places* Christianity	Finding out about the main features of a church building and understanding its significance. Visiting a church.	Whole class for information giving, discussion and visit. Paired work for completion of ground plan.	88
To know that Jews build a sukkah during the festival of Sukkot. To understand some of the reasons why a sukkah is a special place for Jews.	Year 1/P2 *RME: Other World Religions – festivals and customs* Judaism	Learning about the importance of the Sukkah during the Jewish festival of Sukkot.	Whole class for information giving and discussion. Group work for activity.	90
To understand why some Christians go to Lourdes. To identify places which make us feel contented.	Year 2/P3 *RME: Christianity – sacred places* Christianity	Hearing a story about the visions of Bernadette. Understanding why some Christians make a pilgrimage to Lourdes.	Whole class for story and information giving. Individual drawing, paired discussion.	92
To know the features of a Muslim prayer-mat. To know how a prayer-mat is used by Muslims.	Year 2/P3 *RME: Other World Religions – sacred places, worship...* Islam	Using an artefact to find out about the importance of Makkah, the mosque, the prayer-mat and prayer to Muslims.	Whole class for information giving. Individual completion of photocopiable sheet.	94
To understand why most Hindus have a shrine in their homes. To identify objects of personal value and reasons for their significance.	Year 2/P3 *As above.* Hinduism	Using an artefact to learn about Hindu home shrines. Thinking about personal objects which are important.	Whole class for information giving. Individual completion of photocopiable sheet.	95
Expressing what is important				
To be able to sit quietly while listening to a piece of music and then talk about the experience.	Early Years; Rec/P1 *PSD: Self awareness* Human experience	Listening, in silence, to a piece of music and talking about the experience.	Whole-class listening and discussion.	98
To know that certain items are associated with the Jewish Shabbat meal.	Early Years; Rec/P1 *RME: Other World Religions –ceremonies and customs* Judaism	Using artefacts and a story to learn about the Jewish Shabbat meal.	Whole class for story and information giving. Individual completion of photocopiable sheet.	99
To understand that objects have the power to affect the present by evoking memories of the past.	Year 1/P2 *RME: Symbols* Human experience	Using a story to think about how objects can be reminders of the past.	Whole class for story and discussion. Individual completion of photocopiable sheet.	100
To understand that the use of colour can be a significant medium of expression. To be able to use colour in expressing feelings and ideas.	Year 1/P2 *RME: Symbols* Human experience	Looking at pictures of stained glass windows. Designing pictures/ windows using different colours to express feelings.	Group work/whole class for discussion. Pairs designing a stained-glass window.	101
To know some of the reasons why Christians might pray. To identify some of the sentiments in a Christian prayer.	Year 2/P3 *RME: Christianity – worship* Christianity	Role-play different types of conversations. Learning about different reasons why Christians might pray.	Paired work for role-play and activity. Whole class for information giving. Paired completion of photocopiable sheet.	102
To know that stories convey messages. To identify some of the messages in a particular story.	Year 2/P3 *RME: Other World Religions – sacred writings and stories* Sikhism	Thinking about stories which give messages. Listening to a Sikh story and thinking about its messages.	Group work thinking about stories. Class discussion of story. Individual writing of story.	103

Entries given in italics relate to the Scottish 5–14 Guidelines for Religious and Moral Education, and Personal and Social Development

RELIGIOUS EDUCATION

Living with ourselves

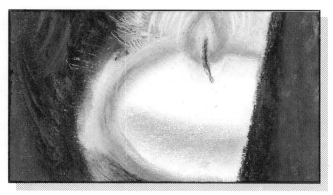

Religious education is not concerned solely with things obviously 'religious'. It is also concerned with addressing and exploring a range of experiences, particularly those which raise issues of belief and value, meaning and purpose. Many of these experiences raise what have been termed 'ultimate questions', such as 'Who am I? What is the meaning of relationships? What is the purpose and meaning of life?'

Thus, in this chapter, the activities give young children the opportunity to explore and respond to a number of key personal experiences. There is the profound and many-faceted experience of loss – of a toy, of a pet, of friendship. There is the experience of change – of ourselves and of the world around us. There is the growing sense of self and its expression in what we do, whom we follow and where we like to be. As in so much work in religious education, the concept of 'specialness' is central and contains within it the notion that, in the blur of daily living, certain things stand out as conveyers of deep meaning.

Though only one of these activities contains explicitly religious material, they touch on experiences and issues which religions address and respond to. The experience of loss and death is the most obvious example of this, for all religions respond in terms of beliefs and rituals which seek to make sense of that which challenges reason and order most of all.

As they grow older, religious education should be providing children with the opportunity to continue exploring these issues for themselves and to examine, in increasing detail, the responses of Christianity and the other religious traditions.

WHAT MAKES ME FEEL THE WAY I DO?

To reflect on personal feelings. To listen with empathy to others reflecting on their feelings.

Emotion. Identity.

†† *Whole class, followed by paired/group work.*
⊕ *Whole class 30 minutes; paired/group work as required.*

Key background information

Much in this activity is not exclusive to religious education but the skills which it is designed to promote are indispensable to work in this part of the curriculum.

Though, as a general rule, the children's responses should be accepted without comment, teachers will need to apply their own judgement about those circumstances when further discussion, at the time or later, is necessary (for example, if a child says 'I feel happy when I make my baby brother cry', it would be appropriate for the teacher to ask the children if this is a good thing to be happy about).

Preparation

Photocopy on to card and cut out the three masks on photocopiable pages 110 and 111. A lollipop stick can be stuck on the reverse to provide a handle. Photocopy (and cut out for the children if necessary) enough copies of the blank mask on page 111 for use in the extension activity.

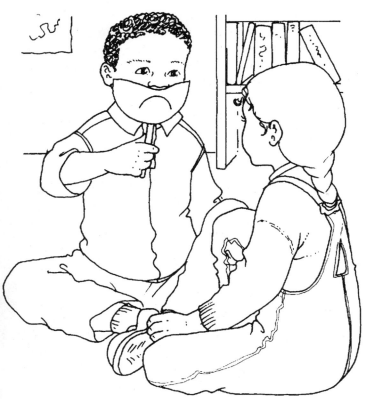

Resources needed

Angry Arthur by H. Oram (Picture Puffin); masks made from photocopiable pages 110 and 111; lollipop sticks; sticky tape. For the extension activity – the blank mask on photocopiable page 111; drawing materials; lollipop sticks; sticky tape.

What to do

Gather the children together in a circle and read them the story of *Angry Arthur* (or another story which focuses on a feeling). Hold one of the masks from photocopiable page 110 or 111 in front of your face and say, 'I feel… (for example, angry) when… (for example, I see people hurting animals).' Pass the mask on to a child and ask her to say what makes her feel angry. Continue passing the mask until every child has had the opportunity to make a response. If any children feel unable to contribute, allow them to pass the mask on without commenting. Repeat the activity with one or more of the other masks, encouraging the whole class to listen attentively to what each child is saying.

Make the masks available to the children to use in role-play for the next few days.

Suggestion(s) for extension

Older or more able children could be asked to think of another feeling or emotion (for instance jealousy, excitement, shyness). They could then be given a copy of the blank mask on photocopiable page 111 and asked to make a mask depicting this emotion.

Suggestion(s) for support

Encourage children to contribute when holding the mask but be aware that not all of them will feel comfortable with this exercise.

Assessment opportunities

Listening to children as they make comments with a mask, and observing them listening to others, will provide evidence of the extent to which they are able to reflect on their own feelings and listen sensitively to others.

Display/assembly ideas

As part of an assembly focusing on a theme such as 'Feelings' or 'Myself', some children can mime actions to the story used in the activity while it is being read by you or other children. Groups of children can then use the four printed masks to say what makes them feel that way. Additional material could include poems and songs about feelings (for example, the song 'When You're Happy and You Know It'). The assembly could end with a reflection such as, 'And now, in a moment of quiet, think about how feelings can affect other people. Help us to control our feelings so that we help and not hurt others.'

A display of masks could also be mounted for the children to look at and refer to over a period of time.

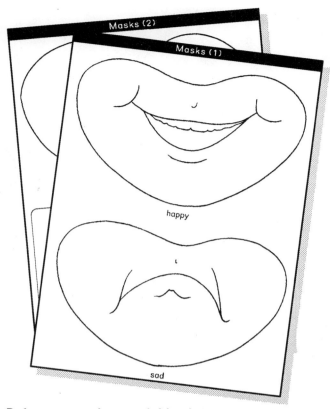

happy

sad

Reference to photocopiable sheets

Photocopiable pages 110 and 111 provide outlines of masks that show three feelings with which the children can identify. The final mask on photocopiable page 111 is blank and some children can use this to depict other emotions.

WHAT IS IMPORTANT TO ME?

To identify physical objects which are of personal value. To understand what makes these physical objects special.

Specialness. Value.

†† *Whole class followed by individual work.*
🕐 *Whole class 20 minutes; individual work 20 minutes.*

Key background information

This activity provides the opportunity for children to reflect on, and learn about, what is special and of value in their own and other people's lives. It also lays the foundation for later work in religious education which will involve investigating the role of special objects within religious traditions. Even at this stage, however, some children might choose to identify religious objects as being special to them.

Preparation

Identify and bring in to school a special object of your own, deciding why it is special to you. Find a copy of *Dogger* by Shirley Hughes (Picture Lions). If this book is not available,

there are many others with a similar theme such as *I've Forgotten Edward* by Susan Hill (Walker Books).

Resources needed

Dogger by Shirley Hughes; drawing materials; tissue-box lid; a special object; collage materials; glue.

What to do

Start the lesson by reading the story of *Dogger* to the whole class. Discuss the story by asking questions, for instance:
▲ How did Dave feel when he lost Dogger?
▲ Why was Dave angry with Bella?
▲ Was the little girl right not to give Dogger back to Dave?
▲ Why weren't Bella's old teddies as good as Dogger?
▲ Did Bella really not miss the new teddy?
▲ How did Dave feel when he got Dogger back?

Show the children the object which you have brought in and explain to them how special it is to you, the reasons why it is special and how you feel about it.

Ask the children if they have any special objects. Listen carefully while each child talks about what is special to them. Ask how they would feel if their object was lost or damaged and how they would want others to look after it.

Suggest that some of the children might like to bring their special object to school to show to the rest of the class. Stress that the object would be well looked after.

Give out the tissue-box lid and the drawing materials. Ask the children to draw round the lid to make a frame. Inside the frame they should draw their special object and then write underneath why it is special to them. They can then use the collage materials to decorate their frame.

Suggestion(s) for extension

Children could make a big book of *Dogger* by retelling the story in their own words. This could then be placed in the class book corner for all the children to read.

RELIGIOUS
EDUCATION

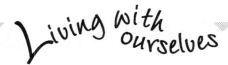

Suggestion(s) for support

Some children might have difficulty in identifying a special object. Use your knowledge of the child to suggest objects which might be special. Questions can then be asked to find out the reasons. Some children may need an adult or another child to scribe what their object is and their reasons for choosing it.

Assessment opportunities

Questioning the children about the object they have drawn in their frame and listening to their response will indicate how far they have understood the concept of something being 'special'.

Opportunities for IT

Ask children to use a word processor to write a label for their special object, explaining in a few sentences why it is important to them. They can then print this out and stand the label next to a display of 'special objects'.

Some children could go on to use a simple art or drawing package to draw their special object.

Display ideas

Display the children's pictures behind a table on which some of the children's special objects have been set out. Title the display 'Our special things' and include a label which says, 'Please look but do not touch. These things are very special.'

WHICH IS MY SPECIAL ROOM?

To understand that some rooms are more special than others. To understand that some rooms require particular kinds of behaviour.

Home. Special place.

†† *Individual work followed by whole class.*

🕐 *Individual work 10 minutes; whole class 15 minutes.*

Key background information

The idea of 'specialness' is as basic to work in religious education as it is to the world of the infant child for whom the notions of 'special place', 'special time', 'special person', and so on come easily.

This activity provides the children with an opportunity to explore a fundamental aspect of their own lifestyle and experience. But it also lays the foundation for understanding key aspects of religion, notably the existence of special places, which are furnished in particular ways and demand appropriate kinds of behaviour.

Preparation

Make or obtain a model house with several rooms (for example, a doll's house or LEGO construction). Collect a selection of items which might be chosen by the children to make the home corner into a special room. These could include:

▲ material to form a barrier between it and the rest of the classroom;

▲ cushions;

▲ a rug;

▲ plants;

▲ teddies.

Make copies of photocopiable page 112, one for each child carrying out the extension activity.

Resources needed

Paper; paints or crayons; model house; items to make home corner special (see 'Preparation'). For the extension activity – photocopiable page 112.

What to do

Ask the children to draw or paint a picture of their home. When they have completed them, gather the children together and look at several of their pictures which show different types of home (flat, bungalow, cottage, detached, terraced, caravan and so on). Talk about the differences.

Using the model house, focus on the different rooms and ask the children what each one is used for. Next, ask the children which room is their favourite and why, concentrating on their feelings associated with these rooms. Discuss which

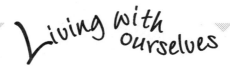

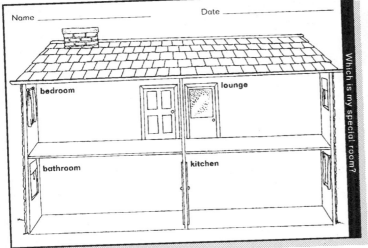

Name _____ Date _____

bedroom   lounge

bathroom   kitchen

Which is my special room?

the room corner should be used and who then behave appropriately when using it will have demonstrated an understanding that some rooms require particular kinds of behaviour.

Opportunities for IT
Encourage children to design their own room using Framework software such as *Moving In* or *My World 2* with the *Design a 3D Bedroom* file. The children can also use a word processor to write about what makes their room special to them.

Reference to photocopiable sheet
Photocopiable page 112, which is used in the extension activity, will enable older or more able children to focus more clearly on the distinct character of each room.

object in their favourite room helps to make it special (a bed gives a feeling of safety, a teddy gives security) and whether there are things that they can and can't do in their favourite room.

Tell the children that they are going to make the home corner into a special room. Over a period of time change the home corner into a special room using the children's ideas. Involve the children in creating the special room as far as possible.

Once the room is made, and before the children use it, agree rules about how the room should be used, for example:
▲ how many children are allowed in at any one time;
▲ who is responsible for keeping it tidy;
▲ what type of behaviour is acceptable;
▲ whether shoes should be removed upon entry.

The children can then use the special room, observing the rules which have been agreed.

Suggestion(s) for extension
Using photocopiable page 112, ask the children to draw objects which are found in the different rooms of the house. On the back of the sheet, they can either draw pictures or make a list of the things which make their favourite room special to them.

Suggestion(s) for support
You may need to encourage some children by asking them direct questions about their favourite room (for example, 'Where do you go when you are feeling ill? Where do you go when you feel angry?') Children who do not come from secure homes may be reluctant to talk about a favourite room. These children could be encouraged to join in the discussion by talking about an object which is special.

Assessment opportunities
Children who can identify their own special rooms will demonstrate that they understand that some rooms are more special than others. Children who suggest ideas about how

HOW DO I FEEL WHEN I WEAR DIFFERENT CLOTHES?

To understand that what people wear can affect the way they feel about themselves.

Identity. Feelings.

†† *Group work, individuals, pairs, whole class, then individual work.*

⏱ *Group work 5–10 minutes; individuals 10 minutes; pairs 5–10 minutes; whole class 15 minutes; individuals 20 minutes.*

Key background information
This activity touches on a number of elements and experiences which are very significant for work in religious education. The exploration of different types of clothing provides a good foundation for other work about how the symbolism of clothing and items worn on the body can create a strong sense of group identity. (As such, it would provide a good preliminary to an exploration of Sikh group identity: see 'Why do we sometimes want to look like other people?', page 32). This activity also provides the opportunity for children to reflect on how their feelings are affected, positively and negatively, by what they wear.

Preparation
Collect a variety of pictures showing children wearing different types of clothing for different occasions (for example school uniform, sports kit, nightwear, party clothes, summer and winter wear). You will need a selection of pictures for each group for the first part of the activity. Make copies of photocopiable page 113, one for each child. If a visitor is going to be invited to a linked assembly, make contact.

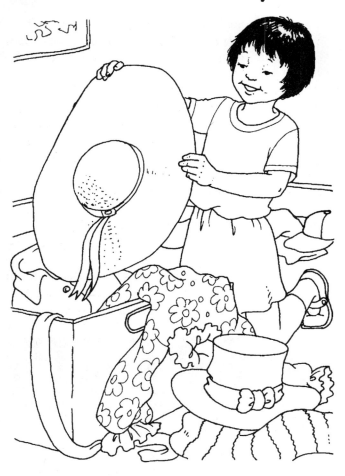

different and, possibly, act differently. You could discuss:
▲ wearing school uniform for the first time;
▲ wearing a wedding dress;
▲ wearing party clothes;
▲ wearing swim wear on a beach.

Give each child a copy of photocopiable page 113 and ask them to draw one set of clothing which would make them feel smart and another which would make them feel uncomfortable. They should complete the sentence for each set of clothes, explaining their reasons.

Suggestion(s) for extension
Ask children to cut out pictures from magazines to make sets of 'clothes that make people feel smart', 'clothes that make people feel relaxed' and 'clothes that make people feel special'.

Suggestion(s) for support
Any child who is having difficulty completing the worksheet could use the magazine pictures to give them ideas. A scribe may be needed to help with the writing on the photocopiable sheet.

Assessment opportunities
Listening to the children when they are working in pairs and talking as a whole class will indicate to what extent they understand that clothes can affect the way people feel about themselves.

Assembly ideas
As part of an assembly focusing on a theme such as 'Feelings' or 'Clothes that people wear', some children could bring different types of clothing from home and describe how wearing them makes them feel. Other children could dress up (as a nurse, a bride, a soldier, a firefighter, a 'super hero') and say how they feel wearing these clothes.

Resources needed
A selection of pictures of children wearing clothes for different occasions; photocopiable page 113; chalkboard/flip chart; drawing materials. For the extension and support activities – magazines.

What to do
Divide the children into groups. Give each group a selection of pictures which they should sort into sets of clothes for different occasions. As the groups are working, discuss with them the reasons for their choices of classification.

Bring the groups together and talk about each of the occasions and the types of clothing which people would wear for them. Make a list on the board of the different occasions and the corresponding clothes. Give each child a sheet of blank paper and ask them to choose one occasion from the list and draw a picture of themselves wearing the type of clothes which would be suitable for that occasion. When they have completed their drawing, ask them to find a partner and talk about their picture, including how they would feel when they were wearing the clothes for this occasion.

Gather the children together and talk about how wearing different types of clothes can make people feel

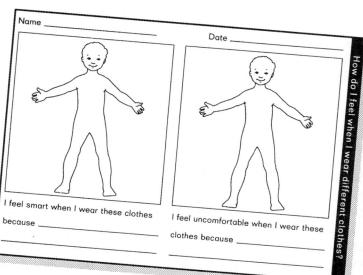

Name _____
Date _____

I feel smart when I wear these clothes because _____

I feel uncomfortable when I wear these clothes because _____

How do I feel when I wear different clothes?

RELIGIOUS EDUCATION

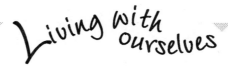
Invite in the school crossing person and interview him about how he feels when he puts his special clothing on and stops the traffic to allow people to cross the road. The assembly could end with an expression of thanks to the visitor for keeping everyone safe when they cross the road.

Reference to photocopiable sheet

Photocopiable page 113 provides outlines for the children to draw clothing which is appropriate for two occasions. It stimulates children to focus on feelings when wearing these types of clothes.

WHO IS SPECIAL TO ME?

To understand that Christians believe that Jesus is special. To identify who is special for oneself.

Specialness. Devotion.

†† *Whole class followed by individual work.*

🕐 *Whole class 20–25 minutes; individual work 15 minutes.*

Key background information

Stories about Jesus were told for 30 years or more before being written down by early Christians. Stories would have circulated in slightly different forms and the Gospel writers crafted them to some degree when they included them in their Gospel books (or *scrolls*, more accurately). The story of 'The stilling of the storm' was included by three of the four Gospel writers; Matthew and Luke probably based their versions on Mark's.

Irrespective of the precise meaning of this story (traditionally classified as a 'nature miracle'), it was preserved because it made a powerful statement about the presence and purpose of Jesus. In the language of this activity, it showed that he was 'special'. The reaction of those who were in the boat with Jesus is fascinating. It has been suggested that when Jesus said, 'Peace, be still!' he might originally have been speaking to them.

There are some groups of children who might find the task of drawing a special person to be against their beliefs. Judgement will need to be exercised. Muslim children who say that they cannot draw the Prophet Muhammad, for example, could be asked to draw a picture of the *Ka'bah* (cube-shaped building in Makkah) instead.

Preparation

Obtain a statuette of Jesus (see 'Useful books and resources', page 107 for contact addresses) and place it in a special bag (see Introduction, page 8). Become familiar with the biblical story of 'The stilling of the storm' in Mark's Gospel, chapter 4, verses 35–41. A retelling of the story might also be consulted.

Resources needed

Statuette of Jesus; a special bag; a version of 'The stilling of the storm' story; paper; drawing materials.

What to do

Tell the children that they are going to see something which is special for many people. Carefully remove the statuette from the bag and show it to the children. Ask the children what they can see. Prompt with questions if necessary:
▲ What is this person wearing?
▲ When do you think this person lived?
▲ What do you think this person was like?
▲ Who do you think this person is?

If the children have not already recognised the statuette as being of Jesus, tell them at this stage.

Explain that Jesus is a special person for Christians and that they tell many stories about him to show why they think he is special. Read or tell the story of Jesus stilling the storm,

including the words at the end of the story, 'Who is this man that even the wind and the waves do as he tells them?'

Next, ask the children who is the most special person for them. This may or may not be a religious figure. Give them several moments to reflect. Let several children share their thoughts with the rest of the class, including the reason or reasons for their choices.

Finish the session by asking the children to draw a picture of their special person and then to give the reasons why this person is special to them.

WHAT MAKES ME SPECIAL?

To identify unique qualities in yourself and others. To increase a sense of personal worth.

Identity. Uniqueness.

†† *Whole class, pairs, then individual work.*

🕐 *Whole class 30 minutes; pairs 20 minutes; individual work 20 minutes.*

Key background information

Religious education has no monopoly on seeking to contribute to the personal development of children. Indeed, much in the school and class ethos, as well as in other aspects of the curriculum, could be seen as contributing to children's sense of personal worth. As such, the achievement of this learning objective is not dependent on this activity alone and, indeed, will only become evident after a considerable passage of time and with close knowledge of the children.

It is giving children the opportunity to reflect upon important qualities in themselves and others that makes this activity particularly relevant to religious education.

Preparation

Find a copy of *But Martin!* by June Counsel (Picture Corgi).

Resources needed

But Martin! by June Counsel; writing and drawing materials; loaded camera; chalkboard.

What to do

Explain to the children that they are going to hear a story which is about a visitor to Earth called Martin. Martin goes to a school and meets several children who all dress, look and act differently. Read *But Martin!* to the whole class, encouraging the children to predict what Martin will do. Ask the children what is special about Martin. Next, ask what is special about the other four characters in the story: Lee, Lloyd, Billy and Angela (for example, colour and shape of face, hair colour, gymnastic ability, number skills). Emphasise that everyone is good at something.

Divide the class into pairs and explain that you would like everyone to think of one thing that makes their partner special. Give the children a few moments to think about what they are going to say and then allow everyone the opportunity to say something about their partner. If there are any children who have nothing to say, make a contribution in their place.

On the board write the starter sentences 'My friend is good at...' and 'I am good at...' Give each child a sheet of paper and ask them to copy the sentences and complete them. They can also draw pictures of their friend and themselves. While the children are completing the sheets, and throughout the remainder of the day, take photographs

Suggestion(s) for extension

Some children could go on to write a short account of 'The stilling of the storm'. This could be done in narrative form or as a series of pictures using speech bubbles.

Suggestion(s) for support

Encourage those children who have difficulty in thinking of someone special. Suggest examples such as:
▲ parents;
▲ friends;
▲ people they admire.

Assessment opportunities

Listen to each child's reasons for choosing a special person. From this it might be possible to assess the extent to which the children have grasped the concept of 'specialness'.

Opportunities for IT

Let the children use a word processor to write some sentences about their special person. These can then be printed out and the children could add a picture of the person they have written about. Alternatively, they could use an art package to draw their special person and add this picture to their writing.

Older or more able children could use a word processor to write their own version of 'The stilling of the storm' story.

Display ideas

The children's pictures of their special person could be made into a class 'big book' and displayed in the class book corner.

wherever possible of the children doing the things or revealing the qualities their partners said made them special. The photographs will be used later for display.

Suggestion(s) for extension

Arrange for individuals to spend some time working alongside children from other classes so that others might benefit from what they are particularly good at. For example, a child who is good at reading could read a story to a younger child; a child who is kind could play with another child during break.

Suggestion(s) for support

Children with low self-esteem might need help with identifying what is special about themselves by being reminded of the quality their partner identified and by suggesting others.

Assessment opportunities

Observing the children while they are working in their pairs and checking their completed photocopiable sheets will provide evidence of the extent to which they have been able to identify unique qualities in themselves and others.

Opportunities for IT

Ask the children to use a word processor to write their two sentences. These can be printed, the photographs added and then used for a class display or bound into a book. If this activity is done with a simple desktop publishing package a 'master page' can be set up with a frame for the photograph and another for the writing.

Display ideas

Mount the photographs and display each one alongside the children's written statements on why they are special, for example a photograph of a child smiling alongside the caption 'I am always happy', a photograph of a child building with construction equipment alongside the caption 'I am good at building things'. The title of the display could be 'We are special because…' Photographs of yourself and classroom assistants, together with captions, could also be included.

HOW DO I FEEL WHEN I ARGUE WITH SOMEONE?

To identify the range of feelings associated with friends arguing.

Separation. Reconciliation.

†† *Session One: individual work. Session Two: whole class.*

🕐 *Session One: whole class 10 minutes; individual work 45 minutes; Session Two: whole class 25 minutes.*

Key background information

It is in relationships with others that people experience some of the most profound and beautiful feelings – and some of the most destructive and disturbing.

Religions have much to say about relationships of all kinds: with oneself, with others, with the world, with God or reality. In Christianity *atonement* (at-one-ment) is a central concept.

This activity gives children the opportunity to explore feelings associated with breaking up and making up. As such, it will make a contribution to their personal and social development.

Preparation

Become familiar with the story *Let's Be Friends Again*, by Hans Wilhelm (Picture Knight).

Resources needed

Session One: chalkboard/flip chart; writing materials. Session Two: *Let's Be Friends Again* by Hans Wilhelm. For the support activity – cassette recorder (optional).

What to do

Session One

Ask the children to think of a time when they have had an argument with a friend. Let several children share their memories with the class. Ask the children how they felt before, during and after the argument.

Then give each child a sheet of paper and ask them to write a story about arguing with a friend, focusing on how they felt. You may like to write the following words on the

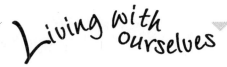

board for the children to refer to while they are writing their stories: 'happy' 'bored' 'pleased' 'sad' 'cross' 'angry' 'upset' 'bothered' 'lonely'. Make additional paper available for the redrafting of their stories.

Session Two
Remind the children of the work they did in Session One by asking two or three children to read out their stories.

Tell the children that they are going to hear a story about two people arguing and falling out. Read the story *Let's Be Friends Again* by Hans Wilhelm. Concentrate on the boy's feelings after he has argued with his sister by asking questions, such as:

▲ Why wasn't it enough that his sister had said sorry?

▲ Why didn't he want a new turtle?

▲ Why didn't he ask his parents to help him?

▲ Why did he want to do horrible things to his sister?

▲ Why did he feel ill?

▲ How did he eventually feel better?

In answering these questions, the children should be encouraged to compare the feelings in their stories with the boy's feelings.

Ask the children whether their stories ended with them making up with their friends. If so, ask them how difficult they found this and how they felt during the process of making up.

Suggestion(s) for extension
Ask children to return to their stories and rewrite the ending to show a different way of making up with their friends.

Suggestion(s) for support
When writing their stories, some children may need additional help with spelling. Alternatively, they may prefer to use a cassette recorder to tape their story.

Assessment opportunities
Through reading their stories and by listening to their responses to *Let's Be Friends Again*, it will be possible to assess the children's grasp of the range of feelings associated with arguing with friends.

Opportunities for IT
Ask the children to use a word processor to write and draft their story. If they save their story they can then return to write a different ending about making up with their friends.

Display ideas
Display a selection of the children's stories under the heading 'Breaking up and making up'. Individual, enlarged words to describe feelings could be placed next to the stories.

HOW DO I FEEL WHEN THINGS CHANGE?

To understand that life is made up of many changes.
To identify feelings associated with these changes.

Change. Feelings.

†† *Small groups followed by whole class, then paired work.*

🕐 *Small groups 10 minutes; whole class 30 minutes; paired work 10 minutes.*

Key background information
The experience of change is fundamental to human life and people respond to it in different ways. In making a response, many find religious beliefs and insights both helpful and satisfying. A Buddhist, for example, might say that nothing is permanent and that it is the attempt to cling on to the appearance of permanence that leads to a feeling of dissatisfaction.

Children of Year 2/P3 age will already have experienced a wide range of changes. For an increasing number of children, the break-up of the home through parental separation is one of the sharpest experiences of change. As such, the teacher will need to be sensitive to individuals for whom this activity might be upsetting.

In having to make the transition from infant to junior – whether within the same school or across different schools – this activity is particularly relevant to children in Year 2/P3. In areas where there is a middle school system, this activity could be adapted for older children moving from their

first school. For children who do not need to move to another building, this activity is still appropriate as moving to a new class can be unsettling.

Resources needed
Chalkboard/flip chart; writing materials.

What to do
Organise the class into small groups and ask each group to make a list of the things that have changed since they began school, for example different classes, teachers, children, topics, displays.

Gather the groups together and make a class list. Then ask questions about the changes in order to identify the range of feelings associated with each change, such as:
▲ How did you feel when this happened?
▲ Which changes made you feel sad?
▲ Which changes made you feel happy?

Ask the children if there have been any changes at home. Again, ask questions about feelings associated with these changes.

Next, talk about the change from infant school to junior school. Children with older brothers or sisters may be able to explain some of the differences in the junior school.

Working in pairs, ask the children to make a list of things which they are looking forward to and things which they are worried about when going to the junior school.

Arrange a visit by some or all of the children to the junior school (or junior department). Each group could have a particular thing to look out for (What happens at playtime? Where is lunch eaten? Where are the Year 3/P4 classrooms?) and then report back to the rest of the class.

If a visit is not possible, ask a Year 3/P4 teacher or the headteacher to come and talk to, and answer questions from, the class.

Suggestion(s) for extension
Ask children to write about one change that they have experienced since starting school. Encourage them to describe their feelings.

Suggestion(s) for support
Be aware of any children who have experienced changes at home which they have found particularly upsetting. Discuss this area sensitively or omit this aspect of the activity altogether.

Opportunities for IT
Ask the children to use a word processor to write about changes they have experienced.

Assembly ideas
As part of an assembly focusing on a theme such as 'Memories' or 'Change' (particularly suitable for the end of the school year), the children can interview each other about the many changes in their lives. (Using a real or dummy hand-held microphone might add to the sense of occasion and fun.) They could also talk about things which they are looking forward to as they grow older. End the assembly with a reflection such as, 'And now, in a moment of quiet, let us think about the time we have spent in the infants and say thank you for the people we have met and the things we have learned. As we become juniors, help us to feel excited that we will meet new people and learn new things.'

HOW DO I FEEL WHEN THINGS DIE?

To understand that loss is a common human experience. To respond to personal experiences of loss.

Loss. Change.

†† *Whole class followed by small friendship groups.*
🕐 *Whole class 20 minutes; small groups as required.*

Key background information
Loss is a key dimension of human life and is experienced in a wide variety of guises – loss of objects, loss of innocence, loss of youth, loss of hope, and so on. But perhaps the most fundamental experience of loss is the death of a close person (or pet). Yet, for many reasons, death is something which many Westerners find difficult to address: it is a 'taboo' subject. It has sometimes been suggested that, while the Victorians were obsessed with death and its attendant rituals but avoided mention of sex, the situation has been reversed today.

If people are to learn to address loss and death in the world and in their lives, then education will play an important role. In that religions respond to the fact of death in a number of ways, through providing beliefs and rituals, for example, so work in religious education will play an important role too.

Some teachers might find this work difficult for emotional reasons. From the children's point of view, great sensitivity is called for in work of this nature. Certain children might not want their poem or picture shown to other class members, for example, and some teachers have developed conventions – a mark in the top corner, perhaps, or a simple verbal request – by which children can indicate that a piece of work is for the teacher's eyes only.

Preparation
Find a copy of *I'll Always Love You* by Hans Wilhelm (Picture Knight). If this book is not available find some other books on the themes of loss and death. These might include *Goodbye Max* by Holly Keller (Walker Books), *Badger's Parting Gifts* by Susan Varley (Picture Lion), *Granpa* by John Burningham (Picture Puffin), *When Uncle Bob Died* by Althea (Dinosaur). Read through the story. Identify any children who have recently experienced a death within the family.

Resources needed
I'll Always Love You by Hans Wilhelm; writing and drawing materials.

What to do
Tell the children that they are going to hear a story about a pet dog who grows older and finally dies. Read *I'll Always Love You* to the children and then allow time for their immediate responses to the story.

Ask questions which will focus the children on elements of the story. These might include:
▲ Why did the boy think that Elfie was the best dog in the world?
▲ How did Elfie change as she grew older?
▲ Why did the boy tell Elfie every night that he loved her?
▲ Why did they put flowers on the grave?
▲ Why did the boy not want a puppy?

Divide the children into small friendship groups and let them talk about something or someone they have lost, how they felt and how they remember them. Encourage the children to write a poem and/or draw a picture of an object, pet or person that they have lost. Some children may prefer to do this with a friend.

Suggestion(s) for extension
Children may wish to read other books which address the theme of loss or death. Have some available so that they can refer to them.

Suggestion(s) for support
Be aware that some children may need comforting and further opportunities to talk.

Assessment opportunities
Because of the personal and sensitive nature of this activity, assessment is not appropriate.

Assembly ideas
The direct use of this activity in an assembly might not be appropriate, but when there has been a loss in the school, the telling of a story such as *I'll Always Love You* or *Badger's Parting Gifts* can be of great benefit.

Living with others

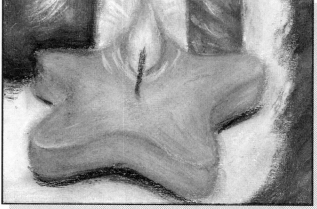

The focal point of the previous chapter, 'Living with Ourselves', is a useful planning device, but is, in a sense, a fiction. For to live as a human being is to live with others in a number of interacting social groups. Even the term 'loner' is a social convention.

This chapter gives children the opportunity to explore and respond to a number of social experiences which give rise to questions of meaning and value. The experience of helping others is explored, for example, but also the issue of whether we should tell others when we do so.

In all but one instance – a general exploration of the nature and purpose of rules – each activity includes material drawn from one religious tradition. The familiar Joseph saga, as well as Jewish Shabbat customs, are used to raise issues about family life. An activity focusing on forgiveness includes looking at the parable of the Prodigal Son drawn from the Christian tradition. The issue of caring for brothers and sisters draws on an annual Hindu festival, and the desire to look like others from an event in Sikh history.

But, of course, the religious material is not used merely as a vehicle to raise issues and questions. As children move through school, religious education should equip them with an increasing knowledge and understanding of the key terms and identity of Christianity and the other religious traditions. At this stage, however, the aim will be to familiarise children with material from a range of religious traditions as a foundation for later, more detailed, learning.

RELIGIOUS
EDUCATION

WHEN DO WE MEET TOGETHER AS A FAMILY?

To identify some of the times when we meet together as a family. To know some of the things that a Jewish family does when sharing the Shabbat meal.

Family. Ritual.

†† *Whole class followed by individual work.*

🕐 *Whole class 25 minutes; individual work 20 minutes.*

Key background information

Much of the practice and ritual associated with the Jewish religion – Judaism – is centred on the home and family. This is certainly true of *Shabbat*, usually called the Sabbath by non-Jews, and Shabbes by Jews of Eastern European origin.

Shabbat is the day of rest which ends the week and which, Jews believe, echoes the rest which God took after the six days of creation (Genesis, chapter 2, verse 3). It begins just before sunset on Friday and ends at sunset on Saturday.

Shabbat has been so important in Jewish history that it has been said that, 'It is not so much that the Jews have kept the Sabbath as that the Sabbath has kept the Jews.'

There will be some variety in how Jews mark Shabbat. Not all Jewish families in Britain will light candles to welcome in Shabbat, for instance. For the observant family, however, the Friday evening meal is an important family occasion which will include a number of ritual elements.

Preparation

Place a white candle in a velvet bag (see Introduction, page 8). Collect together resources to support the activity. These might include posters of Jewish Shabbat, a challah cover, or a video programme such as *Judaism Through the Eyes of Jewish Children* which has a short section depicting the Shabbat meal (see 'Useful books and resources', page 107). It might be possible to ask a Jewish parent or visitor to talk about what happens at the Shabbat meal, or a Jewish pupil if there is one in the class.

Resources needed

White candle in a velvet bag; Shabbat resources (see 'Preparation'); drawing materials.

What to do

Ask several children to feel the object through the bag and to describe what they can feel. Encourage the children to use descriptive language and to build on what their classmates have said about what they can feel through the bag. Ask one child to remove the object from the bag and to tell the class what it is. Then give the whole class an opportunity to talk about times when they have seen candles being used. Explain to the children that they are going to learn about how people called Jews light candles on a special day – Shabbat – each week.

Describe what happens on Friday evening at the beginning of Shabbat. Include the following:

▲ the lighting of two candles by the mother to welcome in Shabbat;

▲ the saying of special words over wine (*kiddush*) by the father;

▲ saying thank you to God for food;

▲ the father cutting specially shaped bread (*challah*), sprinkling salt on it and giving a piece to each member of the family;

▲ the wearing of best clothes including *kippot* (skullcaps) by men and boys.

This could be supplemented by looking at posters, watching a short extract from a video or meeting a Jewish visitor and listening to her or him talk.

Finally, ask the children about times when they meet together with their family (be aware of children from non-nuclear family groups) and discuss what is done to make these times special. Do they wear special clothes? Eat together? Light candles and blow them out?

Children could paint a picture of either a Jewish family welcoming in Shabbat, or their own family meeting together at a special time.

Suggestion(s) for extension

Ask children to write an account of a time when their own family meet together and describe what happens.

RELIGIOUS EDUCATION

Suggestion(s) for support

Children could paint a picture of a Shabbat meal. You may need to remind them of what happens and of the objects that are used for this occasion.

Assessment opportunities

Children who take part in the whole class discussion will demonstrate whether they can identify special family times. Children who have chosen to paint a Shabbat picture can be asked about their painting in order to determine how much information they have retained.

Opportunities for IT

Encourage the children to use a simple CD-ROM encyclopaedia to search for more information about the Jewish Shabbat.

Assembly ideas

As part of an assembly focusing on a theme such as 'Families' or 'Special times', ask the children to talk about special times they spend with their families and to demonstrate how a Jewish family celebrates the beginning of Shabbat. The assembly could end with a thanksgiving reflection such as, 'Thank you for my family and the special times we have together.'

WHY DO WE HELP OTHERS?

To know the Buddhist story of 'The monkey king'. To identify times when they have helped other people.

Self-sacrifice. Compassion.

†† *Whole class.*

🕐 *30 minutes.*

Key background information

Siddhartha Gautama, an Indian prince who was born in the sixth century BCE, left his palace home in order to discover the truth about the meaning of life. He became the *Buddha* – a title meaning 'Enlightened' or 'Awakened One' – when he experienced the truth. He began to teach how others could follow the path to Enlightenment, for he taught that all people have it within themselves to reach this goal.

There are many kinds of Buddha image. Traditionally, there were a number of bodily indications of Buddhahood, such as elongated earlobes, a pointed crown to the head, and long arms. The hand gesture – *mudra* – of an image is important. If the hands are resting in the lap, for example, it shows that Buddha is meditating.

In Buddhist teaching, compassion for all other beings is of central importance and many stories highlight this. The story given in this activity is taken from the Buddhist collection of stories called the *Jataka*.

Preparation

Become familiar with the story on photocopiable page 114.

Resources needed

A picture or statuette of a seated Buddha (see 'Useful books and resources', page 107); photocopiable page 114. For the extension activity – writing and drawing materials.

What to do:

Tell the class of a time when someone has been helpful. This could be an example from school, home life, or an item of local or national news.

Ask the children for examples from their own experience. Talk about several of these examples, focusing on why the helpers acted as they did.

Show the children a picture or a statuette of a Buddha figure sitting in a meditative or peaceful posture (see 'Resources needed'). Explain that the Buddha, a special person for people called Buddhists, wanted everyone to be kind and to help each other. Buddhists tell stories to help us understand this more.

Read or tell the children the story of 'The monkey king'. Ask questions which focus upon the monkey king's act of loving kindness, for example:
▲ Why did the monkey king make a bridge with his own body?
▲ Why didn't he stop when it began to hurt?
▲ How long did he stay as a bridge?
▲ Why did the king of the city go home to rule with care and kindness?

27

Suggestion(s) for extension

Children may like to draw or paint a picture of their favourite part of 'The monkey king' story and then dictate or write a sentence describing the scene.

Suggestion(s) for support

Some children may have difficulty in thinking of occasions when someone has been helpful or they have helped another person. These children can be prompted by an adult helper or teacher suggesting times when they have helped or been helped in the classroom or in the playground.

Assessment opportunities

The ease with which children enter into the whole-class discussion will indicate to what extent they have assimilated the story and are able to relate it to their own experiences.

Assembly ideas

As part of an assembly focusing on a theme such as 'Helping others' or 'People who help us', the story of 'The monkey king' can be acted by the whole class. Masks could be made to distinguish the characters. Several children may like to talk about when they have helped or been helped by others. The assembly could end with a reflection such as, 'And now, in a moment of quiet, let us say thank you for those people who have helped us and remember how we felt when they did those things for us.'

Reference to photocopiable sheet

Photocopiable page 114 has a copy of the story of 'The monkey king', which should be read to the children during the activity. This can be used to illustrate the concepts of kindness and compassion to other beings.

SHOULD WE TELL PEOPLE WHEN WE GIVE TO OTHERS?

To understand that feelings are associated with giving. To know that people called Muslims give because God wants them to.

Charity. Motive.

†† *Whole class.*

🕐 *20–30 minutes.*

Key background information

Within Islam, the religion of the Muslim, there is a strong sense of community, of giving and charity. The third of the five 'pillars' of Islam, those basic duties which uphold the Muslim life, is *zakah*. This is the duty to purify your wealth through giving a proportion of it away each year. A *hadith* (a 'report' of what the Prophet Muhammad did or said) commends 'a person whose one hand did not know what the other hand was doing'. Muslims tell many stories about the Prophet which portray his generosity and kindness to animals and people alike.

The Muslim story of 'The two brothers' referred to in the activity develops as follows:

▲ Two brothers owned a farm.

▲ One was married with a family.

▲ The other was not married.

▲ They shared everything equally.

▲ After a good harvest, the unmarried brother decided he would secretly give some of his crops to his brother.

▲ The married brother thought the same.

▲ By night, they both carried six bags of corn to the other brother's store.

▲ Next morning, they were both surprised to find that they had the same number of sacks as the evening before.

▲ Neither brother talked about what had happened because they did not want to boast of their generosity.

Preparation

Become familiar with the outline of the story of 'The two brothers' (see 'Key background information').

Resources needed

An example, or examples, of badges given out in street charity collections; collection box; sheet of sticky badges; money. For the extension activity – writing and drawing materials.

What to do

Show the children a badge from a street charity collection. Ask them if they, or anybody in their family, have ever given money to someone collecting in the street and if they wore the badge that they were given. Ask the children how they

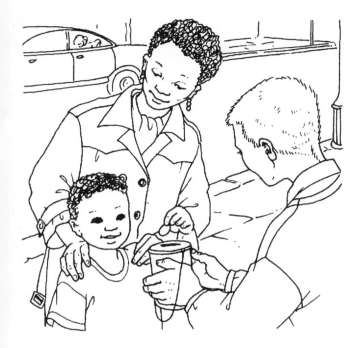

felt when they put the money in the collecting tin and when the badge was stuck on to their coat and ask them how long they kept the badge. Tell the children about people who would not want to wear the badge and ask them if they can think of any reasons for this, such as:

▲ they do not want to spoil their coat;
▲ they do not like the design of the badge;
▲ they do not want other people to know that they have given money.

Explain that, for people called Muslims, giving to others is very important because they believe that God wants them to do this. However, they are taught that they should not boast when they give.

Next, explain that the story they are about to hear is often told by Muslims. Tell the story of 'The two brothers'. For several days after this, provide a collection box, money and a sheet of sticky badges to give children the opportunity to role-play 'collector' and 'giver'.

Suggestion(s) for extension
Encourage children to think of a time when they or a member of their family gave money to someone collecting in the street. They could draw the badge they were given and say how they felt when they were wearing it.

Suggestion(s) for support
Children who find it difficult to role-play the situation can work with an older child or an adult who could suggest ideas and increase their confidence.

Assessment opportunities
Observing the children during role-play will provide an opportunity to assess the extent to which they understand that feelings are associated with giving.

WHY DO WE NEED RULES?

To understand the role of rules within social groups.

Authority. Order.

†† *Session One: small groups of three or four followed by whole class and then a return to small groups. Session Two: whole class followed by small groups of three and a return to whole class.*

🕐 *Session One: small groups 5 minutes; whole class 15 minutes; small groups 10 minutes. Session Two: whole class 5 minutes; small groups 30 minutes; whole class 20 minutes.*

Key background information
Within any social group, rules are all-pervading and probably affect life and thinking more than any group member will realise. Rules are one way in which a sense of order is established and chaos held at bay. Through imposing limits, rules create the possibility of freedom.

One way of understanding schooling, particularly in the case of younger children, is that it inducts them into the sets of rules which apply within a particular society or social group.

This activity provides children with the opportunity to begin to understand the role of rules and, particularly with the board game, to experience rule-making.

In identifying examples of rules followed by religious groups, it will be important to seek a balance between using language that the children can understand and not over-simplifying the material. For example, fasting during the month of Ramadan is one of the five pillars or basic duties of a Muslim. But:

▲ not all adult Muslims in Britain will fast during daylight hours (though most probably will);
▲ Ramadan observance is more than fasting and includes an attempt to lead a better life – not to quarrel, and so on.

Again, though the laws of *kashrut* forbid pork and certain other types of food (such as shellfish) to Jews, it is not unknown for people who call themselves Jews to eat such food. In the same way, some people who call themselves vegetarians will, no doubt, 'break the rules' occasionally for a number of reasons.

Preparation
Session Two: make copies of photocopiable page 115 onto thin card, one copy per group. If possible, collect together pictorial material to show the rules followed by people of different faiths.

Resources needed
Session One: chalkboard/flip chart; writing materials; large sheet of paper. Session Two: photocopiable page 115; counters and dice; writing materials; pictures (optional).

What to do

Session One

Organise the children into groups of three or four and ask them to agree on and list three rules for their class. (Children may need the assistance of an adult helper or support teacher when writing out their lists.)

Gather the children together and, using the ideas from the groups, make one main list of classroom rules. Look at each rule in turn and discuss its importance. It may be decided to discard some rules at this point.

Ask the children to prioritise the remaining rules. This can be done either by a show of hands or by the children writing the numbers of the rules in order of importance on a piece of paper. Write the final list of rules on a large sheet of paper.

Next, working in the same groups as before, tell the children to decide:

▲ what would happen to anyone who broke the rules;

▲ whether the punishment would be the same for each rule;

▲ if some rules are more important than others;

▲ where the list of rules should be displayed;

▲ how newcomers would be told about the rules.

Session Two

Remind the children of the previous session by showing them the list of agreed classroom rules. These could then be displayed in a place decided upon by the majority of groups.

Ask the children where else they have found rules, for instance:

▲ at home;

▲ in board games;

▲ in television game shows;

▲ in sporting activities.

Divide the children into groups of three and give each group one copy of photocopiable page 115. Tell the children that they are going to make up some rules to play this game, for example people take turns, you must throw a six to start, if you land on a shaded island you go back to the beginning. Ask the groups to write their rules down and then play the game. While the children are playing, go round each group and talk about the rules they have invented and why there is a need for them. Give the children a time limit for this activity.

When the time is up, gather the class together and explain to them that some religious groups of people have rules which they try to follow. For example:

▲ Many Jews will not eat pork.

▲ Many Muslims will behave in a special way for each day of the month of Ramadan.

▲ Many Christians will give up something during the time of Lent.

▲ Many Christians will go to church each Sunday.

If you have managed to obtain some pictures of the rules observed by people of different faiths, show these to the children. To finish, ask the children if they observe any rules which affect the way they live their lives.

Suggestion(s) for extension

The children can play each other's games and, in so doing, decide whether the rules are clear, helpful and fair.

Suggestion(s) for support

The groups in each session will need to be mixed ability so that someone can take the lead in writing. Some groups will need teacher support in identifying the rules for their game.

Assessment opportunities

When observing the children working in groups, note their capacity to understand and develop rules.

▲ What are the rules for this game?

Why do we need rules?

Opportunities for IT

Ask the children to use a word processor to create a list of classroom rules. Tell the children to draft them first and then move them into order of priority using 'cut and paste' or 'drag and drop' commands. They can then be printed out for display in the classroom. Rules for the board games could also be written up in the same way and presented to other groups to use. For both activities children may need to be introduced to simple formatting commands to help them lay out their work and to make it easier to read. Demonstrate how to use bold and italics, and how to increase the type size when writing headings.

Display ideas

A display could include the following elements:

▲ a list of classroom rules;

▲ children's board games and rules, together with comments from other groups;

▲ statements about the rules which different religious groups follow.

Reference to photocopiable sheet

Photocopiable page 115 provides a simple outline of a board game, for which the children devise their own rules.

RELIGIOUS
EDUCATION

HOW CAN I SHOW MY BROTHERS AND SISTERS THAT I CARE FOR THEM?

To know how the Hindu festival of Raksha Bandhan is celebrated. To understand that brothers and sisters relate to each other in different ways.

Family. Responsibility.

✝✝ *Whole class followed by small group work.*

🕐 *Whole class 20–25 minutes; small groups 10 minutes.*

Key background information

Though the festival of *Raksha Bandhan* (literally 'protection tying'; sometimes also called 'Rakhi' or 'Raakhi') is essentially a Hindu festival, many other groups in India also celebrate it and follow traditional customs.

Usually occurring in August, it is the time when sisters tie a *rakhi* around their brother's right wrist to symbolise the bond between them. In return, the brother will give his sister a gift, usually money. The rakhi itself might be a simple red thread. More often, it will be ornate with a round decoration made of tinsel, plastic and beads attached to the thread.

A story which is sometimes told tells of a king who was about to invade a queen's territory. Hearing of this, the queen sent him a rakhi, which suggested that, rather than attacking her, he should protect her as a brother. He did not invade.

In Britain, this custom of sisters giving their brothers a rakhi is keenly followed and rakhis are sometimes sent through the post. Rakhis and gifts might also be exchanged between male and female cousins.

The making and giving of 'friendship bands' comes in and out of fashion in Britain and clearly bears some resemblance to the giving of rakhis.

Preparation

Obtain or make a rakhi or rakhis (see 'Useful books and resources', page 107) and place in a special bag. Become familiar with details of the festival of Raksha Bandhan.

Resources needed

Rakhi in a special bag; drawing and craft materials.

What to do

Talk to the children about brothers and sisters, asking who has them and whether they are younger or older. Encourage children with brothers and sisters to talk about times when they have been looked after by them, or when they have done the looking after. Make sure that contributions are as constructive as possible.

Tell the children that they are going to see something special that some sisters give to their brothers. Carefully take the rakhi out of the bag and show it to the children. Ask the following questions to encourage the children to look at it more thoughtfully. What is this made of? What do you think you could do with it? Where might you wear it? Why?

Next, tell the children how the rakhi would be given by a sister to her brother at the Hindu festival of Raksha Bandhan and explain the brother's actions in return (see 'Key background information'). Role-play 'brothers and sisters', with the children inventing situations in which they can look after each other. Help the children to understand that, though brothers and sisters often fight and argue, they can also be very protective towards each other.

Children may like to design a wrist or friendship band for a brother, sister or someone special, giving the reasons why that person has been chosen. The band could be made using various craft materials.

Suggestion(s) for extension

Some children could go on to write their own account of what happens at the Hindu festival of Raksha Bandhan.

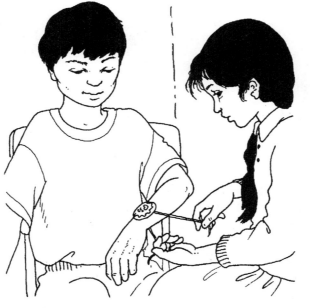

Suggestion(s) for support

Children who do not have brothers or sisters may find the concept of protection in this context difficult to understand. Ask them to think about a special friend or relative instead.

Assessment opportunities

Listening to and observing children during role-play will give some indication of the extent to which they have understood the differing relationships between brothers and sisters. The accounts of the festival written by children in the extension activity will provide evidence of their knowledge of what happens at the festival of Raksha Bandhan.

Assembly ideas

As part of an assembly focusing on a theme such as 'Caring' or 'Families', the children could talk about the festival of

RELIGIOUS EDUCATION

Raksha Bandhan and what it means for the people who take part in it. Groups of children could then act out situations between brothers and sisters which demonstrate both aspects of the relationship: arguing and protecting. The assembly could end with a reflection such as, 'And now, in a moment of quiet, let us think about people who are close to us and how we can protect and look after them.'

WHY DO WE SOMETIMES WANT TO LOOK LIKE OTHER PEOPLE?

To know why the five K's are important to Sikhs. To understand the function of uniform in developing group identity.

Identity. Symbolism.

†† *Whole class, then pairs.*

🕐 *Whole class 30 minutes; paired work 30 minutes.*

Key background information

Groups in society might want to adopt a common appearance for a variety of reasons. A uniform, for example, makes a declaration to others while at the same time reminding the wearer of a number of things such as role, tradition and appropriate behaviour. But, fundamentally, it reminds wearers that they are part of a group.

The role of uniform is particularly marked in Sikhism. The end of the seventeenth century marked the beginning of great persecution for the Sikhs, at the hands of the rulers of India. Each year the *Guru*, leader of the Sikhs, called members of the Sikh community together. The meeting of 1699, when the tenth Sikh Guru, Gobind Singh, called the community together in Anandpur was to have a profound effect on the Sikh community. It marked the emergence of the *Khalsa*, the brotherhood of baptised Sikhs who, sharing common names, were reminded of their beliefs and ideals through a 'uniform' consisting of five elements. Like all symbolism, that of the five K's can be explained in a variety of ways:

▲ the *kirpan* or sword, a reminder that Sikhs must fight for justice;

▲ the *kachera* or undergarment, a reminder that Sikhs must be clean-living;

▲ the *kangha* or comb worn in the hair, a reminder that Sikhs must lead disciplined lives;

▲ the *kesh* or uncut hair, a reminder that Sikhs must devote their lives to God;

▲ the *kara* or steel band worn on the right wrist, a reminder that Sikhs must be strong.

The story of what happened on that day in 1699 is repeated each year by Sikhs at the festival of *Baisakhi*. When

Sikhs decide to be baptised and to take even more seriously their Sikh way of life, including wearing all the K's (most Sikhs will wear some), the ceremony is presided over by five men representing those who offered their lives to their God and Guru in 1699.

Preparation

Read through the story of Baisakhi given on photocopiable page 116. Collect together examples of the five K's (see 'Useful books and resources', page 117) and make enlarged copies of photocopiable page 107. Check that your school library has books about people who wear uniform.

Resources needed

A copy of photocopiable page 116; enlarged copies of photocopiable page 117; examples of the five K's; writing and drawing materials.

What to do

Gather the children together and tell them the Sikh story associated with the festival of Baisakhi (see photocopiable page 116). Ask the children questions related to the last part of the story. How do you think the Sikhs felt when they were given the same name? Why did the Guru choose the name *Singh* for the men? Why did the Guru choose the name *Kaur* for the women? Why do you think that the Guru wanted the Sikhs to look the same?

Talk about each of the five K's in turn, showing a picture (as on the photocopiable sheet) and, if possible, the actual item. Discuss why Sikhs would want to wear some or all of the five K's. Discuss types of uniform that the children have seen, and ask questions about the kinds of uniform that the children wear.

▲ What does it look like?

▲ When is it worn?

▲ How did they feel the first time they wore it?

▲ What does it feel like to be in a group of people, all of whom are wearing the same uniform?

Working in pairs, ask the children to design a uniform which could be worn by pupils attending an imaginary new school called Four Trees Infant School.

Give each child an enlarged copy of photocopiable page 117 and ask them to link each label to the correct picture. After they have done this they can go on to complete the sentence 'Guru Gobind Singh wanted Sikhs to wear the five K's because...' at the bottom of the page.

Suggestion(s) for extension

Arrange for the children to go to the school library in order to find a book about someone who wears a uniform, such as a police officer or a nurse. Using the books which they have chosen, tell the children to draw a picture of the uniform and label the various parts.

Suggestion(s) for support

Suggest the items of uniform to be designed to those children needing support work.

Assessment opportunities

The range and subtlety of the symbolism used by the pairs when designing a school uniform will indicate the extent of their understanding of symbolism and the function of uniform in developing group identity. Photocopiable page 117 could be used for summative assessment in order to ascertain the children's knowledge and understanding of the five K's.

Opportunities for IT

Let the children use an art or drawing package to design their own school uniform. Show them how to draw lines and shapes, fill them with colour and select or change the colours. If children are drawing their own shapes, for example a skirt or trousers, tell them to check that their shapes have no gaps in them before they fill them with colour, to avoid the colour affecting the whole drawing area. Alternatively, children could use an art or drawing package to design a school badge for Four Trees Infant School.

Children could go on to use a simple CD-ROM encyclopaedia to research more information about the five K's or Sikhism.

Display ideas

Make a large display of uniforms worn by different groups of people, including Sikhs. The display could also contain the library books used in the extension activity, the completed photocopiable sheets and examples of the five K's.

Reference to photocopiable sheets

Photocopiable page 116 tells the story of Baisakhi, which is read to the children in the activity. Photocopiable page 117 shows the five K's and is used to reinforce the children's knowledge.

SHOULD WE FORGIVE OTHERS?

To know a well-known parable told by Jesus. To understand the concept of forgiveness.

Forgiveness. Love.

✝✝ *Whole class, followed by small groups, returning to whole class.*

🕐 *Whole class 15 minutes; small groups 20 minutes; whole class 15 minutes.*

Key background information

Jesus, like many Jewish teachers before and since, often expressed his message through vivid language and story. His parables (literally, stories with a twist in them) were remarkable for their number and quality. They would have left some listeners confused, some changed and others deeply angry.

The parable of the Prodigal Son – prodigal means 'spendthrift' – is only recorded in Luke's Gospel (Luke, chapter 15, verses 11–32). It is sometimes renamed 'The parable of the Loving Father', in recognition of the fact that the father is the central character. The story is one of a series of three 'lost' parables which Jesus told as a response to those who criticised the 'bad' company that he kept.

The parable of the Loving Father

Name _____ Date _____

1 Should the father have given the young son what he wanted?

2 Why didn't the son go home straight away when his money was all gone?

3 Why did the father go out to meet the young son?

4 Did the young son deserve his party?

5 Why didn't the older brother go to the party?

6 What was Jesus trying to teach when he told his story?

The parable contains a number of interesting details. What a horrible fate for a Jew, for instance, to have to look after pigs!

This activity will make a number of demands on children. The small group work, in particular, will require various skills (such as those relating to evaluation), and attitudes (including being able to listen to the views of others).

Preparation
Make copies of photocopiable page 118, one copy per small group. Become familiar with the parable of the Prodigal Son (see 'Key background information').

Resources needed
A children's Bible; photocopiable page 118; writing materials.

What to do
Explain to the children that Jesus, a special person for Christians, told stories to explain how people should live their lives. Many of these stories, called parables, were written down in the Christian Bible. Show the children a copy of the Bible and tell them that they are going to hear a parable. Tell or read to them the parable of the Prodigal Son.

Organise the children into small groups and ask each group to choose a leader to act as scribe. Give each group a copy of photocopiable page 118 and ask the children to talk about each question in turn and to decide on a group answer. You may need to help the children to read through the sheet. Explain that the scribe should write the group's answers in the spaces provided. Give the groups a time limit and remind them, at regular intervals, of the time they have left to complete the task.

Gather the class back together, and ask each group to report their answer to the final question. Make sure that all the children understand what is meant by the word 'forgiveness'.

Conclude the session with a general class discussion about the question, 'Should we always forgive others?' Note the children's answers for display later.

Suggestion(s) for extension
Ask the children to work in pairs and to tell each other their own parable about forgiveness.

Suggestion(s) for support
As the groups are working, circulate in order to encourage all children to participate in the discussion.

Assessment opportunities
Listening to individual contributions to the group discussions and final class discussion will indicate the extent to which the children have understood the concept of forgiveness.

Opportunities for IT
Put the children into pairs and ask them to write out one of the class's answers to 'Should we always forgive others?' Using a word processor they should select an appropriate font and enlarge it to an appropriate size to make a label that can be used as part of the class display.

Display ideas
Make a display of the questions and answers from the photocopiable sheet, together with the children's answers to the question 'Should we always forgive others?' The children can add further responses if they wish.

Reference to photocopiable sheet
Photocopiable page 118 is used as a record of each group's discussion about the parable of the Loving Father.

WHAT ARE THE 'UPS' AND 'DOWNS' OF FAMILY LIFE?

To know a story familiar to Christians, Jews and Muslims. To relate aspects of the story to their own experience.

Session One: Family. Relationships. Session Two: Fairness. Destiny. Session Three: Forgiveness. Reconciliation.

†† *Session One: paired work followed by whole class activity and then individual work. Session Two: whole class followed by small group work. Session Three: small group work followed by whole class activity and then individual work.*

🕐 *Session One: paired work 10 minutes; whole class 20 minutes; individual work 10 minutes. Session Two: whole class 20 minutes; small group 30–40 minutes. Session Three: small group 10 minutes; whole class 20 minutes; individual work 10 minutes.*

Key background information

It is easy to see why the biblical story of Joseph has captured people's imaginations down the ages. As characters such as Potiphar and his wife, often sketched in the briefest of details, enter and leave the stage, the story has been compared to a modern-day pantomime. As such, the story had as much appeal to the writers of the medieval mystery plays as it has had for modern musician and lyricists, most notably Andrew Lloyd Webber and Tim Rice who wrote the musical *Joseph and the Amazing Technicolor Dreamcoat*.

The story has a certain childlike quality, with much that children should be able to relate to their own experiences. But it should not be forgotten that the story is part of the sacred literature of three major religions. As part of the Jewish *Torah*, it teaches Jews about their Hebrew ancestry. For Christians, the story comes early on in the first part of their Bible, the Old Testament (see Genesis, chapters 37–46). Surah 12 of the Qur'an contains a story similar in many ways to that found in the Bible, Muslims regarding Yusuf (Joseph) as one of their prophets.

Preparation

Session One: make copies of photocopiable page 119 and 120, enough for each child. Become familiar with the first part of the Joseph story (as told in Genesis, chapter 37 in the Bible). Find a recording of *Joseph and the Amazing Technicolor Dreamcoat* if applicable. (You will need to ensure that your school or LEA has an Educational Recording Agency Licence if you wish to play music in class or at an assembly.) Session Two: become familiar with the second part of the Joseph story, as told in Genesis, chapters 39–41 in the Bible. Set up music, if applicable. Make copies of photocopiable page 121, one for each child. Session Three: become familiar with the third part of the Joseph story, as told in Genesis, chapters 42–46 in the Bible. Make copies of photocopiable page 122, one for each child.

Resources needed

Session One: children's Bible; recording of *Joseph and the Amazing Technicolor Dreamcoat*; photocopiable pages 119 and 120; writing materials. Session Two: music; children's Bible; photocopiable page 121. Session Three: children's Bible; photocopiable page 122.

What to do
Session One

Divide the children into pairs, asking each pair to talk about times when they have felt jealous of someone in their family – of a brother, sister or cousin, for example. Then gather the children together and ask for volunteers to share their experiences with the whole class.

RELIGIOUS EDUCATION

Show the children a copy of the Bible and remind them that it contains many stories. One of these stories is about a family in which the older brothers were jealous of a younger brother. Using photocopiable page 119 tell the children the first part of the story. Play some excerpts from *Joseph and the Amazing Technicolor Dreamcoat* if available.

Ask the children questions about aspects of the story.
▲ Should Jacob have given each of his sons a coat?
▲ Why did Joseph tell his brothers about his dreams?
▲ Why did Reuben say that Joseph should not be killed?

To complete this session, give each child a copy of photocopiable page 120 and ask the children to complete it.

Session Two
Remind the children of the first part of the Joseph story by using an excerpt from *Joseph and the Amazing Technicolor Dreamcoat* as a stimulus. Tell the second part of the Joseph story (Genesis, chapters 39–41).

Ask the children questions which focus on the injustice in the story.
▲ Why was Joseph put in prison?
▲ Why did the butler forget about Joseph when he got out of prison?
▲ How would Joseph have felt when he realised that the butler had forgotten him?

Give each child a copy of photocopiable page 121 and ask them to complete it.

Gather the children together and divide them into small friendship groups, asking them to share experiences of times when they have been blamed for something they have not done. Each group should choose one of these times, role-play the situation and then perform it to the rest of the class.

Session Three
Divide children into friendship groups of four and ask them to talk about times when they have argued with their friends or family and how the situation was resolved. Volunteers could then describe their experiences to the whole class. Next, focus on feelings when making up with a friend, such as relief, guilt, excitement, happiness, reluctance, and ask the children which of these emotions feels the best when making up and which the most difficult. Tell the children that they are going to hear the last part of the story of Joseph, in which he meets and makes up with his family. Remind the children of the first two parts of the Joseph story before telling them the final part (Genesis, chapters 42–46).

Ask the children questions focusing on the meeting of Joseph and his family.
▲ How did Joseph feel when he saw his brothers?
▲ Why didn't Joseph tell them who he was straight away?
▲ Why did Joseph order his cup to be put in Benjamin's bag?
▲ How did the brothers feel when they realised that Joseph was alive?

When the children have discussed the story, give out copies of photocopiable page 122 and ask them to complete it.

Suggestion(s) for extension
Session One: ask children to remember the discussion they had with their partner about a time when they felt jealous of someone in their family and to write an account of this time. Session Two: children can develop the role-play situation by creating a series of comic cartoon illustrations with speech bubbles on the theme of being blamed for something that you have not done. Session Three: ask children to write a poem called 'Making Up', focusing on the mixture of feelings involved in making up with a friend. The children can draw on the class discussion at the beginning of the session for ideas.

Suggestion(s) for support
Sessions One to Three: for children needing support work, it would be helpful to divide each session again to make a total of six sessions. This activity is a lengthy one and the breakdown of the work into further sessions ensures that children do not have too much information to assimilate at one time. Some children will need help with reading the photocopiable sheets. They could use the reverse of the sheets for their drawings.

Assessment opportunities
The accuracy with which children complete each of the photocopiable sheets will provide evidence of the extent to which they know the details of the Joseph story. The extension activities for the more competent children and the results of small group work will provide evidence of the children's ability to relate aspects of the story to their own experiences.

Assembly ideas
As part of an assembly focusing on a theme such as 'Families' or 'Feelings', the Joseph story can be read and acted. Individual children can talk about, dramatise or read their experiences of the 'ups' and 'downs' of family life after each section of the story. You may like to end the assembly with a reflection such as, 'And now, in a moment of quiet, let us think about people in our family and how, although we get really annoyed with them sometimes, it is still good that they are there.'

Reference to photocopiable sheets
Photocopiable page 119 tells the first part of the Joseph story. Photocopiable pages 120, 121 and 122 are for completion by the children and will provide evidence of how much they know of the complete story. An alternative way of using photocopiable pages 120, 121 and 122 is to give them to the children at the beginning of the following session or all together at the beginning of Session Three.

Living in the world

Human beings construct and inherit their own world of meanings and values but also live within the world of nature. This century has witnessed an increasing sensitivity to the 'environment' and awareness of the destructive as well as creative role which human beings might play. Environmental issues have assumed an increasingly important place in the curriculum and culture of schools. 'Environmental education' has been identified as a cross-curricular theme within the National Curriculum and a grouping for subject areas within the Scottish 5–14 guidelines.

This chapter gives children the opportunity to explore a number of issues related to the world of nature and to the human place within it. In all but one instance – an exploration of the Christian harvest festival – the activities use a story as a context for learning. Some of these stories will already be familiar to most primary teachers, such as Raymond Briggs' *The Snowman* and Michael Foreman's *One World*. Some are drawn from mainstream religious traditions, such as the story of 'St Francis and the wolf of Gubbio'. The story of the forget-me-not, on the other hand, is based on a story told by a Native American tribe.

In that this chapter allows children to respond in ways other than cognitive – in ways that have often been described as the 'awe and wonder' dimension of religious education – there is a clear contribution to their spiritual development. Religious education gives children the opportunity to respond in a range of ways, including silence, to the experience of seeing a bud blossom or a butterfly emerge from a cocoon, for example.

RELIGIOUS
EDUCATION

WHY DO THINGS CHANGE?

To understand that, within the natural world, processes of transformation occur.

Transformation. Process.

†† *Whole class, then individual observation, returning to whole class.*

⏲ *Whole class 10 minutes; individual observation ongoing; whole class (at a later date) 15–20 minutes.*

Key background information

At first glance, this activity might appear to be one related to science. Though it overlaps with aspects of curriculum science, it is the approach which makes it a religious education activity.

▲ The central concept is 'transformation' rather than (mere) 'change'.

▲ As well as using their rational minds, the children are encouraged to respond with their feelings and imagination.

It has been said that, whereas science probes the 'how' of things, religion (and poetry) searches out the 'why'.

In that transformation and resurrection are related concepts, this activity would link well with work on Easter.

Part of the power of Eric Carle's book *The Very Hungry Caterpillar* is the final illustration, which is a magnificent butterfly over a double-page spread. The butterfly has been called a universal symbol in that it 'speaks' to people of all ages, times and cultures. It is sometimes used as a symbol of everlasting life.

Children's sketches of butterflies were found on the walls of some of the huts in which, during the Holocaust, children were kept before being sent to the gas chambers.

Preparation

Obtain a twig with dormant buds or a flower in bud, or cress seeds. Find a copy of *The Very Hungry Caterpillar* by Eric Carle (Picture Puffin).

Resources needed

Twig, flower or cress; *The Very Hungry Caterpillar* by Eric Carle.

What to do

Explain to the children that they are going to look at a twig cut from a tree (or a flower in bud or cress seeds). Show them the twig and encourage the children to talk about it: some will think that it is dead. Put the twig in water and leave it in a warm, light spot where it can easily be seen. Encourage the children to look at it regularly over the next few days and to talk about their feelings as they observe changes in the twig.

When the twig is in full leaf, ask the children questions which will encourage them to respond to the changes in an imaginative way.

▲ How did the leaves get into the twig?

▲ How did the twig come alive again?

▲ Does the twig look better with leaves?

▲ What will happen to the leaves next?

Tell the children that many other things change and that what they change into sometimes looks different. Read the story of *The Very Hungry Caterpillar*. Looking at the picture of the butterfly at the end of the story, again ask questions which encourage an imaginative response.

▲ Why did the caterpillar need a cocoon?

▲ How does the caterpillar feel now that it is a beautiful butterfly?

▲ Where did its wings come from?

▲ How will the butterfly change?

Suggestion(s) for extension

Ask a group of children to continue observing the twig until they see more changes. They can report back their observations and responses to the rest of their class. Ask questions to focus their thinking, for instance:

▲ When does the twig stop changing?

▲ Why do the leaves have to die?

RELIGIOUS EDUCATION

▲ Where do the leaves go to?
▲ Will the twig come alive again?

Suggestion(s) for support

Those children who find it difficult to develop a response using their imagination and feelings can be prompted by the use of further questions addressed directly to them and their emotions.
▲ What did the twig look like before the leaves came?
▲ If you were a twig, would you want to have leaves?

Assessment opportunities

The children's answers to the questions will reveal the extent to which they understand the process of transformation in the natural world.

Opportunities for IT

Children could use an art package to create their own butterflies. This is an ideal activity for exploring different tools, such as the spray cans or rollers. Show the children how to alter the brush size to create large bold lines, and how to change or make their own colours. With some software, children may be able to draw one wing of their butterfly and then copy it and flip it to make a symmetrical matching wing. The completed butterflies can then be printed out in colour and displayed in the classroom.

young and old alike. Its power lies undoubtedly in a number of underlying concepts, particularly that of 'transformation'. It also touches on the parallel worlds in which young and old can often exist: while the little boy is flying through the air, his mother and father are sleeping 'safely' in bed.

Preparation

Obtain the video and soundtrack of *The Snowman*. (Ensure that your school or LEA has an Educational Recording Agency licence.) Cut Mod-Roc into small pieces.

Resources needed

Video of *The Snowman*; *The Snowman* music; loaded camera; foil; Mod-Roc; trays to hold water. For the extension activity – writing and painting materials.

What to do

Show all or part of the video *The Snowman* (if only showing part of the video, stop at the end of the flying through the air section).

Ask the children questions about their own experiences of snow and encourage reflection on what they have seen in the video.
▲ How does seeing snow make you feel?
▲ What's the first thing you do when you go out to play in snow?
▲ Why couldn't the little boy sleep when he went to bed?
▲ Why wasn't the little boy frightened when he was flying through the air?

During a PE lesson, build up a dance sequence using the music from *The Snowman* video. Take photographs (where appropriate). This could include getting the children to:
▲ walk, then skip, then run through deep snow;
▲ roll a large snowball to make the snowman's body;
▲ roll a smaller snowball to make the snowman's head;
▲ move like the snowman when he first comes alive;
▲ fly through the air with a snowman looking at all the wonderful scenes;
▲ dancing with the snowman at the party and then melting in the sunshine (if this part of the video has been viewed).

Back in the classroom, let the children model snowmen using foil. When they are satisfied with the shape, they can cover their model with Mod-Roc and add features.

Suggestion(s) for extension

Following the dance sequence, ask the older or more able children to paint a picture of the part of the dance they

WHY DOES SNOW MAKE THE WORLD A SPECIAL PLACE?

To understand that snow transforms the appearance of the world and people's behaviour.

Transformation. Wonder.

†† *Whole class followed by individual work.*
🕐 *Whole class 40 minutes; (watching video 15–20 minutes; dance sequence 20 minutes). Model-making as appropriate.*

Key background information

The animated cartoon based on Raymond Briggs' book *The Snowman* has rightly achieved a unique place at home and at school. It has rapidly become a Christmas 'classic'.

In its interplay of music and movement, colour and ethereal light, the cartoon has a magical quality which fascinates

enjoyed the most and write (or an adult could scribe) their feelings associated with it.

Suggestion(s) for support

If some children appear diffident at expressing themselves through dance, encourage them to watch other children for a short while.

Assessment opportunities

The answers to the questions about the video and the degree of imagination with which they express themselves in dance will indicate the extent to which the children understand the transformative power of snow.

Opportunities for IT

Using an art package, ask the children to adapt the ideas from the video to create their own snow scene. One option is to limit the children to a small number of colours, possibly working in black and white only, to give the effect of snow-covered trees and buildings.

Allowing the children to use the video camera and control the play-back themselves gives them experience in the control aspect of information technology.

Display ideas

Display the children's paintings and sentences, together with photographs of the children dancing. In front of the display place a table covered with polystyrene chips and the model snowmen. Give the display a title such as 'Snow makes the world a special place'.

WHY IS ST FRANCIS SPECIAL FOR SOME CHRISTIANS?

To know a story associated with the life of St Francis. To identify an animal with which they have a special relationship.

Sainthood. Relationship.

†† *Whole class followed by individual work.*

🕐 *Whole class 15 minutes; individual work 10 minutes.*

Key background information

In early Christianity, the word *saint* was used of all Christian believers. As time passed, however, it came to be a title applied to Christians of outstanding virtue or holiness.

St Francis of Assisi (*c.*1181–1226: feast day 4 October) was the son of a wealthy cloth merchant who exchanged a life of material comfort for one of poverty and chastity. Others who also wanted to lead such a life joined him and so began the 'Order of Friars Minor' – the Franciscans or Grey Friars (though their habits are now brown).

St Francis had an intimate relationship with nature. He is often depicted in art among birds and animals whom he called his 'brothers' and 'sisters'. In his famous canticle (hymn) to the sun, he referred to the sun as his 'brother'. The Roman Catholic Church has designated him the patron saint of ecologists, and statues of St Francis are frequently found in Roman Catholic churches and homes.

It was St Francis who is said to have first thought of setting up a nativity scene, using a cave mouth and real people.

Preparation

Become familiar with the details of St Francis' life and the story of the wolf of Gubbio.

Resources needed

Writing and drawing materials.

What to do

Gather the children together and tell them that they are going to learn about a man called Francis who loved God and lived a long time ago in Italy. Continue by telling them more about St Francis, including the story of Francis and the wolf of Gubbio.

In this story, St Francis hears about a fierce wolf that is attacking the people who live in the city of Gubbio. Many people had tried to catch and kill the wolf but it was too clever for them. St Francis decided that he would go to Gubbio to see if he could help. He took one friend with him and waited outside the city walls for the wolf to come. When the wolf was near him, St Francis held up his hand and made the sign of the cross. The wolf stopped snarling and sat down next to St Francis. St Francis knew that the wolf was hungry and promised that the people would feed him if he stopped being fierce. The wolf followed St Francis back into the city and the people promised to feed him. The wolf lived peacefully in the city with the people.

Ask the children to think about animals which they are very fond of. Give each child a sheet of plain paper and tell them to draw a picture of themselves standing alongside their special animal. At the bottom of the sheet ask them to write the sentence 'My special animal and me'.

Suggestion(s) for extension
Children could tell an adult their favourite parts of the story of St Francis and the wolf of Gubbio and draw or paint a picture to illustrate them. The paintings and children's comments could then be made into a book which could be placed in the class book corner.

Suggestion(s) for support
Children who do not come into regular contact with animals may need help in identifying an animal that they can relate to. Offer suggestions, such as a neighbour's cat or dog, a school pet, a soft animal toy in the classroom.

Assessment opportunities
The picture which each child draws, together with an ability to retell the main events in the story, will provide evidence of the extent to which children have been able to identify an animal which they feel attached to and can remember the story.

Opportunities for IT
Encourage the children to use a CD-ROM encyclopaedia to search for further information about the story of St Francis.

Using multimedia authoring software, the class can work together to make an electronic version of the story of St Francis. This software allows children to mix text, pictures and sound. Groups of children could each work on one section of the story, incorporating pictures and adding appropriate text using one or two screen pages. Pictures can be included from a variety of sources. They can be taken from collections of clip art, scanned from the children's own line drawings or created using an art or drawing package. The children could include a simple soundtrack of the story using a microphone attached to the computer.

Display ideas
Make a class 'big book' using the children's completed drawings and display them in the reading area.

IN WHAT WAYS DO WE HELP AND HARM OUR WORLD?

To understand that human beings have a relationship with the natural world.

Nature. Relationship.

†† *Whole class followed by individual work.*

🕐 *Whole class 25 minutes; individual work 25 minutes.*

Key background information
The power of many stories and myths lies in what they have to suggest about the relationship between humankind and the world. Many of them imply that there is a subtle balance in the world which humans forget to their cost.

This story, adapted from *Creation Stories* by Maurice Lynch (see 'Useful books and resources', page 107) was told by the Comanche tribe of North America. It contains many familiar motifs: restoration through an act of self-sacrifice, the superior wisdom of a child, and so on. Like many myths, it also explains the origin of familiar but puzzling names – such as 'forget-me-not'.

The words quoted in the 'Assembly ideas' section is taken from 'Chief Seattle's Testimony'. This testimony, or declaration, was supposedly delivered by Chief Seattle at the great tribal ceremony of 1854 prior to the signing of the Indian treaties. Chief Seattle (or Sealth), after whom the city of Seattle is named, was a member of the Duwamish Tribe of Washington territory.

The first part of the activity consists of a short 'stilling exercise' which is intended to create the right atmosphere for the main part of the activity. (For more about stilling exercises, see 'Useful books and resources', page 107.)

The girl who saved the people

The sound of the prayer drum filled the air but still the rain did not fall. The plain had become dusty and dry, the crops had withered and died and now the people were dying too. The wise man prayed to the Great Spirit. 'What wrong have we done? Why does the rain not fall?' But still the rain did not come.

Then one evening the wise man came running down the hill from the place of the fire. He waved his arms and called for the people to listen. 'At last the Great Spirit has spoken. We have grown selfish. We have taken from the earth and never given anything back in return. We must offer the most precious thing in our camp, then the rain will come and life will return to the earth.'

The people gave thanks and tried to find the most precious thing in the camp. Some said it was the tepee which sheltered them from the winds and rain. Others said it was the blankets which kept them warm in winter. The young braves thought it was the bow and arrow that gave them food to eat and furs to wear. All night they talked but they could not agree.

Sitting at the edge of the camp fire was a young girl. The people called her 'The Girl Who Has No Name' because her family had all died when the crops had failed. She listened, holding her doll in her lap. The doll was the only thing she had left. Her grandfather had found a piece of wood in the forest and had carved it into the shape of a doll. Her grandmother had used berries from deep within the forest to make dyes to colour the wood and give the doll eyes and lips. Her brothers had used soft leather to make a jacket and leggings. Her father had found blue feathers from the jay bird and had made them into a deep-blue head-dress for the little doll.

The girl knew what was the most precious thing in the camp. She took her doll and, without saying a word, thrust it into the fire. She watched as the flames licked round it till it was only a black shape and finally it disappeared into ashes. When the ash had grown quite cold she stopped and gathered all of it in her hands. She turned and scattered the ash to the homes of the wind, to the North, the South, the East and West. Then she lay down and fell asleep.

The sun woke her early next morning. When she opened her eyes she could not believe what she saw. The hillside was covered with tiny blue flowers rippling in the wind. They looked like waves on a lake. The people came to her and danced around her and, as they danced, the rain began to fall.

That day the people changed her name. No longer was she 'The Girl Who Has No Name', for now they called her 'The Girl Who Saved the People'. They asked her to name the blue flowers. She called them 'forget-me-nots'.

Preparation

Become familiar with the story on photocopiable page 123.

Resources needed

A copy of photocopiable page 123; bunch of flowers (preferably blue – forget-me-nots, if possible) in a vase; A4 paper; writing and drawing materials; chalkboard/flip chart.

What to do

Sit the children where they can all easily see the vase of flowers. Let them sit in silence for a short time looking at them. Ask the children what the flowers make them think of.

Explain that the story they are about to hear was told by a North American Indian tribe called the Comanches. Read or tell the story.

Let the children talk about what they think the Comanches might have done wrong to stop the rains falling, for instance, making the river dirty, pulling up flowers by their roots and so on. Then ask them what else people do today which could harm the world.

Give the children a piece of folded A4 paper. On one half ask them to write 'If we do not look after the world it will look like this' and on the other 'If we look after the world it will look like this'. (You may need to scribe these for the children to copy.) Ask them to illustrate both sides.

Suggestion(s) for extension

Ask the children what the most precious thing is that they own. Would they be prepared to give it up to save their world? Allow each child the opportunity to talk about their most precious item. Have a variety of drawing materials available (crayons, pencils, felt-tipped pens and pastels) and allow

the children to choose one medium with which to draw their most precious thing. When the drawing is finished, they should write what it is and the reasons why it is so precious.

Suggestion(s) for support

Make available some illustrated books showing the results of people's neglect of the world to show to children who might find it difficult to think of ideas.

Assessment opportunities

The children's discussion about ways in which the world is harmed should enable you to assess the extent of their understanding of the issues involved.

Assembly ideas

As part of an assembly focusing on a theme such as 'Our world', ask a group of children to dramatise the story told by the Comanches. Other children could talk about ways of looking after our world. You may like to end the assembly with a reflection such as, 'And now, in a moment of quiet, listen to the words of a Native American chief talking about the world in which we live: 'We are part of the earth and it is part of us. The perfumed flowers are our sisters; the deer, the horse, the great eagle – these are our brothers. The rocky crests, the juices of the meadows, the body heat of the pony, and man – all belong to the same family' (for source, see 'Key background information'). Music taken from *Sacred Spirit: Chants and Dances of the Native Americans* (Virgin Records) could be integrated into the assembly.

Reference to photocopiable sheet

Photocopiable page 123 has a version of the Comanche story for use in the activity.

WHY DO SOME CHRISTIANS SAY THANK YOU AT HARVEST TIME?

To understand why harvest time has been important for many Christians.

Thankfulness. Celebration.

✝✝ *Whole class followed by individual.*

🕐 *Whole class 30 minutes; individual work 20 minutes.*

Key background information

In agricultural communities, the successful completion of harvest was a time of natural celebration. The back-breaking work was over for another year and, with the knowledge of stored food, the winter months could be faced with slightly less foreboding.

RELIGIOUS EDUCATION

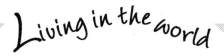

The 'harvest home' and 'harvest supper' – feasting and festivity-making at the end of the harvest in pre-mechanised days of farming – is embedded in British folk tradition. The idea of a church harvest festival is often credited to the Reverend R.S. Hawker, vicar of Morwenstow, Cornwall, in 1843. The practice of offering harvest gifts and decorating the church with fruit and vegetables, bread and corn, soon spread. Today, many schools celebrate harvest festival and express thanks by giving to those in need.

Many festivals celebrated within the different religious traditions – such as Sikh Baisakhi and Jewish Sukkot – have harvest links within their origins.

Preparation

Collect examples of types of food. These could include a tin of carrots, piece of fruit, packet of rice, loaf of bread. Make copies of photocopiable page 124, one for each child. Contact the local priest or minister and arrange a date for a visit, if applicable. Identify a Christian harvest hymn.

Resources needed

Some foodstuffs; photocopiable page 124; drawing materials. For the extension activity – an example of a Christian harvest hymn.

What to do

Show the children a range of different types of food, and talk about where each one comes from and how it is eaten.

Ask the children what their favourite foods are, encouraging them to think about where the food originally came from. Explain, for example, how the carrots were grown on a farm before being picked and transported to a supermarket. Discuss what else was needed for the food to grow:

▲ water;

▲ light;

▲ warmth.

Explain to the children that some people, called Christians, want to thank God for providing the conditions to enable food to grow. A good time for Christians to say thank you is in the autumn, because that is when farmers collect the food that is grown in their fields and fruit is ripe and ready to be picked. This is called the harvest. Many Christians go to church for a special celebration called a harvest festival. They often take food and flowers with them to decorate the church building. Sometimes a loaf of bread in the shape of a sheaf of corn is placed at the front of the church to remind Christians that much of their food comes from the earth.

Give each child a copy of photocopiable page 124. Ask them to think about foods for which they might feel thankful and then draw these in the spaces on the photocopiable sheet.

Invite the priest or minister of a local church, which celebrates harvest festival, in to school. Ask him or her to talk about what happens in the church at harvest time, and to answer questions from the children about this.

Suggestion(s) for extension

Children could look at the words of a Christian harvest hymn, for example 'We plough the fields and scatter', to explore further why some Christians say thank you to God at this time of year.

Suggestion(s) for support

Children who have difficulty in identifying four foods that they would say thank you for could be asked to draw their four favourite foods.

Assessment opportunities

Listen to the questions the children ask the visitor. This will allow you to assess the degree of their understanding about why some Christians celebrate harvest.

Opportunities for IT

Ask the children to use a word processor to make labels for the display of foods. Working either individually or in pairs, the children should select a food they like and write a label saying where the food comes from, how it is eaten and why they like the food. Explain to the children that the labels need to be easy to read, so they must select appropriate fonts and sizes. Alternatively, the children could use an art package to design their own food labels.

Display ideas

On one half of a large sheet of paper mount a picture of a corn sheaf together with the words 'Some Christians say thank you to God at harvest time'. On the other half, mount pictures drawn by the children together with the words 'These are the foods for which we say thank you'. Display these under the general title 'Saying thank you at harvest festival'. A collection of real foods could be placed on a table in front of the display.

Reference to photocopiable sheet

Photocopiable page 124 will reinforce the children's understanding of why some Christians celebrate harvest festival. It will also encourage them to identify foods for which they are grateful.

WHY WAS MUHAMMAD SAD WHEN HE HEARD A CAMEL CRY?

To know that Muslims have beliefs about the relationship between humans and animals. To encourage a caring attitude towards animals.

Relationship. Kindness.

†† *Small groups followed by whole class then individual work.*

🕐 *Group work 10 minutes; whole class 20–30 minutes; individual work 15 minutes.*

Key background information

Though Muhammad is not worshipped, he holds a special place for Muslims. Much of the Muslim life, the way that people greet each other, for example, follows the practice of Muhammad himself. For Muslims, the story used in this activity would have implications for the way in which people should live their lives.

In class, teachers will need to be particularly aware of Muslim sensitivities and perceptions. Muslims would find it objectionable to be asked to represent Muhammad in drama (the film *The Message* was about Muhammad's life but he was never shown – only his voice was heard) or in art form. Generally speaking, the Muslim artistic impulse has shown itself in calligraphy (the beautified Arabic of the Qur'an) and Arabesque (symmetrical patterns such as you might find on a Persian carpet or a prayer-mat).

Preparation

Obtain a picture or model of a camel. Become familiar with the story 'Muhammad and the crying camel' on photocopiable page 125.

Resources needed

Picture or model of a camel; photocopiable page 125; writing and drawing materials.

Muhammad and the crying camel

The sun had been shining for days. Everywhere was dry and dusty. Muhammad walked in the shade of the trees but he was still hot and thirsty.

Suddenly, he heard the sound of a camel crying. Muhammad followed the sound and saw a thin camel standing in the full heat of the sun with no food to eat or water to drink. Muhammad looked around for the camel's owner. He was laughing and drinking with his Muslim friends in a cool, shady spot nearby.

Muhammad walked over to the camel and began stroking its nose. After a while, the camel stopped crying but it still panted with thirst.

'Why is this camel tied in the full sun with nothing to eat or drink!' Muhammad shouted to the camel owner. 'Look how thin and unhappy this camel is. Allah has given the camel to help us in our work, but in return we must look after it and give it food to eat and water to drink.'

The owner of the camel saw how thin and unhappy his camel was and felt ashamed.

'I have done wrong,' he said. 'Muhammad has reminded me that the camel is one of God's creatures. I am sorry for what I have done.' He ran to untie his camel and led it to the shade. He gave it cool water to drink and food to eat. From that day the camel owner cared for all his camels and showed them great kindness.

What to do

Divide the children into small groups. Ask each group to discuss what it is that animals need to stay healthy and happy. Choose someone from each group to keep a pictorial or written record of the group's discussion. Move from group to group ensuring that recording is taking place.

After a specified time, gather the children together and, in turn, let each group show what they have done.

Using either a picture or a model of a camel, ask the children what they know about this animal. Then tell them the story of 'Muhammad and the crying camel'. (If the children are not used to talking about Muslims, a brief explanation of the importance of Muhammad will need to be given before the story is told.)

Ask the children why the owner of the camel was sorry for not giving the animal food and water and what made him change his ways.

When you have finished discussing the story with the children, give each child a blank sheet of paper. Ask the children to draw two animals and then to write about the ways they could be looked after.

Suggestion(s) for extension

Some children may be able to give reasons why humans should look after animals. Ask them to write their reasons on the back of their drawing.

Suggestion(s) for support

For the first part of the activity, mixed ability groups will allow all children to take a full part in formulating ideas without having to worry about recording. When drawing their pictures of the animals, teacher input for the first animal will give children requiring support the confidence to attempt the remaining one.

Assessment opportunities

Listening to the children's answers to the question 'Why did the camel-owner feel sorry for what he had done?' will give an indication of the extent to which they have grasped the importance of the story for Muslims. Answers which indicate such a grasp might be, for example, 'Because Muhammad told him that he was wrong' or 'God cares about camels'.

Assembly ideas

As part of an assembly focusing on a theme such as 'Animals' or 'Our world', the story of 'Muhammad and the crying camel' could be told and a group of children asked about the animals they look after, and how and why they take care of them. End the assembly with a thought such as, 'And now, in a moment of quiet, let us think about how animals make the world a better place to live in.'

Reference to photocopiable sheet

Photocopiable page 125 tells the story of 'Muhammad and the crying camel' and is read to the children during the activity.

HOW CAN WE LOOK AFTER OUR WORLD?

To demonstrate that the children themselves can have a personal impact on the environment. To encourage a responsible attitude to the physical world.

Responsibility. Protection.

†† *Whole class followed by individual or paired work.*
⏱ *Whole class 60 minutes; individual/paired work as required.*
▲ *If the children are going to be practically involved in cleaning up the environment, health and safety issues will have to be addressed.*

Key background information

It has been said that the current environmental 'crisis' is more a spiritual than a physical one – that is, it is rooted in how people regard and relate to the environment. It is in exploring attitudes to and relationships with the physical world that work in religious education complements work in other curriculum areas such as geography.

Using the dictum that 'small is beautiful', this activity begins with the school environment. It is here that environmental improvements can be both suggested and achieved. Using a Michael Foreman story *One World*, the activity then moves from the local to the global.

Preparation

Obtain rubber gloves and other material if required. Find a copy of *One World* by Michael Foreman (Andersen Press).

Resources needed

Rubber gloves or other protective clothing; *One World*; loaded camera; writing and drawing materials.

What to do

Talk with the children about aspects of the outdoor school environment that they like and dislike. Take them on a walk around the school site, encouraging them to point out features which spoil the environment, for example:
▲ litter;
▲ graffiti;
▲ broken glass;
▲ trampled flowers.

Take photographs of these features. Returning to the classroom, make a list of the things that have been noted on the walk. Ask the children what they can do to improve the school site. You might suggest:
▲ picking up litter;
▲ involving the school keeper in removing glass and graffiti;
▲ putting up signs;
▲ talking to pupils in assembly.

You may like to take a further set of photographs, after the improvements have been made.

Show the children the book *One World*, explaining that it is a story about two children who are concerned about the environment. Read the story and then talk about ways in which the children can look after the planet. If the children need prompting, ask questions such as:
▲ How would they feel if they saw the sea covered in oil?
▲ What do people do to look after birds affected by oil?
▲ What material could be recycled?
▲ Is there anyone they could write to about pollution?

Working individually or in pairs, ask the children to design a poster for display in school, reminding the school community to look after their environment.

Suggestion(s) for extension
Children could write to the local environmental office explaining their concerns about the local environment, or to the letters page of a local newspaper asking people in the local community not to drop litter.

Suggestion(s) for support
Some children may need help with ideas for their posters. Suggest various aspects of the environment which it is important to protect.

Assessment opportunities
The learning objectives will have been achieved if, in general, the children respond positively to this activity and are keen to suggest and act upon ways in which the environment can be improved.

Opportunities for IT
The children could use an art or drawing package to create their poster about the school environment. Show them how to use and combine the various text facilities of the package, including appropriate fonts, sizes and colours in order to communicate their message effectively.

Alternatively, children can use a word processor or desktop publishing package and add pictures. These can be drawn with an art package, taken from clip-art collections or scanned from their own line drawings.

Display ideas
Choose some of the posters to display in prominent areas around the school. The remainder of the posters can form part of a classroom display, together with the 'before and after' photographs. (Photographs could also be taken of areas being cleaned or improved.)

HOW DID THE WORLD COME TO BE?

To know a story from the Judaeo-Christian tradition. To relate this story to their own experience of creating.

Creation. Destruction.

†† *Whole class followed by individual work.*
○ *Whole class 30 minutes; individual work as required.*

Key background information
One of the 'ultimate questions' which humans have asked and sought to answer is 'How and why did the world come to be?' Cultures, as well as religious traditions, have sought to respond to this question – through art and ritual, symbolism and imagery, hypothesis and investigation. Stories which seek to provide at least a satisfying response to the question abound.

The Jewish Torah/ Christian Bible begins with the book of Genesis, at the start of which is found a creation story which has had a profound effect on Western thought (chapters 1–2). A second, even more ancient, creation story follows.

The first creation story tells of six days of creation, and a seventh of rest. With the rise of science in the West, a literal understanding of the story became troublesome. In response, some said that the 'days' were periods of unimaginable length, rather than the usual period of 24 hours.

Though some people still maintain that the first creation story of Genesis is literally true, many others regard it as a 'myth' of profound and poetic quality. Among other things, it contains the message that the world is ultimately good (at the end of each day, God declared that what had been created was good) and that its existence is purposeful and planned.

This activity encourages children to move beyond a mere retelling of the Genesis creation story by reacting to the destruction of a product of creation and experiencing the act of creation for themselves.

Preparation
Choose a child to make a model with construction equipment, explaining that you will want to break it up in front of the

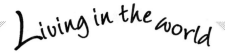

class. Make copies of photocopiable page 126 for those children carrying out the extension activity.

Resources needed

A children's Bible; a modern retelling of Genesis, chapters 1–2 (the creation story), for example 'The Seven Days' in *Creation Stories* by Jon Mayled (Wayland); construction equipment such as LEGO or clay, Plasticine and other modelling material. For the extension activity – photocopiable page 126: writing and drawing materials.

What to do

Show the children the previously made model. Ask the child who made it a number of questions.
▲ Are you pleased with it?
▲ Which part was the hardest to make?
▲ Did you follow a plan?
▲ Are you proud of what you have made?

Turn the model to show different views and 'accidentally' drop it. Allow sufficient time for the children to show and express their reactions before explaining that this had been previously arranged with the child who made it.

Show the children the Bible and explain that you are going to read a story which comes at the beginning of the Bible and is special to both Jews and Christians. Read an account of the first creation story. (You can read the children the story from the Bible or a modern version of it such as the one in *Creation Stories*.)

Ask the children how God felt in the story and why He needed to rest on the last day and wanted people to do the same.

Show the children the different construction materials you have gathered and ask them to choose one medium with which to make something. Once it is made, they should write about it and say how they felt as its creator.

Suggestion(s) for extension

For children requiring extension work, ask them to read the story either in the Bible or in the story book used in the main activity. Give each child a copy of photocopiable page 126 and ask them to write about and draw the different things created on each day.

Suggestion(s) for support

Some of the children may have difficulty in identifying their feelings about what they have made and will need to be prompted by an adult who could also scribe their responses.

Creation

Name _____   Date _____

On the first day God created _____	On the second day God created _____
On the third day God created _____	On the fourth day God created _____
On the fifth day God created _____	On the sixth day God created _____

On the seventh day God _____

Assessment opportunities

What children write and say when they have created something will provide evidence of how they have felt as a creator.

Opportunities for IT

Allow children an opportunity to use the computer and an art package to create their own picture. Older or more able children could use this picture in a word processor so that they could write about how they felt about it as the creator.

Display ideas

Display the children's three-dimensional models on a flat surface in front of a display board. Mount their writing, adding it to the board, and link each child's model and writing with a length of ribbon. Include a globe which is linked to the extension work. Title the whole display 'Look what we have made'. Give the globe and extension work another title, such as 'A story that Jews and Christians tell about how God made the world'.

Reference to photocopiable sheet

Photocopiable page 126, which is for use in the extension activity, gives children the opportunity to summarise and illustrate the creation story found in Genesis, chapters 1–2.

WHAT IS WONDERFUL ABOUT WHALES?

To encourage a reflective attitude towards living things.

Mystery. Relationship.

†† *Whole class, then individual work, followed by whole class.*

🕐 *Whole class 20 minutes; individual work 5–10 minutes; whole class 20 minutes.*

Key background information

The Whales' Song by Dyan Sheldon is one of a growing number of books which, through a combination of evocative text and illustration, have the capacity to 'touch' the reader in various ways. The illustrations, with their play of light and colour, have a haunting quality. The storyline contrasts the broad world of Lilly and her Grandma, who believe that relationship and response extend beyond human

RELIGIOUS EDUCATION

comprehension, with the narrow world of Uncle Frederick, in which material use is the only criterion of value.

This activity allows children to respond to the story – and to the ethereal sounds of whales – each in their own way. In that feelings can be expressed pictorially as well as verbally, they are asked to respond in picture form. Various types of assessment are possible in religious education, but because this activity is seeking to develop a particular type of attitude assessment has not been suggested. This should not prevent the teacher from evaluating the success of the activity as a whole.

Preparation
Obtain a copy of *The Whales' Song* (Red Fox) together with a picture showing whales. Obtain a whale song tape, making sure it lasts a sufficient amount of time for the activity below.

Resources needed
Picture of whales; copy of *The Whales' Song*; tape of whale sounds; drawing materials.

What to do
Show the children a picture of a whale or whales and ask them what they know about these creatures. Tell the children that they are going to hear a story about a girl who had a mysterious meeting with whales and, when the story finishes, they are going to draw a picture of how the story makes them feel. The drawing must be done by themselves without talking with others.

Read the story, making sure that the children can all see the illustrations. As the story ends, fade in the sounds of whales, allowing the children to listen for a few moments before they start their drawing. Leave the whale sounds playing while the children are working.

When the majority of children have completed the task, gather them together and ask some of them to show their pictures, explaining why they drew what they did. Collect the drawings together and ask some questions about the story.
▲ Why did Lilly's grandmother bring the whales something special?
▲ Why did Uncle Frederick not want Lilly to wait for the whales?
▲ Why did the whales come to see Lilly?
▲ Did the whales really call Lilly's name?

To finish the activity, ask the children to think about a special thing they could bring to the whales.

Suggestion(s) for extension
A group of children could write poems about their responses, either to the sounds of whales or to a picture in the story book.

Suggestion(s) for support
Some children may find it difficult to work silently. Give these children extra encouragement.

Opportunities for IT
The children could use a word processor to write their own whale poems. They could then add suitable illustrations, either drawn with an art package or taken from clip-art collections. Encourage them to use an encyclopaedia CD-ROM to search for further information about whales.

A more adventurous project would be to create a multimedia presentation about whales using authoring software. This could be a combination of factual information, a retelling of *The Whales' Song* by the children and their own poems about whales. The title page could contain a list of the different aspects to be covered so that, for example, when children click on 'Whale facts' they are taken to a series of linked pages about whales. A return picture (icon) will take the children back to the title page again. This is a fairly ambitious project and children will probably require extra support and help during the work.

Although aimed at older children, teachers may find some aspects of Topologika's *Whales and Dolphins* study pack useful. The pack contains databases, including some with pictures and whale sounds (Acorn Riscos only) and quizzes.

Display ideas
Use the picture of the whales as a centrepiece and surround it with the children's drawings and poems. You may like to add one or several quotations from the story, such as the first words spoken by Lilly's grandmother.

Following guidance

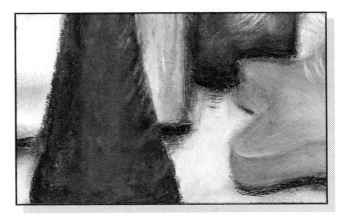

If the concept of 'authority' is significant to human experience in general, it is central to religious traditions of all types and varieties. Authority implies something or someone greater than yourself which directs or influences the way you live and interpret the world, the seen and the unseen. The teacher in the classroom or the guru in the religious community (the word 'guru' itself means 'teacher') carry authority each in their own sphere and in their own way. The same could be said of a book of rules for a game and an ancient sacred text.

The activities in this chapter give young children the opportunity to address a number of issues arising from human experience, such as identifying the books and the people that influence them. The issue of following or not following guidance is addressed through an exploration of a familiar fairy tale.

This chapter also introduces children to sacred texts which carry authority for the adherents of three major religious traditions: Christianity, Judaism and Islam. As they progress through their schooling, children should be able to learn more about such sacred writings and the many different ways in which their authority is expressed and experienced.

At a more difficult conceptual level, perhaps, three of the activities also explore the idea that religious belief has the power to change life or to compel actions. It is in the latter context that the much-loved story of Noah's ark is retold and rescued, some might say, from a frequent tendency to use it for any theme that is in any way remotely wet!

SHOULD LITTLE RED RIDING HOOD HAVE SPOKEN TO THE WOLF?

To understand that there can sometimes be consequences if guidance from elders is not followed.

Authority. Consequence.

†† *Session One: whole class followed by individual work. Session Two: whole class followed by individual work.*

🕐 *Session One: whole class 15 minutes; individual work 15 minutes. Session Two: whole class 15 minutes; individual work 10 minutes.*

Key background information

Little Red Riding Hood must be one of the most familiar fairy tales to the Western child. Even though it has been criticised and parodied (in *Politically Correct Bedtime Stories* by James Finn Garner, Souvenir Press, and *Revolting Rhymes* by Roald Dahl, Picture Puffin), it is unlikely to lose its popularity.

The story of *Little Red Riding Hood* exists in many versions, its first appearance in print being in French in 1697. The most familiar version is that told more than 100 years later by the Brothers Grimm, who called the main character 'Little Red Cap'.

Like all fairy stories, it works on a number of levels. In *The Uses of Enchantment: The Meaning and Importance of Fairy Tales* (Penguin), Bruno Bettelheim explored how this particular fairy story touches on a number of psychological needs and dilemmas of the growing child.

This activity offers an early opportunity to explore the role and place of authority. As such, it lays the foundation for developing an understanding of authority within religion and human experience. In asking the children to think about the consequences of their actions, the activity will also contribute to moral education.

A 'three-character' doll – one which, by moving pieces of fabric, changes to become Little Red Riding Hood, the Grandmother and the wolf – might be a very useful aid to this activity.

Preparation

Session One: make copies of photocopiable page 127, one per child. Make a single A3 copy of this sheet for your own use. Collect a variety of versions of the story of *Little Red Riding Hood* and display. Session Two: Prepare a corrected sequence of pictures. For the extension activity – make copies of photocopiable page 128.

Resources needed

Session One: collection of different versions of *Little Red Riding Hood*; photocopiable page 127; A3 single copy; additional mounting paper, such as coloured sugar paper. scissors; adhesive; drawing materials. Session Two: drawing materials; props. For the extension activity – photocopiable page 128; writing and drawing materials.

What to do
Session One

Show the children the A3 copy of photocopiable page 127, explaining that the pictures of the story have been mixed up and you need some help to sort them out. Look at each picture in turn and ask the children to describe what is happening. Ask them what story they think it is. Give each child their own copy of the sheet. Tell them to re-order the pictures by cutting them out and sticking them on to a second sheet or board, developing the story with each new picture. They could then colour the picture sequence. Make sure that emphasis is put on the first and last pictures – Little Red Riding Hood being told not to talk to strangers and being reunited with her parents. Ask the children whether Little Red Riding Hood should have spoken to the wolf.

Session Two

Use the corrected sequence of pictures from Session One to remind the children about the story of *Little Red Riding Hood*. Refer particularly to Red Riding Hood not doing what she was told by her mother.

Ask the children whether there have been times when they have disobeyed what an adult has told them. Listen to several children's examples, asking whether anything happened as a result.

Tell the children to paint or draw pictures of times when they have not done as they were told. As they are working, ask the children individually to tell you about their painting.

RELIGIOUS EDUCATION

With the addition of a few simple props (including different versions of the story), the imaginative play area could become grandmother's cottage.

Suggestion(s) for extension

Session One: photocopiable page 128 provides a list of sentences in an incorrect order. Give each child a copy of the sheet and ask them to match each sentence to the correct picture. Session Two: instead of just one picture, the older or more able children could draw or paint a sequence of pictures.

Suggestion(s) for support

Younger or less able children may need help with scissor control when cutting out their pictures.

Assessment opportunities

Listening to the children talking about their paintings will give some indication of the extent to which they have understood that it is important to follow the guidance of adults.

Opportunities for IT

Working individually or in pairs, younger children could use a concept keyboard linked to a word processor to create a printed, textual version of the story. The concept keyboard could either contain appropriate pictures so that when the children press the relevant picture a corresponding line of text appears on the screen, or the overlay could contain the sentences themselves in a jumbled order. Children could also use an art or drawing package to create their own Little Red Riding Hood picture.

An alternative approach would be to make a multimedia presentation of the story using authoring software. This could be in the form of a book, with each part of the story illustrated by the children. The pictures can be drawn using an art package, scanned from the children's own drawings or taken from clip-art collections. The children could add the text underneath the pictures and even include a spoken commentary, recorded using a microphone attached to the computer.

Display ideas

Mount the children's paintings and correctly sequenced stories. Write labels to accompany the paintings (what the children said about their paintings). Display these, together with a collection of Little Red Riding Hood story books, under the title 'Should Little Red Riding Hood have spoken to the wolf?' Alternatively, create a class 'big book' and add it to the resources in the reading area.

Little Red Riding Hood (2)
▲ Cut out the sentences and match them to the pictures.

Little Red Riding Hood's mummy said, 'Don't talk to strangers.'

Little Red Riding Hood said, 'What big teeth you have.'

Little Red Riding Hood was sorry

Little Red Riding Hood (1)
▲ Cut out the pictures and stick them in the correct order.

Reference to photocopiable sheets

Photocopiable page 127 is a sequencing activity for the children. One copy should be photocopied on to A3 paper and used to begin Session One. Photocopiable page 128 is for use in the extension activity. It provides a set of sentences for the children to match to the pictures on the first photocopiable sheet.

WHICH BOOKS ARE SPECIAL TO US?

To identify books which are special in our own lives and some of the reasons why. To understand that the way in which some books are treated indicates their special nature.

Specialness. Value.

✝✝ *Session One: whole class followed by individual work. Session Two: whole class.*

🕐 *Session One: whole class 15 minutes; individual work 15 minutes. Session Two: 15 minutes.*

Key background information

Though children are growing up in a world where information is stored and retrieved in an ever-increasing number of ways (the province of 'information technology'), the place of the book remains deeply significant.

A book is more than just a means of storing text. Unlike a floppy disk, the physicality of a book is part of its nature and character. A much-loved book, it has often been remarked, is more of a 'friend' or 'companion' than a 'tool'. As such, the ways in which books are handled express a range of assumptions, ideas, beliefs and values. The strong reaction of many adults against the habit of folding over the corner of a page in a book to mark the place reached is very revealing.

This activity complements work in other curriculum areas such as English by focusing on how, in the total range of books, some become marked out as 'special' for a number of reasons. Even at this stage, some of the children might identify religious books (for example prayer books, stories of religious figures, holy texts) as 'special' to themselves.

Preparation
Session One: display several recently read class books. Choose your own special book (for example, diary, holy book, photograph album, novel). Session Two: make a class 'big book', using the completed work from Session One.

Resources needed
Session One: selection of class books; your own special book; drawing materials. Session Two: class 'big book'.

What to do
Session One
Gather the children together and show them your own special book. Tell them some of the reasons why it is special, perhaps it was given to you by someone special, it is very old, the contents are special to you or the cover is beautifully decorated. Ask the children if anyone has a book which is special to them. Let the children, in turn, talk about their books and the reasons why they are special.

Give each child a blank piece of paper and ask the children to draw a front cover for their special book (if they do not have a special book, let them choose their favourite from books recently used in class). If the children can think of titles for their books, ask them to write them on the covers. They should then write or dictate to an adult scribe or another child a reason why the book is special and write this underneath their drawing of their book cover.

Session Two
Show the children the completed 'big book' from Session One and ask for suggestions as to where it can be kept and how it should be looked after. Ask questions to help the children reach a decision.
▲ Can the book be read during playtime if it is too wet to go outside?
▲ Can it be read by a child drinking milk?
▲ Should it be kept near the paint table?
▲ Should it be kept on the floor?
   Display and treat the 'big book' in the agreed ways.

Suggestion(s) for extension
Older or more confident children can help to make the class 'big book' by writing headings and designing a cover.

Suggestion(s) for support
Use the collection of recently read books in school to suggest ideas to those children who cannot readily identify their own special books.

Assessment opportunities
Listening to the children during the class discussion and looking at their completed drawings will show that the children are able to identify which books are special to them and

RELIGIOUS
EDUCATION

why. Observing the way in which the class 'big book' is used and treated will indicate the extent to which the children understand the importance of treating books respectfully.

Opportunities for IT
Let the children use an art package to create a picture for the cover of their special book. If necessary, demonstrate how to use the text facilities of the package so that the children can include the title and author of the book on their front cover.

Alternatively, children could use a word processor to write a brief account of why their particular book is special to them. Tell the children to select a suitable font and enlarge the type size so that the printed copy can be used as part of the display about special books.

Display ideas
Ask the children to bring their special books into school for a class display. The children may decide to include their class 'big book' in the display. It is important that the children understand that the books on display are special. Ask them to agree on a set of rules for the handling and treatment of the books.

but, because tax-collectors received no official pay, he obtained money for himself by adding his 'cut' to the tax amounts he had to collect. This was a system open to abuse.

Because he was small, Zacchaeus climbed a tree in order to see Jesus.

People have always had views about what 'holy people' should or should not do. The consternation can be imagined when Jesus not only addressed Zacchaeus but invited himself to his home!

The significance of the story for the early Christians who passed it on lies at the end. The meeting with Jesus transformed the world and the values of Zacchaeus. He gave away half of his belongings to the poor and more than amply repaid those he had cheated.

Preparation
Make copies of photocopiable page 129, one for each child. Make copies of photocopiable page 130 for those children carrying out the extension activity. Choose a version of the story of Zacchaeus.

Resources needed
Story of Zacchaeus (this can be found in *People Jesus Met* retold by W. Owen Cole and Judith Evans-Lowndes, Heinemann); photocopiable page 129; drawing materials; plain paper; scissors; adhesive. For the extension activity – photocopiable page 130; writing materials.

What to do
Read or tell the story of Zacchaeus, making sure that the children realise that the story comes from the Christian New Testament. Encourage the children to recount the events of the story in the correct sequence, then discuss with them:
▲ why Zacchaeus would want to see Jesus;
▲ why Jesus chose to eat with Zacchaeus;
▲ how the crowd would have felt when Jesus spoke to Zacchaeus;
▲ why Zacchaeus gave people their money back.

Divide the class into two groups with the task of dramatising the story. The characters that each group will need to choose are:
▲ Zacchaeus;
▲ Jesus;
▲ several disciples;
▲ the crowd in Jericho.

HOW DID JESUS CHANGE THE LIFE OF ZACCHAEUS?

To know a story associated with the life of Jesus. To understand that Christians believe that knowing Jesus can change people's lives.

Repentance. Redemption.

†† *Whole class, followed by large group work, ending with individual work.*

🕐 *Whole class 20 minutes; large group work 20 minutes; individual 20 minutes.*

Key background information
The story of Zacchaeus' meeting with Jesus is exclusive to Luke's Gospel (chapter 19). Luke places the event in the ancient Jordan valley city of Jericho as Jesus was passing through on the way to Jerusalem for the last time.

As a tax-collector, Zacchaeus would have been a despised outcast. Not only did he work for the Roman occupying forces

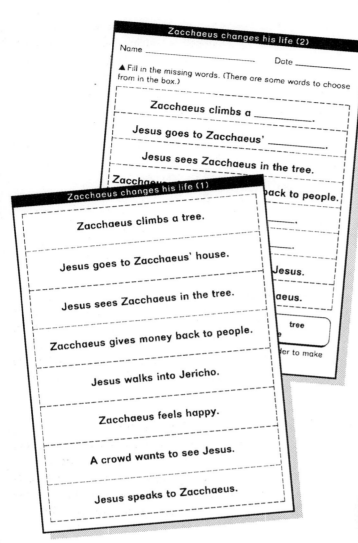

Zacchaeus changes his life (2)

Name _____ Date _____

▲ Fill in the missing words. (There are some words to choose from in the box.)

Zacchaeus climbs a _____.

Jesus goes to Zacchaeus' _____

Jesus sees Zacchaeus in the tree.

Zacchaeus changes his life (1)

Zacchaeus climbs a tree.

Jesus goes to Zacchaeus' house.

Jesus sees Zacchaeus in the tree.

Zacchaeus gives money back to people.

Jesus walks into Jericho.

Zacchaeus feels happy.

A crowd wants to see Jesus.

Jesus speaks to Zacchaeus.

the story. The final sentence in the sequence links directly with the belief that knowing Jesus can change people's lives.

Opportunities for IT
Using a concept keyboard linked to a word processor, children can write a printed, textual version of the story.

Assembly ideas
As part of an assembly focusing on a theme such as 'Special people' or 'Bible stories', one group of children can perform their dramatisation of the Zacchaeus story. The remaining children can ask, and give answers to, the four questions discussed in the activity and show paintings illustrating the story. You may like to end the assembly with a reflection such as, 'And now, in a moment of quiet, let us think about Zacchaeus and how we might show others that we are sorry for things we have done.'

Reference to photocopiable sheets
Two versions of the photocopiable sheet for this activity are provided. Photocopiable page 129, for use in the main activity, requires the children to sequence the sentences in the correct order. Photocopiable page 130, for use in the extension activity, requires the insertion of missing words as well as sequencing.

WHEN DO JEWS DANCE IN THE SYNAGOGUE?

To understand how the festival of Simchat Torah shows how special the Torah is for Jews.

Celebration. Scripture.

†† *Whole class followed by individual work.*
🕐 *Whole class 25 minutes; individual work 15 minutes.*

Give each group a time limit, at the end of which they must perform to the other half of the class. After the performances, give each child some plain paper, crayons, a copy of photocopiable page 129, scissors and adhesive. Ask them to cut out the sentences, place them in the correct order and then illustrate each one.

Suggestion(s) for extension
If children require extension work, give them a copy of photocopiable page 130 and ask them to fill in the missing words, sequence the sentences and then draw a picture of Jesus and Zacchaeus on a separate sheet.

Suggestion(s) for support
If children are not confident about what to do, discuss the sheet with them first and let them number the sentences before cutting them out.

Assessment opportunities
Sequencing and illustrating the story on photocopiable page 129, which might be undertaken at a later time, provides an assessment of the children's knowledge (and retention) of

Key background information
The *Torah* – sometimes translated 'Law' but better translated as 'Teaching' or 'Instruction' – refers to the first five 'books' of the Jewish Bible: Genesis, Exodus, Leviticus, Numbers and Deuteronomy. The words and teachings in these books, Jews believe, are from God. (NB Many Jews would write this word as 'G-d' because of its sacredness.) They form the basis of Jewish belief and practice and are a focus of intense study.

Each of the five books of the Torah is written by hand in Hebrew on to a scroll. The Torah scrolls are treated with great care and honour and are dressed in special ornamented covers. Together with scrolls of other books from the Jewish Bible, they are kept in a special cupboard called an *ark* at the front of a synagogue.

RELIGIOUS EDUCATION

It takes a year to read out the Torah from beginning to end during synagogue services. *Simchat Torah* ('Rejoicing in the Torah', the 'ch' in Sim<u>ch</u>at Torah being pronounced like the 'ch' in the Scottish lo<u>ch</u>) marks the end of one cycle of readings and the beginning of the next.

The Torah has sometimes been described as the 'bride of Israel'. The mood at Simchat Torah has been compared to that at a Jewish wedding.

Preparation

Obtain a miniature copy of a Torah scroll (see 'Useful books and resources', page 107). Become familiar with what the Torah is and what happens at Simchat Torah. Make copies of photocopiable page 131, one for each child. Make copies of photocopiable page 132 for those children carrying out the extension activity.

Resources needed

Miniature copy of Torah scroll; photocopiable page 131; writing materials. For the extension activity – photocopiable page 132.

What to do

Gather the children together and tell them that they are going to see something that is special for a group of people called Jews. Show the children the Torah scroll, handling it carefully so as to emphasise the respect with which Jews treat it.

While the children are looking at the scroll, explain the importance of the Torah to Jews – the fact that it is special because it tells them stories about God and important people.

Ask the children about things that are special to them – where they keep them and how they look after them.

Tell the children that the Torah is kept in a special cupboard called an ark at the front of a synagogue. The Torah scrolls are so important to Jews that they have a special day when they are celebrated every year. Explain that this day is called 'Simchat Torah' and the following things happen:

▲ Jews meet together in the synagogue.

▲ All the Torah scrolls are taken out of the ark.

▲ The scrolls are carried around the synagogue seven times.

▲ While the scrolls are being carried, people show how happy they feel – there is singing, the people carrying the scrolls may dance, children may wave little flags which sometimes have apples attached to the top of the flag-sticks.

▲ Someone reads out the very last words of the Torah, followed by another person reading out the very first words.

Give each child a copy of photocopiable page 131 and ask them to fill in the missing words.

Suggestion(s) for extension

Give each child a copy of photocopiable page 132 and ask them to complete the description. There are words to help them at the bottom of the page.

Suggestion(s) for support

Some children may need a further explanation of why Simchat Torah is important for Jews before completing photocopiable page 131.

Assessment opportunities

Watching the children handling the Torah scroll will reveal their sensitivity towards its specialness for Jews. The completed photocopiable sheets will give some indication of their knowledge of what happens at Simchat Torah.

Display ideas

Display the miniature Torah scroll on a piece of cloth (or within a small cardboard cupboard to represent the ark). Mount the children's work and arrange around the Torah scroll. You may like to use a heading such as 'At the festival of Simchat Torah, Jews show how special the Torah is for them'.

Reference to photocopiable sheets

Photocopiable page 131 requires the children to fill in missing words in a simplified account of Simchat Torah. Photocopiable page 132 is more demanding in that, although there are key words to help them, the children have to identify how Jews show their love of the Torah at Simchat Torah.

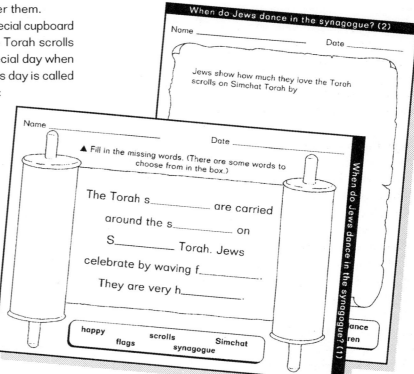

FOR WHOM IS THE BIBLE A SPECIAL BOOK?

To know that the Bible is a special book for Christians.
To know that the Bible is divided into two parts.

Special book. Holy book.

†† *Whole class.*
🕐 *30 minutes.*

Key background information

This straightforward activity could be linked to other activities focusing on certain parts or aspects of the Bible (see 'Who is special to me?', page 19; 'How did the world come to be?', page 46; 'Why did Noah build the Ark?', page 61; 'How did Jesus change the life of Zacchaeus', page 53; 'What special story is told at Christmas?', page 82).

The Bible is in reality a collection of writings, the word itself coming from the Greek for 'books'. The first Christians believed that they were building on and completing the truths revealed in the Jewish sacred writings – what Christians came to call the 'Old Testament'. To this were added 27 other specifically Christian writings – the 'New Testament'. Thus, the Christian Bible consists of both Old and New Testaments.

The Jewish sacred writings were originally mostly written in Hebrew, while the whole of the Christian New Testament was written in Greek. In time, and as Christianity spread, there came a need to translate the Bible into other languages. Some passages of the Bible were translated into the languages of England in Anglo-Saxon days but the first officially authorised version (the word 'version' technically means a translation) was that produced at the command of King James I in 1611 – the 'Authorised Version'. Many English versions of the Bible have appeared in the twentieth century, each trying to make its language and spirit accessible to its readers.

The story of Jesus' boyhood visit to the Jerusalem Temple referred to in this activity is unique to Luke's Gospel (chapter 2, verses 41–50) and is the only boyhood story of Jesus contained in the New Testament. Other stories of what the child Jesus said and did were told but were not included in the New Testament Gospels.

Preparation

Obtain and display a selection of different kinds of Bible, for example children's version, leather-covered, large, small, family.

Resources needed

Different types of Bibles (including a children's Bible).

What to do

Begin by showing the children a copy of the Bible. Tell them that it is a special book for many people and remind them how carefully special books should be treated. Ask if anyone knows anything about the Bible. Listen to the answers, emphasising any that give particular information about the Bible (it's about God, it's about Jesus, it contains stories). If no one has mentioned that the Bible is special for Christians, introduce this now. Show the children the two parts of the Bible – the Old Testament and the New Testament – and tell them that Christians can read stories about Jesus in the second part – the New Testament. Using a children's version of the Bible, read a story about Jesus from the New Testament, for example Jesus visiting the Temple as a boy.

Suggestion(s) for extension

Ask children to look through the different types of Bible on display to find the story they were told during the activity.

Suggestion(s) for support

Some children may need a further explanation of, and a closer look at, the children's version of the Bible and its two sections – the Old and New Testaments.

Assessment opportunities

Children could be asked, at a later stage, who the Bible is special for and how many parts it has, which will allow you

RELIGIOUS EDUCATION

to assess whether they have understood its significance for many people and that it is divided in to two parts.

Display ideas
Leave the Bibles on display for the children to look through at a later stage.

WHY IS THE QUR'AN A SPECIAL BOOK FOR MUSLIMS?

To understand why Muslims believe that the Qur'an is special. To understand why the use of a Qur'an stand indicates the special status of the Qur'an for Muslims.

Holy Book. Message.

✝✝ *Whole class followed by individual work.*
🕐 *Whole class 30 minutes; individual work 30 minutes.*

Key background information
Muslims believe that *Allah* (God) made his will known down the ages through a succession of prophets (messengers). Sometimes the message was written down, but never perfectly. It was left to Muhammad (570–632 CE), the final prophet, to receive the message and deliver it without error.

Muslims believe that the words of the Qur'an are the Arabic words which Muhammad was given and told to recite. The first words that he was given at the cave Hira near Makkah, traditionally by the angel Gabriel, are to be found in Surah (chapter) 96 of the Qur'an and begin with the Arabic word 'iqra' meaning 'recite'. It is from this word that the title *Qur'an* derives which can therefore be translated as 'recitation'.

The Qur'an is revered by Muslims as the words of Allah. Because the words were delivered in Arabic, the Qur'an itself is always the Arabic Qur'an. Translations are useful for those who cannot speak Arabic, but they are translations, not the Qur'an itself.

Muslims honour the Qur'an in many ways. It is handled with great care and, before reading from it, Muslims will wash their hands. When being read from, it will be raised off the floor. A wooden Qur'an stand might be used for this. A familiar design consists of a rectangular piece of wood, carved with floral patterns, which is hinged at the centre so that it opens out in an X-shape.

Because of respect for Muslim beliefs about the Qur'an, teachers will usually handle the Qur'an with care and dignity. If they possess a copy of the Qur'an, they might keep it wrapped and on a high shelf, above other books – as would Muslims. Some teachers will wash their hands before handling the Qur'an in class and inform the children that they have done so. For Muslim children, this can be particularly reassuring.

Preparation
Obtain a Qur'an stand (see 'Useful books and resources', page 107) and place it in a special bag, for example velvet, satin, silk. Make a copy of photocopiable page 133.

Resources needed
Qur'an stand (see 'Preparation'); special bag; photocopiable page 133; writing and drawing materials.

What to do

Sit the children in a circle and tell them that they are going to see something which is special to a group of people called Muslims. Pass the velvet bag to several children in turn and ask them to describe what they can feel through the bag. Carefully remove the Qur'an stand from the bag and ask questions to encourage the children to look at it carefully.

▲ Does it move?

▲ Can it be opened?

▲ What is it made of?

▲ What are the patterns on it?

▲ What could it be used for?

If there are Muslim children in the class, this will be an opportunity to share their experiences of using or seeing a Qur'an stand being used. If there is no child with previous knowledge, then explain how and why a Qur'an stand is used (see 'Key background information'). To indicate further the importance of the Qur'an to Muslims, use photocopiable page 133 to read the Muslim story of how Muhammad received the first words of the Qur'an. When you have finished, ask the children to draw a picture of a Qur'an stand. On the board write the starter sentence 'Many Muslims use a Qur'an stand because...'. Ask the children to copy this underneath their drawing and then complete the sentence.

Suggestion(s) for extension

If children require extension work, ask them to write their own account of Muhammad receiving the first words of the Qur'an.

Suggestion(s) for support

Some children may require a further explanation of why the Qur'an stand is used before completing the starter sentence.

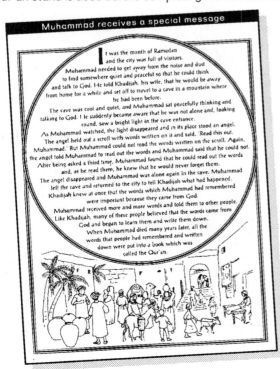

Assessment opportunities

The explanation which children write underneath their drawing will provide evidence of the extent to which they have understood why the use of a Qur'an stand indicates the special status of the Qur'an for Muslims.

Reference to photocopiable sheet

Photocopiable page 133 gives a simplified version of the story of Muhammad receiving the first words of the Qur'an and is for the teacher's use.

WHY DID JOAN OF ARC LEAD AN ARMY?

To know about the life of Joan of Arc. To understand that some people are prepared to die for their belief in God.

Authority. Mission.

✝✝ *Whole class followed by group work.*

🕐 *Whole class 30 minutes; group work 45 minutes.*

Key background information

Joan of Arc (Jeanne d'Arc), sometimes called the 'Maid of Orléans', was born at Domrémy in the Champagne region of France in about 1412 and died in 1431. She was canonised – officially declared to be a saint by the Roman Catholic Church – in 1920. (For the use of the title 'saint', see 'Why is St Francis special for some Christians?', page 40.) Her feast day, the day each year when Roman Catholics celebrate her life, is 30 May.

Joan has been an object of great interest down the ages – George Bernard Shaw's play *St Joan* (1923) was his

greatest box-office success – and her state of mind much questioned. She was not unique in Christian history in claiming to have seen visions and heard voices. In this, and in her poor village background, there is an obvious parallel with St Bernadette (see 'Why do some Christians go to Lourdes?', page 92).

Preparation
Make a copy of photocopiable page 134 and become familiar with the story. Gather collage materials together to make the frieze.

Resources needed
Photocopiable page 134; collage materials.

What to do
Ask the children the question, 'Have you ever been told to do something you didn't think you could do?' Listen to the children's answers. Tell them they are going to hear a story about a young girl who was told to do something that she didn't think she could do. Read or tell the story of Joan of Arc.

After the children have heard the story, ask them questions about it to deepen their understanding.
▲ What did Joan's friends think when she told them about her voices?
▲ Why did Joan not want to do what the voices told her?
▲ What made Joan change her mind?
▲ Why did Joan carry a flag with the names Jesus and Mary on it?
▲ Why did Joan refuse to say that the voices had not come from God?
▲ Why do some Christians believe that Joan was a saint?

Divide the class into four groups. Ask the four groups to make a frieze of Joan of Arc leading her army to Orléans, each group making one part; Joan riding her horse, the soldiers marching, the buildings of Orléans, a large flag with the words 'Mary' and 'Jesus' on it.

Suggestion(s) for extension
Ask the children to rewrite the story of Joan of Arc's life in their own words. These can then be used to accompany the frieze.

Suggestion(s) for support
Some children may like to work with an adult helper or support teacher when discussing the story.

Assessment opportunities
An indication of the extent to which the children have understood the story of Joan of Arc, and the fact that some people will not deny their religious beliefs, may be ascertained by:
▲ listening to the answers to the questions following the story;
▲ listening to the children's conversations while they are making the frieze;
▲ reading and discussing the written accounts.

Opportunities for IT
Children could use a word processor when writing their stories of Joan of Arc to accompany the frieze. Remind them that their stories will be on display, so they will need to be in a type size large enough to be read from a distance.

RELIGIOUS
EDUCATION

The story of Joan of Arc

Many years ago, in a village in France, a baby girl was born called Jeanne d'Arc. She grew up in the village and, although she didn't learn to read or write, she helped her father look after his sheep and helped her mother in the house. Jeanne knew many people who had gone to fight in a war with England. Many of them had been hurt or killed.

When Jeanne was 13, she began to hear voices speaking to her in her head, but no one else heard them. After a while, Jeanne began to see visions of the people who were speaking to her. Jeanne said that they were all people who loved God. Sometimes the voices told her that she must go to church. At other times, the voices told her that she must help France fight the war against the English. Every time Jeanne heard the voices, she would say that she was only a poor village girl and she couldn't possibly do as she was being asked. But the voices didn't stop, and when they said that God was telling her to help France she decided that she must try.

Jeanne travelled to the nearest town where French soldiers were staying. She asked to see the person in charge of the army. When Jeanne told him that God wanted her to help him fight, he just laughed at her and sent her away. But Jeanne did not give up and eventually she

was taken to see Prince Charles, the son of the French king. The prince listened to Jeanne and believed what she told him about hearing voices. He gave her an army of soldiers to lead, a black horse to ride, a suit of white armour to wear and a flag with the names 'Jesus' and 'Mary' on it. He also gave her a sword, but Jeanne said that she would never use it.

Jeanne led her army to the town of Orléans, which had been captured by the English, listening to the voices which spoke to her all the way. In less than two weeks Orléans was free and Jeanne led her army to the city of Rheims, where Prince Charles was crowned king of France. Jeanne told the king that she had done what God had wanted her to do.

Jeanne didn't hear the voices again but carried on leading her army. After one battle, she was caught by her English enemies and put in prison. Her guards told her that she would be set free if she said that the voices she heard had not come from God. Jeanne kept on saying that the voices had come from God so she was taken to the market place in the town of Rouen, tied to a post and burned to death.

The story of Jeanne's bravery has been told by French and English people ever since. The English call her 'Joan of Arc'. Many Christians believe she was a saint.

Display ideas

Mount the written account of Joan of Arc's life and display it with the assembled frieze.

Reference to photocopiable sheet

Photocopiable page 134 gives a simplified version of the Joan of Arc story and is for the teacher's use.

WHO HAS INFLUENCED YOU MOST?

To understand that significant people can shape and influence the lives of others. To identify a person who has influenced your life.

Authority. Leadership.

†† *Session One: whole class. Session Two: individual and paired work.*

🕒 *Session One: 15 minutes. Session Two: individual and paired work 40 minutes.*

Key background information

All people, whether they consider themselves religious or not, are influenced by others – consciously or otherwise. In one sense, each person is a kind of mosaic consisting of the influences and imprints of others.

Within religious traditions, the role of the 'authority figure' is particularly marked. Such figures might, for example, be 'founders', models of belief or action, or contemporary leaders. Within a certain tradition, some people might consider themselves to be 'disciples' – those who follow the 'discipline' exemplified in the life of, or taught by, an authority figure.

This activity provides an opportunity for children to begin to reflect on those people whom they admire and who are therefore probably influencing them. Some of the children might choose religious figures. If this happens, teachers need to be sensitive to feelings about depicting them in art.

RELIGIOUS EDUCATION

Muslims, for example, would not wish to draw the prophet Muhammad, and a Muslim child who chooses Muhammad in this activity might be asked to draw something else instead (a picture of a mosque, the Ka'bah in Makkah, or to do some calligraphy perhaps).

Preparation

Session One: find a photograph or picture of someone who has influenced your life. This may be an author, religious leader, teacher, parent, friend, politician and so on. Gather together a selection of pictures and photographs for those children carrying out the support activity.

Resources needed

Photograph or picture of a person who has influenced you; art materials. For the support activity – collection of pictures and photographs.

What to do

Session One

Show the class a photograph or picture of a person who has had a positive influence on your life. Talk about the ways in which your life has been affected by the influence of this person.

Ask the children to bring in to school a picture or a photograph of a person who has influenced their lives.

Session Two

Using the photographs or pictures brought in by the children as a stimulus, ask the children to make a list of things they do as a result of knowing that person (for example, things they wear, food they like, how they behave, how they treat others). When they have finished, they can tell a friend about the person.

Choosing from a variety of art materials, for example pencil, paint, charcoal, pastels, the children can create their own portrait of the person they have written about.

Suggestion(s) for extension

More confident children can interview a number of adults associated with the school community about the people who have most influenced them. Prior to doing this, they should agree on a set of questions to ask.

Suggestion(s) for support

Have a supply of pictures and photographs ready, for instance previous teachers, classroom assistants, current pop stars,

television personalities for those children who do not provide their own.

Assessment opportunities

Achievement of the learning objectives will be indicated by children being able to identify a person who has influenced them and being able to give at least one way in which that influence reveals itself.

Opportunities for IT

Ask the children to use a word processor to write about how their chosen person has influenced their life, or to write the list of things that they do as a result of knowing that person. When these are completed, print them out and mount them alongside the children's portraits or photographs of their chosen people.

Display ideas

Mount the children's portraits. Display the portraits, together with the lists about how these people have affected the lives of the children, under a heading such as 'People who have influenced us'.

WHY DID NOAH BUILD THE ARK?

To understand that some people believe that God wants them to do certain things. To reflect on the experience of being told to do something without understanding why.

Obedience. Conflict.

†† *Groups, followed by whole class, returning to groups.*

🕐 *Group work 15 minutes; whole class 15 minutes; group work 30 minutes.*

Key background information

Probably few other biblical stories have so gripped people's imaginations down the ages as the story of Noah's Ark. Few modern Western toy shops will be without a Noah's Ark jigsaw, picture or wooden toy.

Like the Christmas Nativity story, the biblical account (Genesis, chapters 6–9) is far more complex and varied than the story of popular imagination. (Genesis intertwines various

strands of the story, including Noah being told to take into the ark seven of every kind of clean animal – see Genesis, chapter 7, verse 2.) The story of Noah is also referred to in the Muslim Qur'an and there are many other flood stories in world literature and folk traditions.

The story of Noah has a firm place in primary school practice. Yet there are many in the field of religious education who would wish to see it banned from the primary school. What view of God, they would argue, does the story perpetuate – a God who drowns all living things on earth except for a select few?

This activity uses a simplified version of the story to achieve two learning objectives. In encouraging children to reflect on the consequences of following or not following instructions, this activity will make a contribution to their moral and social education.

Preparation
Make a copy of photocopiable page 135 and become familiar with the Noah's Ark story. Decide on membership of role-play groups.

Resources needed
Photocopiable page 135.

What to do
Divide the children into groups of between six and eight. Tell them that they are going to do some role-play which involves the following characters:
▲ one or two parents;
▲ a child;
▲ several friends of the child.

Next, outline the situation they are going to role-play: the child is going on an educational visit to a zoo. It is a very hot day with blue skies. The child wants to wear trainers or sandals, whereas the parent says that the child must wear wellingtons. Let the children role-play the situation to its outcome. As they are working, go round each group and make a note of how each situation develops.

Gather the children together, making no reference to their role-play. Explain that there is a story in the Bible about a man called Noah who was told to do something which his friends probably thought was very silly. Read the story of Noah on photocopiable page 135.

Ask the children what happened in their role-play situation, letting each group explain to the others. Then reveal that, when the children got to the zoo, the sky turned grey and it began to rain. So the children who wore wellingtons were allowed to walk around the zoo, while the children who wore sandals and trainers had to stay in the reptile house.

Regroup the children as before and give them time to decide whether they want to change their role-play in the light of what they have just learned. Once they have agreed on their role-play, let the groups perform to each other.

Suggestion(s) for extension
Ask the children to consider the question, 'Should people always do as they are told, even if they don't understand the reason?' and draw up a list of reasons for and against.

Suggestion(s) for support:
Make sure that each role-play group includes more confident as well as less confident children.

Assessment opportunities
Listening to the children working in their role-play groups, particularly at the stage at which they decide whether to change their scenario, will indicate the extent to which they have reflected on the experience of being told to do something without understanding the reason for the request.

Assembly ideas
As part of an assembly focusing on a theme such as 'Doing as we're told' or 'My favourite story', make a display of objects and pictures with a Noah's Ark theme to serve as a visual focal point. After the story of Noah's Ark has been told, ask a group of children to explain what they did in class. This could be followed by another group performing their role-play. Play relevant music, such as part of Benjamin Britten's *Noye's Fludde*, as the children enter and leave.

Reference to photocopiable sheet
Photocopiable page 135 gives a simplified version of the Noah's Ark story, focusing on Noah's obedience to God, and is read to the children during the activity.

RELIGIOUS
EDUCATION

Encountering special times

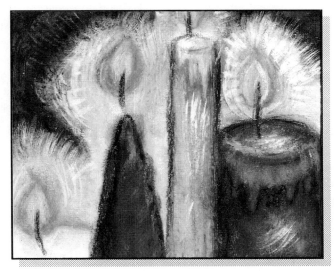

To be human, it could be said, is to celebrate. If there were no religion in the world, people would still feel the need to celebrate and to mark out special times as festivals. If there were no religious education in the curriculum, teachers in infant schools would still ritualise birthdays in order to focus on the individuality and specialness of each child.

Thus, the notion of 'special time' is part of general human experience, and several activities in this chapter are provided to give specific opportunities for children to begin to explore and understand what this means. Creating a birthday party for Teddy is the vehicle for the youngest children, while for the oldest it is designing an 'Elmer's Day' festival based on the well-known story by David McKee.

For both cultural and religious reasons, Easter and Christmas are firmly established in the lives of infant schools. There has been a frequent concern, though, that classroom work focusing on them has lacked continuity and progression. In outlining a different but increasingly complex way of exploring each of these festivals across Key Stage 1, this chapter provides a remedy for this concern.

The remaining activities in the chapter focus on a special time drawn from each of the principal religious traditions: Buddhist, Christian, Hindu, Jewish, Muslim and Sikh.

HOW IS CHRISTMAS CELEBRATED?

To understand what celebration means. To know that Christmas is celebrated in a range of ways, including the giving of presents.

Celebration. Special time.

†† *Whole class followed by individual work.*
🕐 *Whole class 15 minutes; individual work 15 minutes.*

Key background information

Even in their first four or five years, children will have experienced a range of special times. In this activity, they can begin to develop an understanding of how and why special times are celebrated.

As they grow older, children should have the opportunity to explore the Christmas festival in deeper and more complex ways. In this activity, the main focus is on presents but with the children as present-givers rather than present-receivers.

It will need to be remembered that Jehovah's Witness families will probably not want their children to participate in Christmas-related activities. Because the Christmas festival is not explicitly mentioned in the Bible, Jehovah's Witnesses do not acknowledge it.

Preparation

Find a picture of Father Christmas. Write the word 'celebrate' on a piece of card.

Resources needed

Picture of Father Christmas; card with the word 'celebrate' written on it; chalkboard/flip chart; writing and drawing materials.

What to do

Sit the children in a circle and show them a picture of Father Christmas. Ask the children questions about the picture.
▲ Who is this?
▲ When do you see him?
▲ How do you feel when you see him?
▲ Why is he special?
   Ask the children what other special things they see and

do at Christmas, for example decorating Christmas trees, putting up decorations, writing cards, giving presents, opening Advent calendars, looking at Nativity scenes, eating special food, wishing people 'Happy Christmas'. Make a list on the board as children give their answers. Read through the list with the children.

Display the card with the word 'celebrate' written on it. Read it and ask the children what they think the word means. If the children find this difficult, help them by referring back to the list and explaining that these are all ways in which people celebrate Christmas.

Remind the children that one way in which people celebrate Christmas is by giving presents. Ask them to think about a special present they would give to someone at Christmas time. When they have thought of a present, give each child a plain sheet of paper and ask the children to draw a picture of their present. While the children are drawing, visit each table and ask them who their present is for and why they have chosen it. Ask them to write their answers on their sheet. You may need to scribe for some children.

Suggestion(s) for extension

Older or more able children can choose one of the ways of celebrating Christmas from the list, copy it and draw a picture to illustrate it.

Suggestion(s) for support

Children who are having difficulty in identifying a person or a present may find it helpful to hear what other children are doing. Encourage children with good ideas to share them with the rest of the class.

Assessment opportunities

The suggestions for the list will show whether the children understand that Christmas is celebrated in a range of ways. The discussion focusing on the word 'celebrate' will show whether they have grasped the meaning of the concept.

Display ideas

Wrap a variety of boxes in Christmas paper. Write a large label for each box using information from the children's work. For example, 'This is a scarf for my granny because she likes to keep warm.' Add the child's name to each label. Display the boxes together with the title 'We give presents to celebrate Christmas'.

HOW CAN WE CELEBRATE TEDDY'S BIRTHDAY?

To understand the nature and purpose of group celebration.

Celebration. Special time.

✝✝ *Session One: whole class followed by group work. Session Two: whole class.*

🕐 *Session One: whole class 15 minutes; groups as appropriate. Session Two: 60 minutes.*

⚠ *If birthday candles are lit during the activity, warn children of potential dangers.*

Key background information

This activity provides a foundation for understanding the place and purpose of celebration within religious traditions. It also provides a context for social education and development, in that the children, regardless of the religious commitment of their families, will be drawn into many forms of celebrating special times – such as parties. This activity includes customs and conventions that they will encounter socially.

It will need to be remembered that Jehovah's Witness families, because they do not recognise birthday celebrations, will probably not want their children to participate in birthday-related activities.

Preparation

Session One: choose a teddy to show to the class. Make copies of photocopiable page 136, one for each child. Gather ingredients and materials for party preparation. Session Two: display the majority of birthday cards made in Session One. Arrange the room for a party. Put up decorations, including those made by the children in Session One. Choose games and music to use in the party. Put candles on to a birthday cake being aware of health and safety. Wrap up a present for Teddy.

Resources needed

Session One: teddy; craft materials; party food; photocopiable page 136; writing and drawing materials. Session Two: birthday cake; music; materials for party games; loaded camera; cards and decorations made by the children in Session One.

What to do
Session One

Sit the children in a circle and introduce them to your teddy. Tell them a little bit about Teddy's background, for instance:

▲ where he came from;
▲ his name;
▲ where he is kept;
▲ how old he is.

Say that it will soon be his birthday.

Explain that Teddy wants to have a birthday party and would like to invite all the children's teddies to help him celebrate. Teddy needs some help in planning his birthday party.

Ask the children for their ideas about how Teddy's birthday party can be celebrated. Their list should include invitations, decorations, birthday cards, birthday hats, food, songs, games, presents, candles on a cake.

Divide the children into groups, giving each group one task:

▲ making birthday cards;
▲ making birthday hats for their own teddies;
▲ making decorations;
▲ filling in the party invitations on photocopiable page 136 before decorating them and cutting them out;
▲ making party food – such as making small cakes, decorating biscuits, pouring orange squash into party cups.

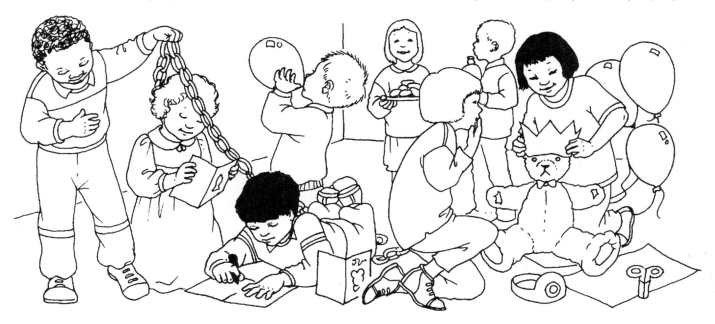

Allow each child to have the opportunity to work at each task. Let the children take their invitation home to give to their own teddy or other cuddly toy.

Session Two

Sit the children in a circle with their teddies wearing their party hats. Seat the birthday teddy where he can easily be seen and begin the birthday party. The party could include:

▲ playing party games;

▲ singing 'Happy Birthday';

▲ giving Teddy some of his birthday cards (the majority of these having already been displayed);

▲ giving Teddy a present;

▲ letting Teddy blow out his birthday candles (with some help!);

▲ eating party food.

Take photographs throughout the party for later display.

Assessment opportunities

The focus of this activity is engaging the children in the spirit and rhythm of celebration. The children's understanding of the nature and purpose of group celebration can be established when they are older.

Opportunities for IT

Let the children use an art or drawing package to make a birthday card for their teddy. They should use the software to draw their design, add a happy birthday message and then print it out. The picture can then be stuck on to a folded piece of card to make a birthday card. The children may also like to word-process a short verse or greeting to go inside the card.

Alternatively, children could use a word processo simple desktop publishing package to design a p invitation. The emphasis here should be on the essen information of th invitation, so th keyboarding time can b kept to a minimum. Th children can the concentrate on the presentation of their invitation. Encourage them to experiment with different features of the computer, such as using different fonts and sizes, formatting using the centre command, and adding colour to make the invitation more interesting. It may even be possible to put a border around the invitation or to include pictures taken from suitable clip art.

There are also several packages available specifically for making invitations and cards and these could be used for either activity. (These include Clare's *Celebrations* pack and Intuit's *Announcements*.)

Display ideas

Under the heading 'We celebrated Teddy's birthday', display the birthday cards, invitations, decorations and photographs of the party. Additional headings could be used, such as 'We made birthday cards', 'We played games', 'We ate party food'. Alternatively, create a book of photographs and captions and add it to the resources in the book corner.

Reference to photocopiable sheet

Photocopiable page 136 provides a blank invitation for the children to complete, decorate and cut out.

WHY DO WE HAVE EGGS AT EASTER?

To understand the link between eggs, new life and Easter.

Symbolism. New life.

✝✝ *Whole class followed by individual work.*

🕐 *Whole class 15 minutes; individual work 20–30 minutes.*

Key background information

Though Christmas is firmly embedded within primary school practice, the same cannot be said of Easter. Many teachers feel ambivalent or awkward about the central Easter story focusing, as it does, on death and resurrection. Yet Easter is the key Christian festival. It celebrates an experience without which there would be no Christians.

This simple activity, which focuses on new life rather than on the Easter story itself, lays a foundation for later work on Easter and the Easter festival.

Preparation

Make a collection of different types of egg. These could include chocolate, hens, wooden, marble, painted and so on. Obtain a decorative fluffy chick. Make copies of photocopiable page 137 on to thin card (or mount on to card) and cut out one chick shape and two egg shapes for each child.

Resources needed

Collection of eggs; decorative fluffy chick; photocopiable page 137; material to make the pop-up cards: yellow cotton or kapok, card, lollipop sticks, adhesive, felt-tipped pens or crayons.

What to do

Show the children a collection of different kinds of egg. Ask some of the children to sort them and explain their criteria for sorting. If no one has sorted into 'real' and 'not real' (hens' eggs and the rest), demonstrate how the eggs can be sorted in this way.

Ask the children what comes from hens' eggs, showing them a decorative fluffy chick to help or reinforce their answers.

Explain that many people think of eggs at Easter time because they are thinking about new life.

Tell the children that they are going to make a pop-up chick Easter card. Give each child one chick shape and two egg shapes (see 'Preparation'). First let them decorate the egg shapes, using crayons or felt-tipped pens, and cover the chick with yellow cotton wool or kapok. Then explain that they should fix a lollipop stick to the back of the chick

and paste the sides of the egg together, leaving a gap at the bottom of the egg to allow the chick to be pushed up and down using the lollipop stick. This shows new life emerging from the egg.

Suggestion(s) for extension

Ask children to think about other forms of new life at Easter time such as daffodils, lambs, buds on trees, and to draw each one.

Suggestion(s) for support

Some children may have difficulty in making the pop-up card, particularly the cutting-out. You may find it useful to have an adult helper or support teacher on hand to give extra support where necessary.

Assessment opportunities

While the children are making their cards, they could be asked why they are putting a chick and an egg on their Easter card. Their answers will reveal the extent to which they have understood the link between Easter and new life.

RELIGIOUS EDUCATION

Why do we have eggs at Easter?

Display ideas

Display the children's Easter cards alongside the collection of eggs with the title 'Easter and new life'.

Reference to photocopiable sheet

Photocopiable page 137 provides templates for a chick and a broken egg. These are used to enable the children to create a pop-up chick Easter card.

HOW DO WE KNOW THAT CHRISTMAS IS COMING?

To be aware of the variety of ways in which people prepare for Christmas. To know that the period leading up to Christmas is called Advent.

Custom. Preparation.

†† *Whole class followed by individual work.*

🕐 *Whole class 20 minutes; individual work 20 minutes.*

⚠ *Ensure that children are aware of the dangers of a lighted candle.*

Key background information

The period leading up to Christmas is called *Advent* ('Coming') and is the first part of the Christian year. It is a time when Christians look forward to remembering the birth of Jesus at Christmas. During the four weeks of Advent, the passage of time is marked in different ways. In Britain, where Christmas is recognised as a national holiday, Advent

calendars and candles are often used to mark the days in December leading up to Christmas. In some churches, an Advent wreath or ring – a circle of evergreens with four red candles, one for each Sunday in Advent, and a large white candle in the centre for Christmas day itself – might be lit.

Preparation

Make copies of photocopiable page 138, one for each child. Obtain an Advent candle and a picture or poster of an Advent wreath (see 'Useful books and resources', page 107).

Resources needed

Photocopiable page 138; Advent candle, holder and matches; picture or poster of an Advent wreath; large sheet of paper; drawing materials.

What to do

Ask the children what they do as their birthday approaches. Do they count the days, tell people, think about presents? Continue by asking how they feel as their birthday gets closer. Are they excited, impatient? Do they want to know what will happen?

Ask the children what special time is coming soon and/or how they know when Christmas is approaching. List their answers on a large sheet of paper. These might include:

▲ Christmas decorations in streets, at home and at school;
▲ people buying presents;
▲ cards being written and sent;
▲ special food being bought and cooked;
▲ visiting Father Christmas;

▲ carol-singing;

▲ rehearsing for Christmas plays at school.

Explain that, for Christians, Christmas is a very special time of year because it is the celebration of the birth of Jesus. Christians look forward to this special time and do things to help them count the days leading up to Christmas. Christians call this time 'Advent'.

Show the children an Advent candle, paying particular attention to the marks which represent the days of Advent. Tell the children that they are going to count the days to Christmas by burning a segment of the Advent candle each day. Light the candle and, while the first segment melts, show the picture of the Advent wreath and explain how some Christians use it (see 'Key background information'). Then light the candle at a convenient time each day, such as registration or storytime. Finally, give each child a copy of photocopiable page 138 and ask them to draw a different picture in each bauble showing the different things that let them know Christmas is coming.

Suggestion(s) for extension

Ask the children to choose one of the drawings on their sheet and write about it.

Suggestion(s) for support

Give those children who have difficulty in finding five examples the list made in the activity during the discussion. This will help them to complete the photocopiable sheet.

Assessment opportunities

Looking at the pictures drawn by the children, and asking for their reasons for drawing them, will indicate to what extent they have understood that people prepare for Christmas in a variety of ways.

Opportunities for IT

Encourage children to use pictures taken from a collection of Christmas clip art to make their own Advent calendar. Prior to the lesson, design a template using a desktop publishing package and save this to disk for the children to use. They can then select relevant pictures from the clip art to fit each of the spaces. Once they have printed out their 'calendar' tell them to attach flaps to each of the pictures. The children could also use Framework software such as *My World 2* with the Christmas Ideas Pack for similar work.

Christmas is coming

▲ Draw five ways in which you know that Christmas is coming.

Display ideas

Under the title 'Christmas is coming', display Christmas cards, Christmas decorations, photographs of the children rehearsing for their Christmas play, an Advent calendar and the Advent candle.

Reference to photocopiable sheet

The outline of a Christmas tree on photocopiable page 138 contains blank baubles. Inside these the children draw different things which demonstrate how they know that Christmas is coming.

WHAT HAPPENS TO SOME BABIES WHEN THEY ARE CHRISTENED?

To know what happens at a traditional Christian christening.

Belonging. Ritual action.

†† *Whole class followed by individual work.*
🕐 *Whole class 30 minutes; individual work 30 minutes.*

Key background information

Within the worldwide family of Christian Churches, there is great variety in practice and custom. This applies particularly to 'rites of passage' – those rituals which mark stages of transition in people's lives.

Many in Britain will be familiar with the custom of *christening* new-born babies. With the change in patterns of religious belief and observance, this has become for some an expected or welcome way of marking the arrival of a baby into the community of family and friends.

Technically, a christening is a form of baptism (a word deriving from the Greek 'to dip' in water). Within churches that practise infant baptism, other rituals will follow later in life. 'Confirmation', for example, marks that point in life at which people who were baptised as infants confirm the promises made on their behalf at that time

The account of a christening contained in this activity is much-simplified.

Preparation

Obtain a baptismal candle (available by post – see 'Useful books and resources', page 107). Write the words 'Christian', 'font', 'godparents', 'priest', 'cross', 'christening', 'gown', 'water' on to pieces of card. If possible, obtain some pictorial material of a christening, for example posters, pictures, video extract.

Resources needed

Baptismal candle in a velvet bag; word cards; pictorial material if available; writing materials.

What to do

Gather the children together and tell them that you are going to show them something which is special to many people. Carefully remove the candle from the bag and let the children look at it closely. Tell them that a candle like this is given to some Christian parents to help them remember a special day in their baby's life. Explain that some Christian parents take their baby to church to celebrate the new baby with their friends and to make the baby part of the group of people who go to church.

Tell the children what happens at a christening, using pictorial material if available. As specific terms are used and explained, show the children the word cards. The account should include the following:
▲ The baby is often dressed in a special christening gown.

RELIGIOUS EDUCATION

▲ Several people called godparents are chosen by the parents to help the baby learn about God and Jesus as he grows older.

▲ The baby, the parents and the godparents stand by a font (raised container for water) with the priest.

▲ The baby is given to the priest who says special words over him.

▲ The priest puts his or her fingers into the water in the font and draws a cross on the baby's forehead with the water, while saying the baby's name.

▲ The priest gives the parents or godparents a candle to help them remember this special day.

Enquire whether children who have been christened would be able to bring to school photographs of their christening or the special clothes they wore.

Give each child a sheet of plain paper and explain that they are to write an account of what happens at a christening, using the key words on the cards.

Suggestion(s) for extension

Children could interview one or more adults in school who have been to a christening. Ask the children to compare what they are told about the christening with what they learned during the activity. Which aspects were similar and which were different and in what ways?

Suggestion(s) for support

Some children may need adult support when writing their accounts of what happens at a christening. A picture or poster will provide a helpful stimulus to these pupils.

Assessment opportunities

The children's written accounts will show to what extent they have understood what happens at a christening.

Opportunities for IT

Show younger children how to use a concept keyboard linked to a word processor so that they can work individually or in pairs to produce a sequenced account of a christening. The concept keyboard could either contain the pictures in the wrong order so that when the children press the relevant picture a matching line of text is placed on the screen, or the overlay could contain the sentences themselves in a jumbled order.

Older children could use a word processor to write a description of a christening. Children who remember attending a christening might like to write a newspaper account of it using a simple newspaper package.

Display ideas

Under the heading 'What happens to some babies when they are christened?', mount some of the children's accounts. If children have brought in photographs of their christening, display these alongside them.

WHY IS DIVALI A SPECIAL TIME FOR HINDUS?

To know in what ways Hindus celebrate Divali. To reflect upon good and evil in the world.

Good and evil. Celebration.

†† *Session One: group work, whole class, then paired work. Session Two: whole class followed by group work.*

🕐 *Session One: group work 15 minutes; whole class 15 minutes; paired work 30 minutes. Session Two: whole class 20 minutes; group work as appropriate depending on time available.*

⚠ *Children should be reminded about the proper use of matches and the danger of an open candle flame. Care will be needed when making the barfi.*

Key background information

Divali (or *Diwali*) is the Hindu festival that is perhaps best-known outside the Hindu community. It is a late October/early November festival, lasting one to five days, which also marks the beginning of a new year. The title itself derives from *Deepavali* meaning 'row of lights'.

There are many customs and stories associated with Divali: there is no 'right' way of celebrating it. Many of the customs are more properly cultural rather than religious and are found throughout India in a variety of contexts. The practice of decorating the hands with mendhi (henna) patterns, for example, is an expression of celebration which is not confined to Divali. It is also associated with weddings.

The making of symmetrical rangoli patterns using coloured powder is a task traditionally performed by women.

Divas, the small pots which hold a light (traditionally, a small cotton wick floating in ghee – clarified butter), can be unadorned brown clay or brightly painted and decorated.

The sending of cards is, of course, a universal expression of celebration. Divali cards come in as many forms and sizes as Christmas cards. A common printed greeting inside the card is 'Divali Greetings and Best Wishes for a Happy New Year'. The front of the card usually has a greeting such as 'Happy Divali' or 'Divali Greetings' together with an illustration such as a group of divas or a Hindu deity or deities

The story of Rama and Sita, which is often told at Divali time, is found in the Hindu epic the *Ramayana* (pronounced 'ram-eye-ana'). It is a complex story: the incident which leads to Rama's 14-year banishment, for example, originates in the desire of his father's favourite wife to have her son, rather than Rama, succeed to the throne.

For Hindus, Rama is Vishnu, the supreme deity, in human form. He is a manifestation ('avatar') of Vishnu as, too, was Krishna. Lakshmi, goddess of wealth and prosperity, is also connected with Divali. Houses are cleaned and lights lit so that Lakshmi will visit and bring prosperity. It is customary for business accounts to be settled for the year at Divali time.

Preparation

Session One: make copies of photocopiable page 140, one for each pair. Put a night-light in a diva. Make a copy of photocopiable page 139 and become familiar with the story. Session Two: choose a section of a video showing Hindus celebrating Divali. A suitable video may be obtained from the BBC Watch 'Festivals' programmes (see 'Useful books and resources', page 107). Gather together materials for the group activities. Make a copy of photocopiable page 141.

Resources needed

Session One: diva, night-light and matches; photocopiable pages 139 and 140; scissors; blank paper; adhesive; writing materials; blank speech bubbles. Session Two: video containing scenes of Hindus celebrating Divali ; television; coloured chalks; black sugar paper; felt-tipped pens; card; clay; paint; recipe ingredients; photocopiable page 141.

What to do
Session One

Ask the children if they know any stories which have 'goodies' and 'baddies' in them (characters such as Little Red Riding Hood and the wolf, Cinderella and the ugly sisters, and heroes and villains from cartoons and comic strips).

Divide the children into groups and ask each group to retell a story which features goodies and baddies.

Let each group briefly retell their story and then focus on the fact that the majority of the stories end with the goody winning and the baddy losing.

Explain that you are going to tell them a story which is special for people called Hindus. It is about goodies and a baddy. Read or tell the story. Light the night-light in the diva (if available) at the point in the story when Rama, Sita and Lakshman are welcomed home by the people of Ayodhya after the defeat of Ravana.

Put the children into pairs and give each pair a copy of photocopiable page 140. Look at each picture with the children, making sure that they know which characters are represented. Point out that the pictures are in the wrong order so the children must cut them out and resequence them to tell the story of Rama and Sita. Finally, give the children the pre-prepared blank speech bubbles and ask them to write in appropriate dialogue.

Session Two

Remind the children of the Hindu story about Rama and Sita. Explain that the story is told at a special time of year called Divali (noting the link with the word 'diva' found in the story), and that Hindus celebrate Divali in lots of ways. Show a video of Hindus celebrating Divali. Encourage the children to talk about what they have seen, and answer questions which arise.

Divide the children into five groups, each group working on an activity associated with Divali. These could include:
▲ rangoli patterns – using coloured chalks and black sugar paper;
▲ mendhi patterns – the children draw round their hands and then use felt-tipped pens to design patterns on the cut-out hand;
▲ divas – using clay, make small thumb pots (the divas can be painted in bright colours when dry);
▲ Divali cards – discuss with the children what symbol or

picture to put on the front and how the greeting 'Happy Divali' can be written inside;

▲ food – make barfi, a sweet enjoyed by many Hindus at Divali time (photocopiable page 141 provides a recipe for this; the groups can be rotated if time allows).

Suggestion(s) for extension
Children could make a book entitled 'The Hindu festival of Divali'. They could use the school library to obtain additional information and watch the video extract for a second time in order to look for details they missed when they first viewed it.

Suggestion(s) for support
Some children may find it easier to retell their story about 'goodies' and 'baddies' in picture format. They may also need the support of a more experienced partner when working on the photocopiable sheet.

Assessment opportunities
The stories featuring 'goodies' and 'baddies' retold by each group will provide evidence of the extent to which the children are able to reflect upon good and evil in the world.

The correct sequencing of the story on photocopiable page 140 and the words the children write inside the speech bubbles will indicate how well they have understood the story.

Opportunities for IT
Encourage the children to use an encyclopaedia CD-ROM to look for further information about Divali.

Let the children use an art package or drawing package to make Divali cards. They can use the software to draw their design, add a Divali message and

then print it out. The picture can then be stuck on to card. The children could also word process a short greeting to go inside the card. Specific card-making software such as *Clare's Celebrations* may be most useful for this work.

The children could also use the BBC *Ramayana Tales* software. This enables children to combine pictures of the story with their own text in a simple desktop publishing format. Alternatively, children could use a simple desktop publishing package to write their version of the story, adding pictures once the story has been printed out.

Display ideas
This activity offers many opportunities for display work. Child-sized figures of Rama, Sita and Lakshman can be made by drawing around three children and then painting and decorating the outlines using a variety of materials. Mount the rangoli patterns and display them with a border of mendhi patterns. The Divali cards could surround a large greeting of 'Happy Divali!' The divas could be displayed on a window-sill with divas painted on the window behind.

Reference to photocopiable sheets
Photocopiable page 139 gives a simplified version of the Rama and Sita story and is for the teacher's use. Photocopiable page 140 is a picture version of the Rama and Sita story. The children are asked to arrange the pictures in the correct sequence and to write appropriate text inside speech bubbles. Photocopiable page 141 provides a recipe for barfi, an Indian sweet traditionally eaten at Divali time.

RELIGIOUS EDUCATION

WHY IS CLOTH SOMETIMES GIVEN TO BUDDHIST MONKS?

To know what happens at the Buddhist festival of Kathina. To identify times when others are thanked.

Thankfulness. Community.

†† *Group work, followed by whole class, finishing with individual work.*

🕐 *Group work 10 minutes; whole class 10–15 minutes; individual work 15 minutes.*

Key background information

Buddhism began on the Indian sub-continent. With its spread, various traditions – ways of living out the Buddhist life – developed. Today, there are many 'schools' of Buddhism, such as Tibetan Buddhism and Zen Buddhism. In the West, the 'Friends of the Western Buddhist Order' have sought to develop a form of Buddhism which is appropriate for Westerners today.

Theravada Buddhism is associated with Sri Lanka and with the lands of south-eastern Asia such as Thailand. Monks in the Theravadin tradition go on an annual retreat which coincides with the rainy season. Kathina Day comes at the end of the retreat or shortly afterwards.

The robes which Buddhist monks wear differs depending on the country and tradition. The robes of Tibetan Buddhist monks are burgundy red in colour, Sri Lankan monks wear saffron orange, while monks in Thailand wear brown-coloured robes.

Meditation, a practice which seeks to move the mind away from ever-changing distractions to find its still centre, is central to the Buddhist life. It is said that the Buddha's last words were, 'With mindfulness strive on.'

It must be stressed that the children, in being asked to sit in silence for one minute, are not 'pretending' to be Buddhists. Rather, they are being given the opportunity to 'don't just do something – sit there' (see 'Useful books and resources', page 107), an experience which can contribute to their spiritual development. There are many who would claim that going through some sort of 'stilling exercise' is often an important prelude to sensitive and focused work in RE.

Preparation

Choose a piece of music (or a picture or a plant) for the minute's silence. This may be particularly helpful for those children requiring support.

Resources needed

Writing and drawing materials. For the support activity – music, picture or a plant.

What to do

Divide the children into groups and ask them to imagine that it is going to rain for the next two weeks and they will not be able to go outside. Encourage them to talk about how they will spend their time while they are indoors for the next two weeks and then to write down some of their ideas. Explain that each group will tell the others what they have decided.

Tell the children that there are parts of the world where it does rain for a very long time each year: this is called the 'rainy season'. During the rainy season people try to stay indoors whenever they can.

Explain that there is a group of people called Buddhist monks who do not usually stay in one place for longer than

three days. When they travel, they often teach others about how to be happy in life. During the rainy season, it is impossible for the monks to travel so they are allowed to stay in one place. They spend much of their time meditating – sitting calmly in silence. Other Buddhists look after the monks by giving them food. They are pleased to do this because they think that what the monks are doing is important.

Ask the children to sit quietly for one minute. At the end of the minute, ask them what they were thinking about.

Tell the children that, near the end of the rainy season, Buddhists bring the monks enough cloth to make a new robe for one of the monks to wear. This is their way of saying thank you to the monks for teaching them. The monks have to make the robe in one day and then choose a monk to wear it.

Complete this section by telling the children that, when the rainy season is over, the Buddhist monks continue their travels.

Ask the children to think about times when they say thank you to other people. They could draw four pictures to represent four different occasions, writing underneath each picture what they are saying thank you for.

Suggestion(s) for extension

More able children could work as a group and design clothes for a special occasion. Ask them to think about how they would present the clothes to the person who would wear them.

Suggestion(s) for support

Some children may have difficulty sitting in silence for a minute. It may help these children if music is played quietly or if they have something to focus on, such as a picture or a plant.

Assessment opportunities

The children's pictures and writing will indicate whether they can identify times when they say thank you to others.

Opportunities for IT

Ask the children to use an encyclopaedia CD-ROM to search for further information about Buddhism.

Assembly ideas

As part of an assembly focusing on a theme such as 'Saying thank you' or 'Clothes', some children may like to talk about the things they say thank you for. Others could present a picture of clothes designed for a special occasion to a chosen person. The remainder could re-enact the giving of cloth to Buddhist monks while explaining about this special day. End the assembly with a reflection such as, 'And now, in a moment of quiet, let us think about people we would like to say thank you to.'

HOW COULD THE ELEPHANTS CELEBRATE ELMER'S DAY?

To understand the nature and purpose of festival. To be able to use symbolism.

Celebration. Festival.

†† *Whole class, followed by ability groups, returning to whole class.*

🕐 *Whole class 15 minutes; group work 60 minutes; whole class 20 minutes.*

Key background information

Involving the children in the celebration of festivals associated with actual religious practice can raise a number of concerns. These concerns are rooted in the understanding that religious education is an educational rather than a confessional activity.

Yet, at the same time, a festival is a phenomenon which engages people actively in a number of ways. Simply looking at how other people celebrate festivals can sometimes appear to deny the very life which is of the essence of festival.

This activity is designed to engage the children actively in the process of 'making' a festival. In so doing, it is hoped that they will begin to understand the many dimensions and aspects of festivals, both religious and secular. For example:

▲ that festivals have the power to bind together a group;

▲ that festivals often focus upon and relive a past event;

▲ that particular ways of celebrating, such as the sending

of cards, the giving of presents and greetings run across a range of festivals;

▲ that festivals can be fun.

Preparation

Obtain a copy of *Elmer* by David McKee (Red Fox).

Resources needed

Elmer by David McKee; craft materials; loaded camera; writing and drawing materials.

What to do

Read the story of *Elmer*, showing the children the illustrations. Stop at the penultimate page where an elephant suggests the annual celebration of Elmer's Day.

Divide the children into small groups and ask them to think about the ways in which Elmer's Day could be celebrated. These could include:

▲ elephants decorating themselves in patchwork patterns;

▲ singing the Elmer song;

▲ playing tricks on others;

▲ eating Elmer cake;

▲ walking round the grey berry tree;

▲ washing in a river (to remember when Elmer showed his true colours).

When the groups have thought of several ideas, ask them to make items such as greeting cards, invitation cards, hats and so on, associated with the festival. Alternatively, children can draw pictures of different scenes of the occasion.

When the groups have finished, ask them to combine their ideas, in order to have a class celebration of Elmer's Day during which photographs can be taken.

Suggestion(s) for extension

Children could go on to collate activities from all the groups in order to produce a record of the class celebration of Elmer's Day. This could be kept for future reference.

Suggestion(s) for support

Children who find the activity difficult may find it helpful to work together, with the support and encouragement of an adult helper or teacher.

Assessment opportunities

The range of ideas which the children generate within their groups, and the extent to which they involve symbolism, will provide evidence of the extent to which the children have understood the nature and purpose of a festival.

Opportunities for IT

Let the children use an art or drawing package to make celebration cards for Elmer's Day, or a word processor to make invitations for the class celebration (see 'How can we celebrate Teddy's birthday?', page 65).

The children could use a simple desktop publishing package or dedicated newspaper software to create a class newspaper about their celebration of Elmer's Day. Set up a simple newspaper format and organise children into groups to write about different parts of the celebration, or why they are celebrating Elmer's Day. Photographs can be added, either by scanning them so that they can be used in the software or by adding them to the pages once they have been printed.

Display ideas

Mount the children's artefacts and illustrations, together with photographs showing the class celebration, under the heading 'Celebrating Elmer's Day'.

WHY IS RAMADAN A SPECIAL MONTH FOR MUSLIMS?

To know what Muslims do during Ramadan. To know that Ramadan is a special time for Muslims.

Duty. Community.

†† *Individual work followed by whole class.*

🕐 *Individual work 20 minutes; whole class 30 minutes.*

Key background information

Islam, the way of life of the Muslim, is a title which derives from an Arabic word meaning 'peace'. It is the Muslim belief that, through doing the will of Allah (pronounced 'Ull-lah': God), a person finds true peace. A Muslim is someone who submits to the will of God. Any person can be a Muslim: it is not limited to a specific racial or cultural group.

The 'Five Pillars' of Islam are a series of basic duties or obligations which support the Muslim life – as pillars do a building. One of these pillars is the obligation to fast during daylight hours of the ninth month, *Ramadan*.

Even Muslims who do not, for example, pray five times daily (another pillar) will be keen to keep to the Ramadan fast. It is an activity which shapes the behaviour of the whole Muslim community during Ramadan. Children, quite naturally, will begin to copy their elders, perhaps by missing several breakfasts or by fasting for one or two days during the month. They will be proud of doing this and will be praised by their elders.

Though an obligation, Muslims will point to many benefits resulting from Ramadan practice. It binds the Muslim community together, encourages self-discipline and sensitises people to those less fortunate, for example.

Ramadan is also a time of heightened devotion to the Holy Qur'an. Copies are often divided into 30 sections so that one can be read during each of the days and nights of the month.

It was the Prophet Muhammad's practice to break the fast each day by drinking, and eating dates. In emulating this, a link is created between the life of Muhammad 1400 years ago and Muslims today.

Preparation

Make copies of photocopiable page 142, one for each child. Make copies of photocopiable page 143 for those children carrying out the extension activity. Display a collection of books/posters on Islam, for example *The Muslim World* by Richard Tames (Simon & Schuster) or the Westhill photo pack on Islam (see 'Useful books and resources', page 107).

Resources needed

Photocopiable page 142; collection of books/posters on Islam; writing and drawing materials. For the extension activity – photocopiable page 143.

What to do

Give each child a copy of photocopiable page 142. Remind the children that there are 12 months in the year and that the months are grouped into seasons. Ask them to think of something special that happens in each month (it may be their birthday, or birthdays of members of their family, Christmas and other festivals, going on holiday, playing in the snow, or spring flowers appearing) and to write or draw their ideas on a separate sheet. When they have completed all the months, or as many as they are able, ask them to put a tick next to their most important month on photocopiable page 142.

Gather the children together and quickly go round the class, giving each child the opportunity to say briefly which is their most important month and why.

Tell the children that they are going to learn about a month which is very important for a group of people called Muslims. Explain that Muslims call the month Ramadan and tell them the following information.

▲ Ramadan is a time when Muslims fast during the hours of daylight. (You may need to explain to some children what the word 'fast' means.) This means that Muslims have to get up very early, while it is still dark, to have a big breakfast which will last them through the day. They do not eat or drink again until it is dark in the evening. As soon as it becomes dark, many Muslims will eat a few dates and drink milk before they have a large meal together as a family.

▲ During Ramadan, Muslims spend more time than usual reading the Qur'an and thinking about Allah (God). Women usually do this at home while men will go to the mosque.

▲ Because Muslims feel hungry during Ramadan, it is easier for them to remember people in the world who do not have enough water or food all of the time.

RELIGIOUS EDUCATION

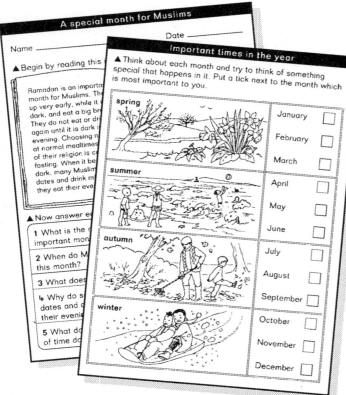

A special month for Muslims

Name _____
Date _____

▲ Begin by reading this

Ramadan is an importa
month for Muslims. Th
up very early, while it i
dark, and eat a big br
They do not eat or dr
again until it is dark i
evening. Choosing n
at normal mealtimes
of their religion is c
fasting. When it be
dark, many Muslim
dates and drink m
they eat their eve

▲ Now answer e

1 What is the
important mon

2 When do M
this month?

3 What does

4 Why do s
dates and d
their eveni

5 What do
of time do

Important times in the year

▲ Think about each month and try to think of something special that happens in it. Put a tick next to the month which is most important to you.

spring

summer

autumn

winter

January	☐
February	☐
March	☐
April	☐
May	☐
June	☐
July	☐
August	☐
September	☐
October	☐
November	☐
December	☐

▲ Muslims try even harder to be kind to other people during this month.

Ask the children how they think Muslims feel at the end of Ramadan. Tell them that Muslims have a party to celebrate the end of this special month. It is called Id-ul-Fitr. Muslims eat lots of food, wear new clothes and give presents and cards. They wish each other 'Id mubarrak' (happy Id).

Leave the books and pictures on display so that children can look at them over the next few days.

Suggestion(s) for extension

Give each child a copy of photocopiable page 143. Ask them to work on their own, read the information on the sheet and answer the questions.

Suggestion(s) for support

The less able children may have difficulty in filling in something special for some of the months of the year. It will be easier for them to think about the four seasons and write something special for each season. They could then, with adult help, narrow down their most important time to a month within one season.

Assessment opportunities

The children's comments and conversations when looking at the book and poster display will reveal the extent of their understanding of Ramadan for Muslims. Photocopiable page 143, which is for use in the extension activity, provides an opportunity to assess how much knowledge children have gained about Ramadan.

Opportunities for IT

Encourage the children to use an encyclopaedia CD-ROM to find out more about Ramadan.

Children could also use Framework software such as *My World 2* with the Id resources pack to create their own hand-painting patterns and greetings cards.

Assembly ideas

Make a display of books and posters for the children to look at before assembly. Choose two or three children to tell everyone what they ate and drank the previous day. Show an empty plate and glass, and explain to the children that most Muslims do not eat and drink during daylight in a month called Ramadan. Briefly explain what Muslims do during this special month. If there are Muslim children in the school, they may be willing to help by explaining what their family does or by reciting a small passage from the Qur'an. The assembly could end with a thought such as, 'And now, in a moment of quiet, let us think – like Muslims do during Ramadan – about those people in the world who do not have enough food or clean water to live.'

Reference to photocopiable sheets

Photocopiable page 142 focuses children's thoughts on a period of time which is important to them and provides a foundation for understanding the significance of Ramadan. Photocopiable page 143 requires the children to answer various questions about Ramadan and may be used as an assessment activity for children requiring extension work.

WHY DO JEWS EAT SPECIAL FOOD AT PASSOVER?

To know what foods are eaten at a Passover Seder meal. To understand that food can form a link with the past.

Tradition. Symbolism.

✝✝ *Session One: whole class. Session Two: whole class followed by individual group work.*

🕐 *Session One: 30 minutes. Session Two: whole class 30 minutes; individual/group work 30 minutes.*

Key background information

The Exodus – the hasty departure of the Hebrews from Egypt under the leadership of Moses – is for Jews the key event in their people's history. It showed, they believe, that God was at work in the events of history and that they had been chosen to have a special relationship with God. The portrayal of the Exodus can be found in the biblical book of that name which is also part of the Jewish Torah.

For Jews, the Exodus is not 'just' an event of history but is relived each year at the week-long festival of Passover (Hebrew – *Pesach*). The *Seder* meal or supper which Jews eat at the start of the festival is structured around a spoken retelling of the events of the Exodus. The symbolic foods recall not only aspects of the Exodus but also the spring timing of the festival. Each person at the meal follows the story of the Exodus in a Passover *hagadah*, a book or booklet which is also produced in a simplified version for children. The description of the Seder food in this activity is much simplified. The lamb shankbone, for example, is usually said to recall the animal sacrifices that took place in the Jerusalem temple before it was destroyed in 70 CE.

There are many designs of Seder plate, some of them with several tiers. The script which is often found at the centre of the plate is sometimes mistaken for the word 'God': it is, in fact, the Hebrew word 'Pesach'.

This activity would link well with the activity based on the biblical story of Joseph 'What are the 'ups' and 'downs' of family life?', page 35, which tells how the Hebrews came to be in Egypt before the Exodus (see Genesis, chapters 37–46).

Preparation

Session One: find a clear retelling of the Exodus story. Session Two: obtain a Seder plate and a copy of a children's hagadah (see 'Useful books and resources', page 107). Buy a pack of matzah (available at most large supermarkets).

Resources needed

Session One: a story of the Exodus. Session Two: Seder plate; matzah; writing and drawing materials. For the extension activity – a children's version of the hagadah.

What to do

Session One

Explain to the children that they are going to hear a story about a group of people called Hebrews who became slaves in Egypt. (If activities related to Joseph have already been undertaken, remind the children of how, according to the Bible, the Hebrews came to be in Egypt.) Show them a copy of the Bible, explaining that the story comes from the first part and is particularly special for Jews because it is about their ancestors.

Read or tell the story of the Exodus, finishing at the crossing of the sea.

Session Two

Tell the children that they are going to see something which many Jews use at the festival of Passover when they remember the story of the Exodus.

Show the children the Seder plate and ask them what they can see on it. As they identify each section, explain the link with the story:
▲ *charoset*: a sticky paste of apples, cinnamon, nuts and wine. This reminds Jews of the mortar which the Hebrew slaves used to make bricks.
▲ a piece of roasted lamb's bone. This reminds Jews of the lamb's blood that was smeared on the door posts at the first Passover.
▲ bitter herbs: usually horseradish. This reminds Jews of the bitter lives of the slaves in Egypt.
▲ roasted or baked egg. This reminds Jews that Passover is a spring festival.
▲ parsley, a symbol of spring which is also dipped in salt water as a reminder of the tears that the Hebrew slaves shed.
▲ lettuce or other fresh vegetables such as watercress, a symbol of spring.
▲ the Hebrew script at the centre of the plate says 'Pesach' (Passover).

Tell the children that the Seder plate is placed on the table during the Seder meal (the first meal to be eaten during the Passover festival). Throughout this meal, Jews refer to the food on the Seder plate to help them tell the story of the Exodus.

Explain that songs are sung and games are played during the eating of the meal. One of the games is played with a piece of matzah (unleavened bread). Show a piece if available. At the beginning of the meal half a matzah is hidden. Midway through the meal the children are sent to look for the missing piece because the meal cannot continue without it. The child who finds the missing matzah often receives a reward for finding it. The matzah reminds Jews of the part of the Exodus story when the Hebrews left Egypt quickly and did not have time to make bread and leave it to rise.

To allow the children to have a closer look at the Seder plate, provide opportunities for them to make observational drawings in small groups. While this is happening, the others could retell their favourite part of the Exodus story and/or write an account of a meal eaten with their family for a special occasion.

Suggestion(s) for extension

Provide a children's version of the hagadah and encourage the children to refer to it in order to discover more about the Seder meal.

Suggestion(s) for support

Ask children to draw a picture of their family celebrating with a meal. Alternatively they could draw a series of pictures to show their favourite part of the Exodus story.

Assessment opportunities

Give the children a list of the six foods found on the Seder plate and ask them to explain the link between the foods and the Exodus story.

Opportunities for IT

Ask the children to write a newspaper account of the Exodus story, using a simple desktop publishing package or dedicated newspaper software.

The children could work together to create an electronic version of the story of the Exodus and the festival of Passover, using multimedia authoring software. This software allows children to mix text, pictures and sound together. Pictures can be included from various sources. They can be drawn using an art or drawing package, taken from collections of clip art or scanned from the children's own line drawings. A simple soundtrack of the story can be made by using a microphone attached to the computer. Groups of children could each work on a different section of the story, drawing

pictures and adding appropriate text using one or two screen pages. A separate section could give all the details about the symbolism of the Seder plate and the way in which families celebrate Passover.

You may find it helpful to set up a structure for the presentation in advance, possibly with a title page with headings such as 'The Exodus', 'Seder plate', 'Celebrating Passover' and so on. When the user clicks with the mouse on one of these they are then taken to the relevant section. This work is best undertaken when other adult support is available.

Display ideas

Mount the children's observational drawings and display them around the Seder plate. Surround them with the retellings of the Exodus story. Use the title 'The Jewish festival of Passover'.

WHY IS EASTER SPECIAL FOR CHRISTIANS?

To know the outline of the Christian Easter story. To identify sad times and happy times in their own lives.

Resurrection. Reversal.

✝✝ *Session One: whole class followed by individual work. Session Two: whole class followed by individual work.*

🕐 *Session One: whole class 30 minutes; individual work 20 minutes. Session Two: whole class 20 minutes; individual work 20 minutes.*

Key background information

Within the Bible, it is in Paul's letters to early Christian groups that we first find the declaration that Jesus not only died but rose again. Later, each of the four Gospel-book writers – Matthew, Mark, Luke and John – gave versions of what happened after Jesus' resurrection. The first Easter was so central to their beliefs, that they went into considerable detail.

The main events that could be included in a summary story are:

Session One

▲ Jesus rides into Jerusalem on a donkey.

▲ The Last Supper takes place on the Thursday evening.

▲ Jesus and a few friends go to the Garden of Gethsemane, where Jesus prays.

▲ Jesus is arrested in the Garden.

▲ Soldiers make fun of Jesus and place a crown of thorns on his head.

▲ Jesus is condemned to die.

▲ Jesus carries the cross-beam (rather than the whole cross) through the streets.

▲ Jesus is crucified on the Friday.

▲ Jesus' body is placed in a cave-tomb and a stone rolled over its entrance.

Session Two

▲ Some women (Mary Magdalene, Joanna and Mary the mother of James) return to the tomb at first light on Sunday (the first daylight after the Sabbath).

▲ They find the stone rolled away and the tomb empty.

▲ They are told that Jesus is no longer there but has risen.

▲ Was Jesus alive again?

What happened at Easter is central to Christianity and explains, for example, the significance of Sunday (the day of Jesus' resurrection) for Christians. The Last Supper, in which bread and wine were shared, has deeply affected the worship of most Christian groups.

The crucifix – a cross with the figure of Jesus upon it – is traditionally associated with Catholic forms of Christianity. In the Protestant tradition, however, it has been more usual to find an empty cross.

The issue of disclosure is raised by this activity. Teachers will need to be sensitive to the fact that some children may not wish others to see their poem about sadness, for example. It is suggested, therefore, that you only display those poems which children are happy for others to see.

Preparation

Session One: set up a display of books, including the Bible, and pictures about Easter. Obtain a crucifix (see 'Useful books and resources', page 107). Session Two: obtain a plain cross.

Resources needed

Session One: hot cross bun; Crucifix; Easter story, for example *The Story of Easter* retold by W. Owen Cole and Judith Evans-Lowndes (Heinemann), *Easter* by Gail Gibbons (Picture Knight); writing materials. Session Two: plain cross; Easter story.

What to do
Session One

Show the children a hot cross bun, and ask them what they can see. Focus on the cross, letting the children tell you

what they already know. Build on this knowledge by explaining that the cross reminds Christians of the sad part of the Easter story.

Read or tell the Easter story, beginning with Jesus' entry into Jerusalem on a donkey and ending with Jesus' body being placed in a tomb. Explain that this is not the end of the story and they will hear the rest in the next session.

Ask questions about the story. For instance:

▲ Why were the people pleased to see Jesus when he came to Jerusalem?

▲ What was special about the last supper that Jesus had with his 12 special friends?

▲ Why did Jesus wait to be arrested?

▲ How did Jesus' friends feel when he was put on the cross?

Show the children a crucifix and explain that this is what some Christians have to remind them of Easter.

Ask the children to think of a time when they have felt sad and to go away quietly and write about how they felt. This can be in the form of a poem if it helps them to express their feelings better.

Session Two

Show the children the crucifix as a reminder of the previous session and tell the rest of the Easter story.

Ask them questions.

▲ How did Jesus' friends feel when they saw Jesus' empty tomb?

▲ How did they feel when they thought that he had come alive again?

▲ Why are Christians happy on Easter Sunday?

Show them a plain cross and explain that some Christians like to look at this to remember Easter.

Give the children back their poems or writing about a time when they have been sad and ask them to write a poem about a happy time in contrast to it.

Suggestion(s) for extension

Using the books on display, ask children to make a timeline showing the events of the last week of Jesus' life.

Suggestion(s) for support

Some children may need help in identifying a sad time. Those who find writing poetry difficult could express their feelings in prose or by drawing a picture.

Assessment opportunities

Leave the books and pictures on display and listen to the children's conversations and comments when looking at them. Note those who have understood the importance of Easter to Christians.

Opportunities for IT

Children could use a simple desktop publishing package or dedicated newspaper software to write a class broadsheet about the Easter story. Different groups of children could be responsible for different parts of the story: the entry into Jerusalem, the Last Supper and so on.

Display ideas

Alongside the display of books, pictures and crosses, display a selection of sad time and happy time poems written by those children who are willing to have them displayed.

WHAT SPECIAL STORY IS TOLD AT CHRISTMAS?

To know the outline of the traditional nativity story. To understand some of the underlying ideas and beliefs which make it a special story for Christians.

Incarnation. Belief.

†† *Whole class followed by individual work.*

🕐 *Whole class 25 minutes; individual work 20 minutes.*

Key background information

The 'traditional' Christmas nativity story is, in reality, a combination of the two accounts given in the Gospel books written by Luke and Matthew (to be found at the beginning of the New Testament). These writers came from very different backgrounds and wrote about Jesus' birth in very different ways. Luke wrote about the angel appearing to Mary, the journey to Bethlehem, the birth in the stable, and the visit by shepherds. Matthew wrote about Joseph's dreams, the birth in Bethlehem, the visit to a house by wise men (Magi) who had followed a star, the trickery of King Herod and the subsequent journey of the holy family into Egypt. Down the ages, both accounts have been harmonised and, often, gaps filled in by people's imagination.

The nativity 'story' is not a simple narrative tale but is suffused with symbolism, belief and interpretation. In his Gospel, for example, Luke placed great stress on poverty and the poor. Jesus' birth in a stable and the visit by shepherds – outcasts in the Jewish society of the time – are consistent with this. Matthew, by contrast, had much to say about kingship and it is in his account that the newborn child is visited, in a house, by magi (astrologers) from the East who bring him gifts fit for a king. But, behind all this symbolism

is the theme of Incarnation – the key Christian belief that God was born (incarnated) in human form.

Part of the purpose of this activity is to begin to move the children beyond a merely literal understanding of the story.

Preparation

Obtain a picture of the traditional nativity scene or an artefact, for example a nativity set or South American retablo (see 'Useful books and resources', page 107). Find a suitable children's version of the nativity story such as *The Birth of Jesus* retold by W. Owen Cole and Judith Evans-Lowndes (Heinemann, two stories as told in Luke and Matthew). Make copies of photocopiable page 144, one for each child.

Resources needed

Picture or artefact; Bible; photocopiable page 144; children's version of the nativity story; scissors; blank paper; adhesive; writing materials.

What to do

Show the children the picture or artefact you have obtained. Ask them what they can see and remind them that Christmas is a special time for Christians. Ask them if they know why it is a special time.

Show them a Bible and tell them that the Christmas story can be read in the second part – the New Testament. Read or tell them the traditional nativity story. Ask questions to ensure that they have grasped the main outline of the story. For example:

▲ Who told Mary that she was going to have a baby?

▲ Why did Mary and Joseph have to go to Bethlehem?

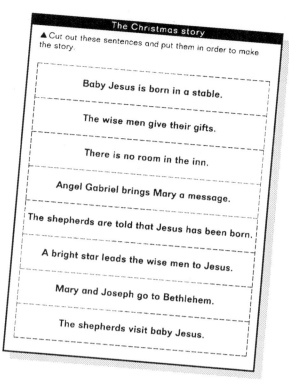

The Christmas story

▲ Cut out these sentences and put them in order to make the story.

Baby Jesus is born in a stable.

The wise men give their gifts.

There is no room in the inn.

Angel Gabriel brings Mary a message.

The shepherds are told that Jesus has been born.

A bright star leads the wise men to Jesus.

Mary and Joseph go to Bethlehem.

The shepherds visit baby Jesus.

▲ Why was Jesus born in a stable?

▲ Who came to visit baby Jesus?

Continue asking questions to develop the children's understanding of the story.

▲ How did Mary feel when the angel told her that she was going to have a baby?

▲ Where did the message come from?

▲ Why is it important to Christians that Jesus was born in a stable?

▲ Why did both wise men and shepherds visit the baby?

When you feel the children have a suitable understanding of the story, give out copies of photocopiable page 144 and ask them to complete the sequencing activity.

Suggestion(s) for extension

Ask children to work in pairs and to make a list of the parts of the story which they think would make it special for Christians, for example an angel appearing to Mary, the star and so on.

Suggestion(s) for support

If children have difficulty with the photocopiable sheet, read through the sentences with them and discuss their correct sequence. Let the children number the sentences before cutting them out.

Assessment opportunities

The ability to sequence the story will give some indication of the children's knowledge of the story. Listening to the children's answers to the second set of questions asked in the main activity will show the extent to which they understand ideas and beliefs contained within the story.

Opportunities for IT

Ask children to work in groups and use a word processor or desktop publishing package to write different parts of the Christmas story; this will help to keep the writing task manageable for younger children. They could then add pictures taken from some of the many Christmas clip-art collections that are commercially available. If a desktop publishing package is used, a master page format can be set up in advance, with a space for the picture and one for the text. The individual pages can then be printed out and bound together to make a class book of the Christmas story.

Assembly ideas

As part of an assembly focusing on a theme such as 'Christmas' or 'Special stories', ask the children to make a presentation in three groups. One group can tell or dramatise the nativity story using Matthew's version. A second group can do the same but using Luke's narrative. The third group could give some of the reasons why the nativity story is so special for Christians. You may like to end the assembly with a reflection such as, 'And now, in a moment of quiet, let us think about the Christmas story and which part of it we like best or which we find special.' The picture or artefact used at the start of the activity could be displayed to act as a visual focus during the assembly.

Reference to photocopiable sheet

Photocopiable page 144 contains a number of sentences about the nativity, which have been placed in the wrong order. The children have to cut them out and then sequence them correctly.

HOW DO SIKHS CELEBRATE DIVALI?

To know that Sikhs celebrate Divali. To know the story associated with Sikh Divali.

Freedom. Celebration.

†† *Paired work, followed by whole class, returning to pairs.*

🕐 *Paired work 5 minutes; whole class 20 minutes; paired work 30 minutes.*

Key background information

The Sikh religion began in the Punjab region of north-west India with Guru Nanak (1469–1539). Before his death, Nanak passed on the leadership of the Sikh community to another person, who became the second Sikh Guru. Of the ten Sikh Gurus, Guru Har Gobind (or Hargobind) was the sixth and lived from 1595 to 1645. After the tenth Guru, the holy book became the Guru of the Sikhs.

By the time of Har Gobind, India was ruled by Muslim Moghul emperors. Some Sikh Gurus enjoyed good relationships with the Moghul emperors while others did not. Har Gobind had an ambivalent relationship with the emperors of the time. The episode described in the story reflects a time when suspicion had become dominant.

Justice and service to others are central tenets of Sikhism. Har Gobind exemplifies these beliefs in his response to the unjust imprisonment of the Hindu princes.

The 'Golden Temple', built by the fifth Guru and renowned for its beauty, stands in the middle of an artificial lake in Amritsar, Punjab. Many Sikhs visit it on pilgrimage.

Preparation

Obtain a picture of a Sikh. Make copies of photocopiable page 147, one for each pair. Make one copy of photocopiable pages 145 and 146 to read to the children during the activity. Make extra copies for those children carrying out the extension activity.

Resources needed

Picture of a Sikh; photocopiable pages 145, 146 and 147; writing and drawing materials.

What to do

Working in pairs, ask the children to tell each other about a time when they have helped a friend.

When they have done this, gather the class together and show the children a picture of a Sikh and explain that Sikhs tell a story about one of their Gurus helping his friends. Tell the story of Guru Har Gobind and his cloak.

Explain that Guru Har Gobind was released with the 52 Indian princes at Divali time and Sikhs celebrate Divali with lights and fireworks as do Hindus (see 'Why is Divali a special time for Hindus?', page 71). The Golden Temple at Amritsar is lit up and sweets are given to relatives and friends.

Ask the children to imagine that they are reporters working for the 'Amritsar Times'. Give each pair a copy of photocopiable page 147 and ask them to prepare a news item to accompany the headline 'Guru tricks Emperor. 52 princes walk free'.

Suggestion(s) for extension

Ask children to imagine that they are one of the 52 princes, giving an interview to the 'Amritsar Times'. They may find it useful to refer to a copies of photocopiable pages 145 and 146, to help them with this task.

Suggestion(s) for support

Put the children into mixed ability pairs when preparing the newspaper article.

Assessment opportunities

The children's newspaper articles and the accounts of the story written from the point of view of one of the princes, will give an indication of the children's knowledge of the story.

Opportunities for IT

Encourage children to use a simple desktop publishing package or dedicated newspaper software when writing their report for the 'Amritsar Times'.

Display ideas

Mount the children's newspaper articles and personal accounts and display under the title 'A Sikh story about freedom'.

Reference to photocopiable sheets

Photocopiable pages 145 and 146, which tell the story of Guru Har Gobind and his cloak, are for use by the teacher initially but also by those children carrying out the extension activity. Photocopiable page 147 provides the title of a newspaper and headlines under which the children write an accompanying article.

RELIGIOUS EDUCATION

Encountering special places

As individuals grow and develop, the number of places which they can consider as 'special' increase in number. They might be 'secret' places of private significance or places associated with life-changing events or encounters with others. Special places will be full of memories and associations.

Societies, too, have a range of special places which carry their own particular associations or resonances. The special place might be an area set apart for the practice of particular activities or rituals. It might be the focus of journeying and pilgrimage because of its association with someone's life or a particular event. It might house an object of great significance.

Within religious traditions, special places can be of various types. They might be associated with worship. They might be temporary but deeply connected with the group past, such as the *sukkot* which Jews build each year in the autumn. They might be a focus of worldwide pilgrimage because of events that happened there – such as Lourdes in France. Within many religious traditions, too, there will be some who are deeply suspicious of an overemphasis on the physicality of the special place at the expense, they would say, of the 'inner' and most precious special place of all.

The activities in this chapter provide children with the opportunity of beginning to understand the concept of special place. For the youngest children, this involves them in identifying their own special place and looking at what a journey involves. For the older children, an example drawn from Christianity or one of the other principal religions provides the focus of each activity.

RELIGIOUS
EDUCATION

WHERE IS YOUR SPECIAL PLACE?

To understand that some people have places which have special significance for them. To understand what makes these places special.

Special place. Identity.

♦♦ *Whole class followed by individual work.*
🕐 *Whole class 15 minutes; individual work 10 minutes.*

Key background information

This activity begins to lay a foundation for developing understanding of the significance of 'special places' within human experience in general and within religious traditions in particular. As they progress through school, children can be introduced to specific religious examples (see 'When do Jews eat in a special place?', page 90, for Year 1 work on the Jewish *sukkah*).

The book *A Place for Ben* is well-established in the primary classroom, though some teachers will want to address a certain stereotyping of roles within it – the mother washing up, the father asleep in a chair. The book, of course, is not just about a special place: its power lies in its implicit statement about relationship.

This activity would link well with 'Which is my special room?' on page 16.

Preparation

Identify a special place of your own. Find a copy of *A Place for Ben* or *Sally's Secret*.

Resources needed

A Place for Ben by Jeanne Titherington (Julia MacRae) or *Sally's Secret* by Shirley Hughes (Red Fox); writing and drawing materials.

What to do

Gather the children together and read them one of the books you have selected. Tell the children about your special place – this could be your bedroom, your car, your garden – and give the reasons why it is special for you. Ask the children about their special places, encouraging them to talk about why they are special.
▲ What do they keep in it?
▲ Who do they share it with?
▲ How do they look after it?
▲ When do they go to it?

Let the children draw or paint a picture of their special place. When the picture is completed, an adult should ask the child about the picture and scribe the child's answer.

Suggestion(s) for extension

The older or more able children could write their own sentence when describing their picture.

Suggestion(s) for support

Those children who do not have their own special place can paint a picture of the special place in the story (the garage for Ben, the garden for Sally).

Assessment opportunities

Looking at the children's pictures, and listening to them talking about their special place, will provide evidence of their growing understanding of the significance of special places.

Display ideas

Mount the children's pictures and descriptions, and display them under a title such as 'Where is your special place?'

RELIGIOUS EDUCATION

WHAT DO YOU NEED FOR A JOURNEY?

To understand that a journey is a significant human activity. To understand that feelings are associated with going on a journey.

Journey. Preparation.

†† *Whole class followed by individual work.*
🕐 *Whole class 15–20 minutes; individual work 10–15 minutes.*

Key background information
The concept of 'journey' is a significant one, both within human experience in general and within religious belief and practice in particular.

Pilgrimage – a journey to a special place of religious significance for devotional reasons – can be found in many religious traditions. At another level, life itself is often described as a kind of pilgrimage.

This activity allows children to begin to explore the place of the journey in their own and others' experience. It will also provide a foundation for later work on different types of pilgrimage.

Preparation
Pack a suitcase with a selection of items (see 'What to do').

Resources needed
Packed suitcase; writing and drawing materials.

What to do
Gather the children around the closed suitcase. Talk about when people use suitcases, such as going on holiday, moving house, going into hospital. Tell the children that this suitcase has been packed for a holiday to the seaside. Open the suitcase, taking out the things inside one by one, and talk about why they have been packed. Items in the suitcase could include:
▲ a teddy – a comforter and a reminder of home;
▲ a map – so that you know where you are going;
▲ clothing – suitable for a seaside holiday;
▲ bucket and spade – for playing on the beach;
▲ suncream and sunhat – to protect you from the sun;

▲ a photograph of members of your family or pets – a reminder of home.

Ask the children what things they would take with them on a journey and why.

Give each child a plain sheet of paper and ask the children to draw the items they have thought of.

As they are working, visit each child individually. Write down what the items are on their sheet and talk to them about journeys they have made and how they felt.

Suggestion(s) for extension
Some children may be able to write without the assistance of an adult. Encourage them to write about their feelings when going on a journey.

Suggestion(s) for support
There will need to be an awareness that, for some children, journeys could be very frightening or upsetting and that not all children will have been on holiday. These children may need more teacher time during the one-to-one discussion.

Assessment opportunities
Individual conversations with the children as they are drawing their pictures will provide evidence of the extent to which they are able to associate feelings with going on journeys.

Opportunities for IT
Ask the children to use a word processor to make a list of special items that they might take with them on a particular journey. Show them how to use the return key to make each item appear on a new line. Suggest that they put the list into order of priority, with the most important item at the top. You may need to demonstrate to children how to move items around by using the 'cut and paste' or 'drag and drop' facilities of their word processor. The children can then format the list, possibly using the centre commands, or change the size and style of the print so that the list can be printed out and displayed in the classroom.

Display ideas
Mount the children's completed drawings and display them around the suitcase with its items. Give the display the title 'Going on a journey'.

RELIGIOUS EDUCATION

WHY IS A CHURCH BUILDING SPECIAL TO CHRISTIANS?

To understand why a church building is special to Christians. To know some of the main features of a church building.

Church. Function.

†† *Session One: whole class followed by paired work. Session Two: whole class – visit.*

🕐 *Session One: whole class 25 minutes; paired work 15 minutes. Session Two: whole class – as appropriate.*

Key background information

Strictly speaking, the word *church* does not refer to a building at all but to the people who make up a Christian community. In that a community of Christians might worship in a building which has been set aside for that purpose, this is a church building – or 'church' for short. Many Christians, of course, worship in their own homes or in buildings or rooms which they borrow or hire from others.

There are many types of church building which are given a variety of titles: a 'cathedral' is a church which houses the bishop's throne (*cathedra* in Latin), a 'chapel' might be a very small building or an area in a larger building which contains an altar, a 'meeting house' is used by members of the Religious Society of Friends (Quakers). Design varies, as does the amount of decoration. It is likely that many statues will be found in a Roman Catholic church, but none in a Methodist church.

The features described in this activity belong to a traditional Church of England (Anglican) church building. Each school, however, will have to adapt the activity according to which building is most accessible for the visit.

In order to reinforce the idea that the 'church' is really

about people, it will be useful for the children to meet within the building some of the people who use it.

The activity (which could link with work on a christening, see 'What happens to some babies when they are christened?', page 70) provides an opportunity for the children to begin to understand how religious buildings function within the life of a community. It will also contribute to the children's social education – in learning that different behaviour is needed in different buildings, how to meet and greet people away from school, how to express thanks, and so on.

Preparation

Session One: take photographs of the outside and inner features of the church to be visited. Prepare a large ground plan of the inside of the church showing the main features, with spaces for the children to label them. Session Two: make arrangements for the visit. Check relevant school policies on organising visits outside school.

Resources needed

Session One: photographs and ground plan of the church. Session Two: clipboards; writing and drawing materials.

What to do

Session One

Show the children a photograph of the outside of the church and ask them questions about it:

▲ What is this building?

▲ How can you tell?

▲ Who uses it?

▲ What do they use it for?

▲ Why is it special for them?

Show the children photographs of features inside the church and talk about what they are used for.

▲ altar – a table near which Christians gather when they meet to worship;

▲ pulpit – a high place where a person stands to teach about God and Jesus;

▲ lectern – a stand for the Bible, the Christian holy book;

▲ stained glass windows – windows made of coloured glass which show scenes from stories which are special for Christians;

▲ pews – seats where Christians sit when they meet together to worship;

▲ font – container for water over which prayers have been said, used in a christening;

▲ organ – musical instrument which is played when Christians sing special songs, or for them to listen to during worship.

Tell the children that they are going to visit the church in the photographs to see all these things. Explain that, because this building is special, they must be very well-behaved and respectful. Divide them into pairs and ask them to complete the ground plan, filling in the names of the features.

Session Two

Spend some time looking at the outside of the church building. Point out features which distinguish it from other buildings: the cross, churchyard and graves, tower, steeple.

Take the children inside the church. Depending on the nature of the building and the arrangements agreed for your visit, some or all of the following activities might be appropriate. The children can:

▲ work in their pairs, identifying the features shown on their ground plan;

▲ make observational drawings of features in the church;

▲ take rubbings of carvings or brasses;

▲ listen to the organ being played or a recording of church music;

▲ listen to a Christian who worships in the church talk about why the church is special to him or her;

▲ sit in silence, taking in the atmosphere, and then talk about their feelings and thoughts.

On their return to school, ask the children to write thank you letters to send to the people who use the church. A display of the children's work could also be sent.

Suggestion(s) for extension

Encourage children to find books in the school library about churches. They can then use them to make lists of things they saw on their visit that were the same and things that were different.

Suggestion(s) for support

Children requiring support can be paired with more able children for the work in Session One and the visit to the church building.

Assessment opportunities

Question the children during the visit in order to find out how much they have learned about the main features of a church building. Ask them why they think the building is special for Christians.

Opportunities for IT

Ask the children to use an encyclopaedia CD-ROM to look for information about church buildings.

The children can also create their own class glossary of words connected with churches, using a word processor or simple desktop publishing software. Each child could have responsibility for writing about one particular part of the church building, possibly leaving a space for an illustration

RELIGIOUS EDUCATION

to be added. These can then be printed out and bound together to make a class reference book.

Children could also use framework software such as *My World 2* with the *Places of Worship* pack to design and build their own model church.

Display ideas

Under the heading 'The church building – a special place for Christians', mount the photographs and display them alongside the various pieces of work produced by the children, such as the drawings of features in the church, brass rubbings, ground plans, and so on.

WHEN DO JEWS EAT IN A SPECIAL PLACE?

To know that Jews build a sukkah during the festival of Sukkot. To understand some of the reasons why a sukkah is a special place for Jews.

Special place. Tradition.

✝✝ *Individual, followed by whole class, ending with group work.*
🕐 *Individual work 10–15 minutes; whole class 20 minutes; group work 30 minutes.*

Key background information

The Jewish festival of Sukkot, which takes place in the autumn, is one of the three biblical pilgrim festivals. This activity does not focus upon the festival itself, however, but rather on the *sukkah* which is erected for the festival.

The word 'sukkah' (plural 'sukkot', thus the name of the festival) is variously translated 'booth', 'shelter', 'hut' or 'tabernacle'. The erection of sukkot helps Jews to remember and relive the experience of their ancient ancestors as they hastily left Egyptian slavery and wandered for many years in desert areas before settling in the land now called Israel.

During the eight- or nine-day festival, which was also a harvest festival in ancient days, Jewish families and groups eat their meals, entertain friends and perhaps even sleep in the sukkah. This is set up out of doors, for example in a garden (where the walls of the house will often form one or several walls of the sukkah), on the balcony of a flat, on the flat roof of a house, or outside the entrance of a Jewish school. The roof, which is put in place last of all, is made of cut vegetation such as branches and leaves (the stars must be visible from the inside) and it is decorated inside with flowers and fruit hanging from the ceiling. Children will sometimes hang paper chains and coloured lights. Pictures and posters with Jewish themes also often adorn the inside walls. The sukkah has at least three sides; the fourth can be left open. It is large enough to house a table and chairs, but

might also be large enough for several hundred people to gather in – outside a synagogue, for example.

Apart from those given in the activity, there are, of course, many other ways of understanding the significance of the sukkah. Its temporary and flimsy structure is a reminder, for example, of the fragility of existence.

Preparation

Set up a display of books and pictures about Jews using a sukkah. Make copies of photocopiable page 148, one for each group.

Resources needed

Selection of books and pictures about Sukkot; shoeboxes; paper, pencils, crayons, felt-tipped pens; paint; Plasticine; LEGO; adhesive; string; photocopiable page 148.

What to do

Ask the children to think about times when they eat with their family or friends in an unusual place. These could include camping in a tent, a barbecue in the garden, a picnic in the park, a picnic on the beach, a meal on a ferry. Let the children choose one of these times and draw or paint it. When they have finished, gather the children together with their pictures and ask them questions about their experiences and feelings when eating in these different places.
▲ Why were you eating in this place?
▲ What did you think about when you were eating there?
▲ Did you like eating there? Why?
▲ Did it feel different to where you normally eat? In what way?
▲ Would you want to do it again? Why?

90

Explain that for some part of every year, people called Jews eat their meals in a shelter they have made themselves. Tell the children that this shelter is called a sukkah and is built for the festival of Sukkot. The children can then be told about the festival of Sukkot and why Jews build a shelter during it (see 'Key background information'). Show the children pictures of Jews eating in a sukkah and have books available which give further information.

Make sure that some of the reasons why Jews build sukkot are clearly understood.

▲ It helps them to remember the story of the Israelites (ancient Jews) wandering through the wilderness and building temporary shelters when they left Egypt.

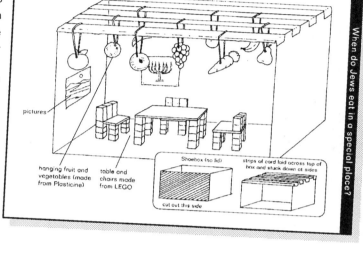

hanging fruit and vegetables (made from Plasticine)

table and chairs made from LEGO

pictures

Shoebox (no lid)

strips of card laid across top of box and stuck down at sides

cut out this side

When do Jews eat in a special place?

▲ The fruit and vegetables decorating the sukkah remind them to be thankful to God for the harvest.

▲ Because Jews everywhere eat in a sukkah during the festival of Sukkot, it reminds them that they are Jews.

Divide the children into groups of five or six and explain that each group is going to make a model sukkah. Give each group a copy of photocopiable page 148. This lists various suggestions which the children can develop when making a model sukkah. Some members of the group can draw small pictures and make miniature fruit and vegetables to decorate the sukkah. Others can make tables and chairs to put inside

it. The rest can use the shoebox to make the framework of the sukkah.

A small climbing frame or other PE equipment can be used to build a play sukkah. It can be decorated with artificial fruit and vegetables and surrounded on three sides by a large piece of material. Twigs and small branches blown down by the wind can be laid over the top and a table and chairs can be placed inside.

Suggestion(s) for extension

Children can use the books you have provided to research further information about sukkot. This can feature as part of the display.

Suggestion(s) for support

Some children may need encouragement when taking part in the class discussion. Ask these children direct questions about their experiences when eating in an unusual place.

Assessment opportunities

Through discussion during and after the making of the model sukkot, the extent to which the children have understood the importance of a sukkah for Jews can be gauged.

Opportunities for IT

Encourage the children to use an encyclopaedia CD-ROM to look for information about Sukkot.

Display ideas

Arrange the model sukkot and the books used in the activity on a table. Display the pictures of Jews in a sukkah, the researched information from the extension activity and the children's pictures from the beginning of the session on a wall behind the table. Give the display the title 'Eating in special places'.

Reference to photocopiable sheet

Photocopiable page 148 gives suggestions which the groups of children can develop when making their sukkot.

WHY DO SOME CHRISTIANS GO TO LOURDES?

To understand why some Christians go to Lourdes. To identify places which make us feel contented.

Pilgrimage. Vision.

†† *Session One: whole class, individual work, ending with paired work.*
Session Two: whole class, followed by individual work.
🕐 *Session One: whole class 10 minutes; individual work 15 minutes; paired work 5 minutes. Session Two: whole class 30 minutes; individual work 30 minutes.*

Key background information

Mary, mother of Jesus, has a special place in the devotional life of Christians of the Catholic and Orthodox traditions. Prayers are offered to the 'Blessed Virgin Mary', and statues or paintings of her will be found in the church building as well as the home.

Several centres of Christian pilgrimage, such as Walsingham in Norfolk ('England's Nazareth'), have grown up around areas where individuals or groups claimed to have received visions or apparitions of Mary. The most famous of these is *Lourdes*, in the Pyrénées region of France, which has become one of the greatest centres of pilgrimage in Christian history.

Lourdes is associated with the life and experiences of the peasant girl, Bernadette Soubirous. It was in 1858 that Bernadette claimed to have a number of visions of the Blessed Virgin Mary at the Grotto of Masabielle, a shallow cave on the bank of the river Gave. Though scoffed at by many, Lourdes soon became a focus of pilgrimage and devotion. News of healings after bathing in the spring water flowing from the cave soon began to spread. The Church authorities, then and now, were reserved about such claims. Bernadette eventually became a nun and died, aged 35, in 1879. She was canonised (officially declared by the Roman Catholic Church to have been a saint) in 1933. Her feast day, when her life is particularly remembered, is 16 April.

While it should be stressed that the purpose of this activity is not to encourage children to believe in visions or apparitions (technically, a vision in which a voice is heard) they should be allowed to engage with the story and to respond in their own way. One seven-year-old child who was asked what he thought a vision might be said that it was like a photograph which had not come out properly!

Preparation

Session One: identify a place which is special to you. Session Two: make a copy of photocopiable page 149.

Resources needed

Session One: drawing materials; peaceful music (optional). Session Two: photocopiable page 149; writing materials; chalkboard/flip chart.

What to do
Session One

Talk to the children about a place which makes you feel peaceful and contented, explaining some of the reasons why it has this effect on you. These might include:
▲ because something happened there which you want to remember;
▲ because you want to be with people who go there;
▲ because of its physical features.

Ask the children to think about a place where they feel peaceful or contented. When they have identified such a place, ask them to draw a picture and write one or two sentences about it. Then they should talk to a friend about the place they have chosen. (While this part of the activity is taking place, some peaceful music, such as that played on pan pipes, could be played to create a sense of atmosphere.)

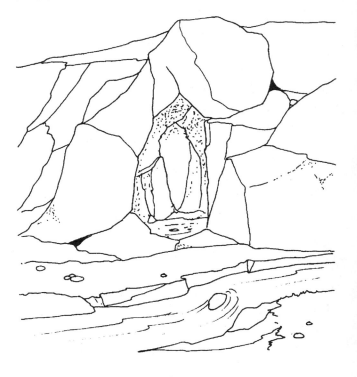

Encountering special places

Assessment opportunities

The children's answers to the questions following the telling of the story and their own written accounts will provide evidence of the extent to which they have understood the significance of Lourdes for some Christians.

Opportunities for IT

Ask the children to use an encyclopaedia CD-ROM to find out information about Lourdes and what has happened there since the time of Bernadette. Using a word processor, the children can then write about Lourdes in greater detail, including in their writing the information they have researched.

Assembly ideas

As part of an assembly focusing on a theme such as 'Special places' or 'Journeys', ask some children to talk about the places which make them feel peaceful or contented. Children or teachers from other classes can also be invited to talk about their special places, and some written accounts could be read out in order to explain why Lourdes is a special place for some Christians. You may like to end the assembly with a reflection such as, 'And now, while we listen to peaceful music, let us think about how we feel when we are in our own special place.' (If you played music during the class activity, you may like to use the same piece of music during this period of reflection.)

Reference to photocopiable sheet

Photocopiable page 149 provides an account of the story of Bernadette for the teacher's use. The final part of the story should be read again to those children carrying out the extension activity to help them focus on the reasons for present-day pilgrimages to Lourdes.

Session Two

Having gathered the children together, tell or read the story of Bernadette on photocopiable page 149.

Ask the children questions about the story to develop their understanding. For example:
▲ Why was Mary important to Bernadette?
▲ Why did Bernadette call Mary a vision?
▲ Why did Bernadette go back to the cave when her mother had told her not to?
▲ Why did some people call Bernadette names? How do you think this made Bernadette feel?
▲ Why do some people go on pilgrimage to Lourdes?
▲ Would a pilgrimage be a waste of time if a sick person was not made better? Why?

When you feel the children have sufficiently understood the story, ask them to imagine that they are one of Bernadette's friends. Tell them to write the story of what happened when they went to gather firewood and came back to find Bernadette kneeling in the grass. Write the following words on the board for the children to refer to while they are writing: 'cave', 'vision', 'Mary', 'rosary', 'mother', 'drink', 'spring', 'water'.

Suggestion(s) for extension

Ask children to add to their story by writing about what has happened at Lourdes since the time of Bernadette. Read the children the penultimate paragraph on photocopiable page 149 again to help them with this part of the activity.

Suggestion(s) for support

More time might be needed with some children in order to make sure that they understand the importance of Mary to Christians and hence the importance of Lourdes.

The story of Bernadette

Bernadette pulled her woollen shawl more tightly round her shoulders. She wished her friends would hurry back. It was getting cold. They were collecting firewood but Bernadette couldn't help them. She knew that if she went in the long grass to pick up sticks, her feet would get wet and she would be ill again. While she waited, she looked around and noticed a small cave in the hillside. As she looked at the cave, a strange light seemed to glow inside it. Bernadette rubbed her eyes and looked again, but the light was still there. It was growing brighter all the time and, as Bernadette watched, she saw a lady appear out of the light. Bernadette felt frightened at first, but when she looked at the lady's face she felt peaceful and happy. The lady was wearing a white dress with a blue sash, and in her hand she held a rosary. Bernadette knew at once that this was a vision of Mary. She sank to her knees, not caring about the wet grass any more, took her rosary out of her pocket and said a prayer as she moved the beads through her fingers.

'Bernadette, get up! What are you doing kneeling in the wet grass!' Bernadette staggered to her feet and, turning round, saw her friends, their arms full of firewood. 'Can't you see her?' Bernadette asked, but the vision had disappeared. Bernadette told her friends what had happened but they didn't believe her. They thought that she had been day-dreaming again.

When her mother saw Bernadette's wet skirt, she was very angry and told Bernadette that she was not to go back to the cave. But Bernadette did go back. She went back to the cave every day, and each time she saw the vision of Mary. On one of her visits, the lady pointed to the earth and told Bernadette to drink. Bernadette used her fingers to dig, and after a while the soil felt damp. As she dug, the hole began to fill with water from an underground spring. Bernadette drank the water, which was cold and clear.

Bernadette told the people in her village about what she had seen. Some of them teased her and called her names, but others visited the cave themselves to see if Mary would appear to them. No one else saw the vision of Mary, but many people drank the water from the spring and some of them who had been ill said that the water had made them better. More and more people came to drink from the spring. People who felt ill, people who felt sad, people who were lonely, came to drink the water and went away feeling better.

After a while, a big church was built near the cave and pools were made to hold the spring water. People came from all over the world to visit the spot where Bernadette had seen the vision of Mary. Today, thousands of people make a pilgrimage and bathe in the water. Many of them come in wheelchairs, some have to be carried on stretchers but there are always people ready to help them. Some of the people who make the pilgrimage say that they have been cured by visiting this special place and drinking the water.

Many Christians call Bernadette a saint, and in their homes have pictures of Lourdes, the village in France where Bernadette saw the vision.

RELIGIOUS EDUCATION

WHY DOES A MUSLIM STAND ON A PRAYER-MAT?

To know the features of a Muslim prayer-mat. To know how a prayer-mat is used by Muslims.

Special place. Prayer.

†† *Whole class followed by individual work.*
🕐 *Whole class 30 minutes; individual work 30 minutes.*

Key background information

Set prayer five times daily is one of the five basic duties (or 'pillars', see 'Why is Ramadan a special month for Muslims?', page 76) of a Muslim. It requires careful preparation, including finding a clean space upon which to perform prayer and establishing the direction in which to face. This direction – the word *qiblah* is Arabic for 'direction' – is towards the Ka'bah in Makkah.

In order to pray to Allah (God) appropriately, a Muslim will stand upon clean ground. The large carpet in the prayer hall of a mosque will provide this. Away from the mosque, however, a Muslim might use a prayer-mat which serves, therefore, as a 'portable mosque'. A prayer-mat is not obligatory, though. A sheet of clean paper would do and ultimately, Muslims would say, it is the intention to worship Allah properly which is the vital part of prayer.

A prayer-mat provides sufficient room to perform the bodily movements of set prayer. A sequence of these movements – several such sequences are performed at each time of prayer – begins with the standing position, but culminates in the full prostration where the forehead touches the ground. In this position, the Muslim is bodily acknowledging that he or she is the servant of Allah.

There is no one 'standard' design of prayer-mat, though they follow the conventions of Muslim art and design. There is a strong tradition against figurative art – producing representations of living things artistically – in favour of symmetrical patterns (Arabesque).

A prayer-mat will usually have tassels top and bottom. It might consist simply of Arabesque and floral patterns. The one described in this activity is a common design and includes

in the top two panels representations of a mosque and the Ka'bah in Makkah. Below is a stylised arch which, when the mat is positioned, indicates *qiblah*.

If away from a mosque or familiar surroundings, a Muslim might use a 'qiblah compass' to establish the direction for prayer. This is a compass with a circle of numbers behind the magnetic needle. By rotating the compass so that the magnetic north end of the needle rests on the number for the part of the world in which you are in (a small booklet informs a Muslim which is the appropriate number), an arrow marked alongside the numbers indicates *qiblah*. Some prayer-mats have a qiblah compass sewn on to them.

Preparation

Make a display of books and pictures about Islam including pictures showing Muslims at prayer. Obtain a prayer-mat (see 'Useful books and resources', page 107). If possible, obtain a qiblah compass. Make copies of photocopiable page 150, one for each child.

Resources needed

Books and pictures about Islam; prayer-mat; qiblah compass (optional); photocopiable page 150; writing and drawing materials.

What to do

Seat the children on the floor in a circle near the display of books and pictures. Tell them that you are going to show them something which is used by many Muslims every day of their lives. Unfold the prayer-mat and hold it up for all the children to observe. Let them spend a few moments looking at it carefully before asking them what they can see. Their answers will give you an opportunity to focus on the different features of the prayer-mat and to explain what they represent.

▲ The building with a dome will be a mosque – a place where many Muslims meet together to pray.

▲ The cube-shaped building standing in the centre of a courtyard is the Ka'bah in Makkah – marking the spot where, Muslims believe, God was first worshipped;

▲ The decorated archway represents the alcove in a mosque wall showing the direction of Makkah – towards which all Muslims face to pray.

▲ The patterns round the outside make the prayer-mat look

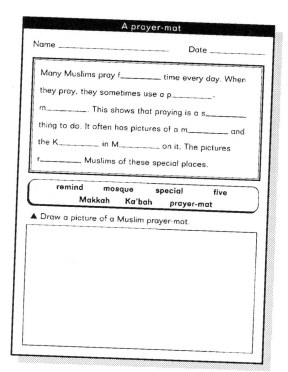

A prayer-mat

Name _____ Date _____

Many Muslims pray f_____ time every day. When they pray, they sometimes use a p_____-m_____. This shows that praying is a s_____ thing to do. It often has pictures of a m_____ and the K_____ in M_____ on it. The pictures r_____ Muslims of these special places.

remind   mosque   special   five
Makkah   Ka'bah   prayer-mat

▲ Draw a picture of a Muslim prayer-mat.

Assessment opportunities
The accuracy with which the children complete the photocopiable sheet will indicate the extent of their knowledge on the features of a Muslim prayer-mat and how it is used.

Opportunities for IT
Let the children use an art package to design their own prayer-mat. They may like to include features of the mat shown to them in the activity.

Display ideas
Add a prayer-mat, and examples of children's work, to the display of books and pictures which have been set up prior to the activity. Label the features of the prayer-mat.

Reference to photocopiable sheet
Photocopiable page 150 provides an account of how a prayer-mat is used, in which the children fill in missing words, choosing from a selection of words given. There is also space for the children to complete an observational drawing, using information gained in the activity.

beautiful and show how special it is to Muslims. They are called Arabesque patterns.

Ask the children how they think Muslims would use a prayer-mat . Some children might think that it is kept on the wall to be looked at. Others will know that it is placed on the ground and used for prayer. Explain further how Muslims use the prayer-mat, stressing that praying is an important and serious activity for Muslims. (Some children may already have a stereotypical view of Muslims at prayer which will need to be addressed.) If a qiblah compass is available, show the children how it is used to find the direction of Makkah. Place the prayer-mat on the ground and, referring to the pictures and books on display, talk about the prayer positions and the significance of removing footwear. Finally, tell the children that many Muslims will pray like this five times a day.

Give each child a copy of photocopiable page 150 and ask them to read through it and fill in the missing words. The lower half of the sheet should be used to complete an observational drawing of the prayer-mat. They can then draw a border on another piece of paper using Arabesque patterns.

Suggestion(s) for extension
Using the missing words from the photocopiable sheet, children can write about a prayer-mat. Allow them to have another look at the prayer-mat used in the main activity.

Suggestion(s) for support
Some children may need the help of an adult when reading through the sheet. Numbering the missing words and spaces when the children have identified the links will allow them to complete the sheet independently.

WHY DO MOST HINDUS HAVE A SHRINE IN THEIR HOMES?

To understand why most Hindus have a shrine in their homes. To identify objects of personal value and reasons for their significance.

Shrine. Devotion.

†† *Whole class followed by individual work.*
🕐 *Whole class 30 minutes; individual work 30 minutes.*

Key background information
Though to the outsider it might seem that Hindus worship a number of gods, many Hindus would wish to assert that there is only one God. They might say that the many images of the gods illustrate different aspects or characteristics of God. This has sometimes been compared to the role of photographs: you might know someone well, but it would take many photographs, each illustrating different aspects of their personality, to capture a full sense of the person.

Hindu gods and goddesses are often illustrated in pictures, but also in three-dimensional images or *murtis*. (The word 'image' should be used rather than 'idol'.) The god Krishna, usually depicted as blue-skinned and holding or playing a flute, will often be prominent in home shrines in Britain.

Hindu worship is as much focused on the home as the temple. Indeed, when they use the word 'temple' (*mandir*), many Hindu children will be referring to the shrine in their own homes.

Home shrines might contain a wide range of pictures of deities and holy people, images and objects of devotional value (such as copper pots containing water from the river Ganges).

This activity provides an opportunity to learn both *about* religion – in this instance, an aspect of Hinduism – and *from* religion.

Preparation
Set up a display of books, pictures and artefacts associated with Hinduism. Obtain a statuette or picture (see 'Useful books and resources', page 107) and place it in a special bag. Make copies of photocopiable page 151, one for each child.

Resources needed
Statuette or picture of Hindu deity or deities; special bag; photocopiable page 151; writing and drawing materials.

What to do
Sit the children in a circle and tell them that they are going to see something which is very special to a group of people called Hindus. Carefully remove the statuette or picture from the bag and ask the children what they can see. (If there are Hindu children in the class, they may be prepared to give some information about it.) Tell the children that the statuette or picture reminds Hindus of God and is therefore very special, and that in most Hindu homes there will be a special place which is always kept clean and where statuettes or pictures like this one are kept. Members of the family pray there each day, having washed first. Explain that this special place is called a *shrine* and that it might be a whole room, a corner of a room, a shelf in a room or a cupboard. Describe some of the things that happen at a Hindu home shrine. For instance:

▲ shoes are removed – to keep the area clean and to show respect;

▲ flowers are placed in front of the statuettes/pictures – to make the shrine look beautiful;

▲ incense sticks are lit – to make the area around the shrine smell pleasant;

▲ candles or lamps are lit and waved in front of each image – to show respect to God;

▲ a bell is rung – to show that worship is about to begin;

▲ prayers are said or sung – an important part of the worship that takes place at the shrine.

Ask the children to imagine that they have a cupboard in their room at home where they can put things which are important to them. Give out copies of photocopiable page 151 and ask them to write about the things they would put in the cupboard and why they would choose them. When the children have written about their items they can draw a picture of each of them in the space provided on the photocopiable sheet.

Suggestion(s) for extension
Ask children to write an account of what happens at a Hindu home shrine. They could use the books, pictures and artefacts on display to help them.

Suggestion(s) for support
Some children may need help in identifying objects which have special significance for them. If possible, arrange for an adult helper or support teacher to support these children.

Assessment opportunities
After a period of several days, show the children the Hindu statuette or picture again and ask them what they remember about the place where it might be found in a Hindu home.

Opportunities for IT
Tell the children to use a word processor to write their own list of items they would put into a special cupboard and why they would put them there. These can then be printed out and either bound as a class book or displayed in the class.

Display ideas
Add the statuette or picture to the display already set up (see 'Preparation') and give it the title 'We have been finding out about Hindus'.

Reference to photocopiable sheet
Photocopiable page 151 allows the children to write a list of items which have special significance for them and then to draw them on the shelves of an imaginary cupboard.

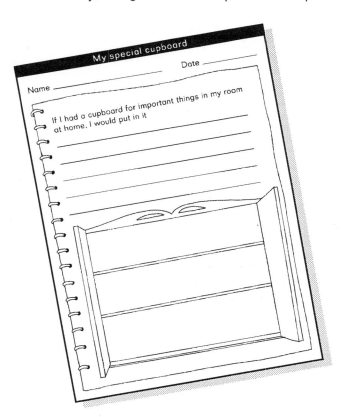

My special cupboard

Name

Date

If I had a cupboard for important things in my room at home, I would put in it

Expressing what is important

In a whole range of intentional and unintentional ways, people express what is of importance and value to them. At the individual level, the painter, sculptor, musician and poet are all striving to express through their chosen medium a range of emotions and interpretations. At the group level, rituals embody a range of meanings (conventions and beliefs, values and ideals) even though these might only be apparent to the knowing observer. Participants, being 'inside' the rituals as it were, might 'feel' rather than understand what is going on. For the individual as well as the group, there will be particular objects – from the holiday souvenir to the crown of state – which evoke memories and associations.

In religious practice there are many ways in which individuals and groups seek to give expression to their highest and deepest beliefs and aspirations: in prayer and worship, in the stories they tell, and in the art forms which all religions have given rise to. In that much is an attempt to express the inexpressible, symbolism abounds. As such, one of the key skills that religious education seeks to develop is the ability to interpret and to use symbolism.

The activities in this chapter give children the opportunity to begin to explore the place of prayer within religion and their own response to silence, the use and value of significant objects and religious artefacts, and the use of symbolism in both art and story.

97

WHAT HAPPENS WHEN I AM STILL AND QUIET?

To be able to sit quietly while listening to a piece of music and then talk about the experience.

Stillness. The inner life.

Whole class.

As appropriate.

Key background information

This deceptively simple exercise is designed not only as an end in itself but also as a basis for later work on the 'inner' aspects of experience, as well as key aspects of religion (such as prayer and meditation). As such, it can be seen as making a contribution to the spiritual development of children. It might also give children skills which they will be able to apply during times of silence and quiet reflection within school or class collective worship.

Some teachers will find that it is an exercise which is worth repeating (after a windy playtime or at the start of an exciting day, perhaps) and that, with repetition, the children will become more adept at 'stilling' themselves. Indeed, once used to it, children often look forward to the experience of this quiet time.

Some thought will need to be given to the transition periods in and out of the activity. After it is over, for example, there will need to be a gradual return to the pace of normal classroom life.

Preparation

Prepare the classroom by moving furniture to provide sufficient space or use another area such as the school hall. Choose an appropriate piece of music, such as flute or pan-pipe music, and check that the equipment to play it on is in working order.

Resources needed

An appropriate piece of music. For the extension activity – writing and drawing materials.

What to do

Explain to the children that they are going to have a quiet time. Ask them to find a big space and make themselves comfortable, either sitting or lying. Tell them that you are going to make the classroom darker to help with the quiet time. Darken the room as much as possible without making it frightening. Then, when the children are still and quiet, play the chosen piece of music. Talk quietly to the children for the first few moments, telling them that they can close their eyes if they want to while they listen to the music. If some children find it difficult to remain still and quiet, ask an adult to sit with them. Play the music for as long as seems appropriate (this period will increase the more the children get used to it). Fade out the music and quietly ask the children to sit up when they are ready. Let the children describe what they felt while they were being quiet or what pictures they saw in their heads. Return the classroom to its normal lighting.

Suggestion(s) for extension

Encourage the children to record what they experienced during the quiet time in words and/or pictures.

Suggestion(s) for support

Some children might need the support provided by an adult presence during the quiet time.

Assessment opportunities

Observing the children during the quiet time and listening to their descriptions of what they felt or 'saw' will provide evidence of the extent to which the children are able to be still during an allocated period and how well they are able to describe their experiences.

RELIGIOUS EDUCATION

WHAT DO JEWS HAVE ON THEIR TABLE AT THE SHABBAT MEAL?

To know that certain items are associated with the Jewish Shabbat meal.

Symbolism. Ritual.

✚✚ *Whole class followed by individual work.*

🕐 *Whole class 15 minutes; individual work 20 minutes.*

⚠ *Care will need to be taken in displaying the knife.*

Key background information

This activity links well with the activity that is based on the Jewish Shabbat (see 'When do we meet together as a family?', page 26) to which it would form a logical sequel.

The items referred to in the activity are:

▲ a kiddush cup – the cup over which, when filled with wine, the blessing (*kiddush*) is said by the father at the beginning of the Shabbat meal;

▲ Shabbat candles – over which the mother says a blessing in the home to welcome in each Shabbat;

▲ challah cover – a decorated cloth cover which is placed over the special braided Shabbat bread (*challah*);

▲ knife – which is used to cut the Shabbat bread;

▲ kappel – sometimes also called a *yarmulke* or *kippah*, which is worn by male Jews during prayer and by many Orthodox male Jews all the time, to indicate that they are in the presence of God.

▲ 'Aleph' is the first letter of the Hebrew alphabet.

The story of Kiddush Cup, loosely based on an American original by Byrd Salop, is not only about Jewish artefacts, of course. It is also a tale with a message familiar in folk tradition: be content with what and where you are. Listening to the story could be said, then, to be contributing to the children's moral education.

Preparation

Gather together and display the five items referred to in the story: kiddush cup, Shabbat candles, challah cover, knife and challah. Place a label next to each artefact. Make a copy of photocopiable page 152 and become acquainted with the story of Kiddush Cup. Place a kiddush cup inside a bag. Make copies of photocopiable page 153, one for each child.

Resources needed

Jewish artefacts associated with the story; special bag; photocopiable pages 152 and 153; writing and drawing materials.

What to do

Gather the children together in a circle and tell them that you are going to show them something which is very special to people called Jews. Remove the kiddush cup from the bag and ask the children what they can see. Tell them that it is a kiddush cup used by Jews at the Shabbat meal each week. If the activity 'When do we meet together as a family?' has already been carried out, ask the children what they remember about Shabbat, prompting them by showing them the artefacts. If this previous activity has not been carried out, explain briefly what happens during a Shabbat meal, using the artefacts as visual aids. Then, tell or read the story of Kiddush Cup.

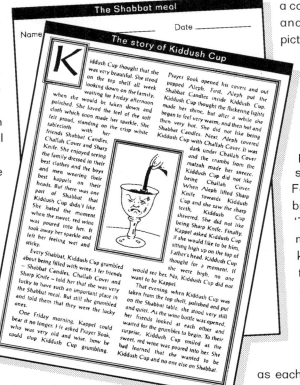

In small groups, give each child a copy of photocopiable page 153 and ask them to match each picture to its correct label.

Suggestion(s) for extension

For children requiring extension work, ask them to use the reverse of their photocopiable sheet to write a sentence about each artefact. For instance, 'The special braided bread is called challah', 'The candles are lit by the mother', 'Red wine is put in the kiddush cup', 'The knife cuts the special bread', 'The challah cover is put over the bread'.

Suggestion(s) for support

Some children may need adult help when matching the words as each artefact begins with either a 'k' or a 'c'. If they experience difficulties, show them how to look at the second or even third letter of each word.

Assessment opportunities

While the groups are matching the labels to the correct artefact, ask each child individually to talk about when and how the objects are used.

Opportunities for IT

Ask the children to use an encyclopaedia CD-ROM to find out further information about the Shabbat meal.

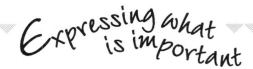

Display ideas

As the children complete their sheets, add these to the display of artefacts. Use a title such as 'The kiddush cup and her friends'.

Reference to photocopiable sheets

Photocopiable page 152 tells the story of Kiddush Cup which is told to the children during the activity. Photocopiable page 153 has the Hebrew letter 'aleph' at the top to link with the story of Kiddush Cup. The children should match each label to the correct artefact.

WHAT DO THINGS MAKE US REMEMBER?

To understand that objects have the power to affect the present by evoking memories of the past.

Remembrance. Identity.

†† *Whole class followed by individual work.*
🕐 *Whole class 20 minutes; individual work 20 minutes.*

Key background information

The enrichment of the present through objects evoking memories of the past is a dimension both of human experience and religious belief and practice. As such, this activity would link well with that exploring the role of food for Jews at Passover (see 'Why do Jews eat special food at Passover?', page 78).

Though the story of *Wilfrid Gordon McDonald Partridge* has little text, it is profound in that it tells of an old lady who is leading a hollow life because she has lost touch with her past. Through the caring and active concern of a small boy taking objects which are full of meaning and memory (a ball, a medal, a shell, a puppet and an egg), she regains a connection with her past and thus becomes complete again. It is this profundity (some might say spirituality) underlying the story that makes it so suitable for use in assembly and collective worship.

Preparation

Borrow an object from the Reception class which will evoke memories for the children in the present Year 1 class. Make copies of photocopiable page 154, one for each child. Find a copy of *Wilfrid Gordon McDonald Partridge* by Mem Fox (Picture Puffin).

Resources needed

Object from Reception class; a copy of *Wilfrid Gordon McDonald Partridge*; writing and drawing materials; photocopiable page 154.

What to do

Show the children the object which has been borrowed from the Reception class (for example, a stuffed toy, a pencil pot, a cushion or a rug) and ask them questions about it.
▲ Where have you seen this before?
▲ Where was it kept?
▲ What do you think about when you see it?
   Explain to the children that you are going to tell them a story about a little boy who helps an older lady remember things. Read to them *Wilfrid Gordon McDonald Partridge*.
   Give each child a copy of photocopiable page 154 and ask them to write or draw the answers to the questions. As the children are working, go round and ask them to describe their own object which evokes a memory that they have drawn or written about. What memories does this object evoke?

Suggestion(s) for extension

Once they have completed the photocopiable sheet, children could draw a picture of the object borrowed from the Reception class and write about what it reminds them of.

Suggestion(s) for support

If children experience difficulties when completing the photocopiable sheet, encourage them to draw their answers when responding to the pictures.

Assessment opportunities

The children's responses, both on the photocopiable sheet and orally when describing their own object, will provide evidence of the extent to which they understand how objects can evoke memories of the past.

Opportunities for IT

Tell the children to use a word processor to write about their own special object. If the children are willing to bring the objects in to school they may also like to create labels for a class display. They could use a drawing program to draw their object.

What do things make us remember?

Name _____ Date _____

▲ What did these things remind Miss Nancy Alison Delacourt Cooper of?

medal
egg
shell
puppet on a string
football

▲ What reminds you of something?

Draw the object or write about it.

RELIGIOUS EDUCATION

Assembly ideas

As part of an assembly focusing on a theme such as 'Memories' or 'Special objects', choose a child to be the leader. Ask the child to collect together the five objects referred to in the story (shoebox of shells, puppet on strings, medal, football, egg) and put them in a basket. The leader could begin the assembly by showing two personal objects and describing the memories they evoke. The story of *Wilfrid Gordon McDonald Partridge* can then be told or read, with the objects being lifted out of the basket as they occur in the story. End the assembly with a reflection such as, 'And now, in a moment of quiet, let us think about the small boy in the story and how good he felt when he made Miss Nancy smile'.

Reference to photocopiable sheet

Photocopiable page 154 provides an opportunity for the children to demonstrate what they have learned from the story read to them in the activity. It also allows them to reflect on their own experience by identifying an object which evokes their own memories.

WHY DO PEOPLE USE COLOUR TO SHOW IMPORTANT THINGS?

To understand that the use of colour can be a significant medium of expression. To be able to use colour in expressing feelings and ideas.

Symbolism. Expression.

✝✝ *Small groups, whole class and then paired work.*
🕐 *Small groups 10 minutes; whole class 20 minutes; paired work as appropriate.*

Key background information

The use of colour to express important ideas and emotions is not confined to religion. As the children progress in religious education, however, they will learn about a variety of artistic and symbolic traditions.

The use of stained-glass windows is particularly associated with church buildings in the West, though the use of such windows is not confined to churches. Particularly when few churchgoers were literate, the stories portrayed in stained-glass windows were an important teaching aid. The colour of such windows must also have been stunning to those living in relative poverty. Early stained-glass windows consisted of individual pieces of coloured glass. Later, glass on to which colours had been applied was used. There are many British artists who have distinguished themselves in their use of stained glass. These include Edward Burne-Jones

(1833–98) and John Piper (1903–92), famous for his work in the new Coventry Cathedral.

This activity would form an ideal link with the visit to the church (see 'Why is a church building special to Christians?', page 88).

Preparation

Obtain pictures and/or take photographs of stained-glass windows in churches or other local buildings.

Resources needed

Six pieces of coloured card (red, yellow, green, blue, purple, white); paper; crayons or coloured pencils (several shades of each colour); tissue paper; adhesive.

What to do

Arrange the children into six groups. Give each group a different coloured piece of card and different coloured pencils. Ask them to choose a scribe and then make a list on the card of anything that their colour makes them feel or think of. Set a time limit for this task. At the end of the time limit, bring the groups together and ask for volunteers to read through each list. Then choose one of the colours and ask the children how that colour makes them feel. Repeat this with each colour. Next, tell the children that for hundreds of years, people have used coloured glass to show how they feel and to tell stories. Show pictures or photographs of stained-glass windows and ask the children what they think the person who made the window was feeling. Explain that the black lines running through the pictures are the strips of lead that are used to hold the pieces of coloured or painted glass next to each other.

Divide the children into pairs and tell them that they are going to design a coloured window to show two of the

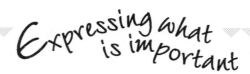

feelings talked about earlier. Encourage the children to use a range of colours and shades in their windows. Remind the children that they can use blank paper strips in between their colours to stick them together. Give each pair drawing materials and black paper. Take the opportunity while the children are working on their windows to talk to each pair about what they are doing. Share interesting ideas with the rest of the class.

When their pictures are finished, suggest that they may like to make the same or a similar picture with tissue paper, which can then be stuck on a window in the classroom.

Suggestion(s) for extension
Encourage children to write a short description of their finished picture or coloured window, explaining what it means to them.

Suggestion(s) for support
Make sure that the groups and the pairs are of mixed ability to ensure that all children are able to participate.

Assessment opportunities
Listening to the children as they work together in pairs, and asking them about the symbolism within their completed windows, will provide evidence of the extent to which they understand the significance of colour, both as a medium of expression and to indicate feelings and ideas.

Opportunities for IT
Let the children use an art package to design their own stained-glass window. They can create the design of their windows using either freely drawn shapes or geometrical shapes filled with colour. Show the children how to draw the outlines with a thick black line to form the leading of the stained-glass window. The children can then use the fill option to add colour to their design and experiment with changing the colours. More competent children can mix or select their own shades of colour. Print the final designs out on paper or, if available, on special overhead transparency sheets designed for colour printers, and attach them to the classroom windows.

Display ideas
Display a range of children's coloured tissue pictures on the window itself. In between the windows, mount some or all of the pieces of coloured card containing the lists of things that these colours made the groups think of. Pictures or photographs of stained-glass windows could also be mounted. Any available examples of real or replica stained-glass work could be placed on the window alongside the children's work (clear plastic pictures to stick on windows, small panels of glass and toy shapes which are filled in with melted plastic are increasingly common). Give the display a title such as 'We use colour to show important things'.

WHY DO CHRISTIANS PRAY?

To know some of the reasons why Christians might pray. To identify some of the sentiments in a Christian prayer.

Prayer. God.

†† *Pairs, followed by whole class, returning to pairs.*

🕐 *Pairs 15 minutes; whole class 15 minutes; pairs 15 minutes.*

Key background information
The association of prayer with religious belief and practice is very familiar, though there is sometimes a tendency to reduce prayer to a series of requests for things wanted. However, the prayer tradition in Christianity, as in other religious traditions, is far broader and more subtle than this.

Beginning with a number of situations which give rise to talk between people, this activity provides an opportunity to understand some of the dimensions of Christian prayer. The most famous and well-loved Christian prayer – called 'The Lord's Prayer' because Jesus gave it to his followers as a model (see Matthew's Gospel, chapter 6; another version can be found in Luke's Gospel, chapter 11) – is rendered loosely on photocopiable page 155.

Preparation
Make copies of photocopiable page 155, one for each pair. Write the four situations (see 'What to do') where the children can see them.

RELIGIOUS EDUCATION

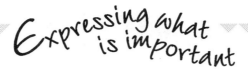

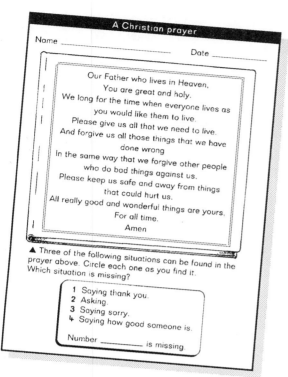

A Christian prayer

Name _____
                                    Date _____

Our Father who lives in Heaven,
You are great and holy.
We long for the time when everyone lives as
you would like them to live.
Please give us all that we need to live.
And forgive us all those things that we have
done wrong
In the same way that we forgive other people
who do bad things against us.
Please keep us safe and away from things
that could hurt us.
All really good and wonderful things are yours.
For all time.
Amen

▲ Three of the following situations can be found in the prayer above. Circle each one as you find it. Which situation is missing?

1 Saying thank you.
2 Asking.
3 Saying sorry.
4 Saying how good someone is.

Number _____ is missing.

Resources needed
Photocopiable page 155; writing materials.

What to do
Ask the children to work in pairs. Tell them that they are going to role-play four different situations. Ensure that the four situations are written where the children can see them and let them work through each one in turn:

▲ saying thank you for something;
▲ asking for something;
▲ saying sorry for something;
▲ saying how good someone is.

As they are role-playing, choose some of the best examples from each situation. Use these as demonstrations to show to the rest of the class at the end.

Gather the children together and explain that people who are Christians want to talk to God about the same kinds of things that they have just been talking to each other about. Tell them that when they talk to God, Christians call it prayer. Sometimes, prayers are already written and can be like poems or songs. At other times, Christians make up their own prayer as they talk to God. (Some children might want to talk about prayers they know or have heard.)

Give each pair a copy of photocopiable page 155. Explain that the words on the sheet are a prayer that Christians might use when they talk to God. Read through the words with the children and explain the task which they have to complete.

Suggestion(s) for extension
More able children could look up the words of the Lord's Prayer in the Bible (see 'Key background information') and

match the form of words and sentiments in that version with those on the photocopiable sheet.

Suggestion(s) for support
Arrange the children in mixed ability groups for the role-play and when working on the photocopiable sheet.

Assessment opportunities
By reading the children's completed photocopiable sheets you will be able to gauge the extent to which the children have understood why Christians pray and whether they have been able to identify some of the sentiments found in a Christian prayer.

Reference to photocopiable sheet
Photocopiable page 155 has a loose rendering of the Christian Lord's Prayer. It has within it three of the four situations in which Christians might want to talk to God (asking, saying sorry and saying how good someone is – saying thank you is absent). Working in pairs, the children have to identify three of the four situations.

WHY DO SIKHS TELL THE STORY OF GURU NANAK BATHING IN THE RIVER?

To know that stories convey messages. To identify some of the messages in a particular story.

Symbolism. Communication.

†† *Groups, followed by whole class, then groups, whole class, ending with individual work.*

⏱ *Groups 10 minutes; whole class 20 minutes; groups 10 minutes; whole class 10 minutes; individual work 20 minutes.*

Key background information
Guru Nanak (1469–1539) was the founder and first guru of the Sikh religion. He is honoured as a guru (literally 'teacher', but sometimes translated as 'prophet') by Sikhs, and many of his words are contained in the Guru Granth Sahib, the Sikh holy book. Stories are told about Guru Nanak's life and travels, many of which convey the message that he was a wise man truly in touch with God.

Story is of great significance both to human experience and to religious belief and practice. It could be said that, in one sense, our lives are about forming and then retelling our own personal stories. Within religious traditions, stories are often used to convey teachings, insights and truths which would be hard to convey in other ways. Clearly, the story about Guru Nanak used as the focus of this activity is

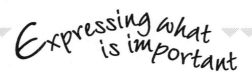

attempting to describe an experience or conviction beyond the limits of everyday language.

Preparation

Make a copy of photocopiable page 156 and become familiar with the story. Make a copy of photocopiable page 157 for those children carrying out the support activity.

Resources needed

Photocopiable page 156; writing materials. For the support activity – photocopiable page 157.

What to do

Arrange the children into groups of five or six and ask each group to think of a story which gives a message. For example Little Red Riding Hood's message could be 'Do as your mother tells you', (see 'Should Little Red Riding Hood have spoken to the wolf?', page 50) the message of *Dogger* could be 'Bella was special because she was kind to Dave', (see 'What is important to me?', page 15) the message in *But Martin!* could be 'People are different but everyone is good at something', (see 'What makes me special?', page 20).

Bring the groups together, giving each one the opportunity to talk about the story they chose and the message(s) it contains. Tell the children that you are going to tell them a story which contains messages. Tell them that it is a story told by a group of people called Sikhs about a man who is very important to them. The man's name is Nanak, but Sikhs call him 'Guru Nanak' to show how important he was. Ask the children to listen carefully to the story and remember the messages they hear. Tell or read the story.

Ask the children to work in their groups again and to choose a scribe who can make a list of the messages in the story they have just heard. While the groups are making their lists, go round and offer prompts when needed.

▲ Was Guru Nanak an ordinary person?
▲ Where did Guru Nanak say that he had been?
▲ Was Guru Nanak different when he came back?
▲ What did Guru Nanak do when he came back?

When the lists are complete, a class list can be made with each message being discussed in turn. These messages could include that Guru Nanak:

▲ was a special person;
▲ is an important person to Sikhs;

▲ was a holy person;
▲ was doing what God wanted him to do.

To complete the activity, ask the children to write the story of Guru Nanak in their own words. They should include at least one of the messages in the story.

Suggestion(s) for extension

Ask children to write their own stories about people who are important and to explain what the message is in their written account.

Suggestion(s) for support

Use mixed ability groups for the two group activities. If children experience difficulties give them a copy of photocopiable page 157 to use during the final part of the activity.

Assessment opportunities

Listening to the children while they are discussing in their groups and reading their accounts of the story and the messages from it, will give an indication of the extent to which they understand how messages can be conveyed in a story.

Opportunities for IT

Ask children to use a word processor or simple desktop publishing package to write their version of the story of Guru Nanak. Alternatively, the story could be split into several parts and groups can write different parts of the story. A class book can then be compiled. Pictures could be added, either drawn on the printed version, or scanned from children's own line drawings.

Display ideas

Using the title 'Many stories contain messages', display the titles of stories and their messages listed by the groups. For example, *But Martin!* – people are different, but everyone is good at something. Mount the children's written stories and photocopied sheets and add them to the display. Surround them with the messages that the children think the stories contain.

Reference to photocopiable sheets

Photocopiable page 156 is a retelling of the Guru Nanak story. Photocopiable page 157 is for use by children who need support work. It provides them with an outline of the story and spaces to fill in missing words.

SHORT GLOSSARY OF RELIGIOUS TERMS

For a full glossary of religious terms, consult the booklet *Religious Education – Glossary of Terms* published by the School Curriculum and Assessment Authority.

Advent	The period in the Christian year leading up to Christmas. The word literally means 'coming'. Some churches use an Advent wreath or ring to mark the four Sundays during Advent.	**Easter**	The centrally important Christian festival in which Christians remember and celebrate the death and rising from the dead of Jesus, the Christ. The events in the life of Jesus which are remembered during 'Holy Week' – such as the Last Supper on Maundy Thursday – are of deep significance for Christians.
Allah	The Muslim word for God. Literally, it is Arabic for 'the God' (pronounced 'ull-lar').		
Baisakhi	Sikh spring festival which commemorates the founding of the Sikh Khalsa by Guru Gobind Singh at Anandpur in 1699.	**Font**	The container used to hold the water used during a Christian baptism.
Bible	The sacred book of Christians which is divided into the Old and New Testaments. It is, in reality, a library of books: the word 'bible' itself derives from the Greek word for 'books'. The term is used also by Jews when referring to what Christians call the Old Testament.	**Gospel**	Literally 'good news'. The term 'Christian Gospel' refers to the central message of Christianity, but when people refer to *the* Gospels they are referring to the four writings at the beginning of the New Testament.
Buddha	A word that literally means 'Enlightened' or 'Awakened One' and applied by Buddhists particularly to Siddhartha Gautama after he received his enlightenment in the sixth century BCE.	**Five K's**	The five symbols which mark out a baptised Sikh. They are given this title because, in Punjabi, they all begin with the sound 'k'.
		Genesis	The first book of the Jewish Torah/Christian Old Testament. It was the ancient practice to name a writing after its opening words: 'genesis' means 'beginning'.
Challah	The unleavened bread which is eaten by Jews during the Friday evening meal at the beginning of Shabbat (often pronounced 'holl-ugh').	**Gurdwara**	A Sikh place of worship, literally the 'doorway to the Guru'.
Christening	A term used for the baptism of infants practised by some Christian groups.	**Guru**	The word means 'teacher'. In many religions, a guru is a spiritual teacher who gathers disciples. The Sikh religion began with Guru Nanak (1469-1539) after whom there were nine other Gurus. Today Sikhs regard their holy book as the Guru from whom they gain guidance and teaching.
Christmas	The Christian festival celebrating the birth of Jesus. For the first few centuries of Christianity, it was not celebrated and has always been secondary in religious importance to the festival of Easter.		
		Hadith	A 'report' of what the Prophet Muhammad said, did or commended. Hadiths have had a great effect on the Muslim way of life.
Divali	The Hindu new year festival, celebrated in late October/early November, at which lights are lit. The title – sometimes spelt 'Diwali' – derives from 'deepavali' meaning 'row of lights'. Sikhs also celebrate Divali but focus on their own stories.	**Hagadah**	The book used during the Passover seder meal which contains, among other things, a brief account of the Exodus. The Hebrew word means 'narration'.

SHORT GLOSSARY OF RELIGIOUS TERMS (continued)

Islam	The title given to the religious way of life of Muslims. The Arabic word means 'submitted', a Muslim being a person who submits him/herself to the will of Allah.
Jataka	Literally 'birth stories'. A collection of stories about the former lives of the Buddha.
Ka'bah	The cube-shaped building in the Holy Mosque in Makkah, Arabia, which is of great devotional significance to Muslims and towards which they face in prayer.
Kappel	Skull-cap worn by male Jews during religious activities and by Orthodox Jewish men all the time. Some Jews call it a 'kippah', others a 'yarmulke'.
Kashrut	Jewish dietary laws which set out what is allowed (*kosher* = pure, clean) and what is forbidden.
Kathina	A festival celebrated by some Buddhists during which monks are offered new material for their robes.
Kaur	A Punjabi word meaning 'princess'. It is the name used by Sikh women.
Khalsa	The 'Pure Ones', the brotherhood of baptised Sikhs.
Kiddush	The Jewish blessing which is said over a cup of wine at the beginning of the Shabbat meal and some other occasions.
Lourdes	A French centre of modern Christian pilgrimage associated with events in the life of St Bernadette during 1858.
Makkah	The birthplace of the Prophet Muhammad in Arabia and the focus of the Hajj or pilgrimage made by Muslims.
Mandir	A Hindu temple.
Mosque	A Muslim place of worship, literally 'a place of prostration'.
Mudra	The position of the hands and fingers of, for example, an image of the Buddha. A particular mudra will symbolise aspects of Enlightenment.
Murti	A three-dimensional representation of a Hindu deity. The word 'idol' is avoided as it can cause offence.
Parable	A story with a message and which often has an unexpected twist. Parables are particularly associated with the teaching of Jesus but many other teachers and religious figures have used them.
Pesach	The Hebrew title for the Passover festival which begins each year on the fifteen day of the Jewish month Nisan (pronounced 'pay-sach', the 'ch' as in the Scottish lo<u>ch</u>).
Pilgrimage	A journey to a place of religious or spiritual significance made for devotional reasons.
Qiblah	The direction, towards the Ka'bah in Makkah, in which Muslims face during set prayer. The word literally means 'direction'.
Qur'an	The sacred book of Muslims. The title means 'recitation'. Muslims believe that the Arabic words of the Qur'an were revealed to Muhammad who was told to recite them. The spelling *Qur'an* is now preferred to the older *Koran*.
Rakhi	The decorative thread which is tied round the wrist of the brother by the sister during the festival of Raksha Bandhan.
Raksha Bandhan	Hindu festival in which brothers and sisters exchange gifts as a recognition of the bond between them.
Ramadan	The ninth month of the Muslim year during which Muslims fast during daylight hours.
Ramayana	The Hindu epic poem which includes the story of Rama and Sita, remembered by Hindus at the festival of Divali.
Rosary beads	Prayer beads sometimes used by Christians of the Catholic or Orthodox traditions.

Glossary

SHORT GLOSSARY OF RELIGIOUS TERMS (continued)

Seder	The meal eaten at the beginning of the Passover festival by Jews (usually pronounced 'say-dur', but sometimes 'sigh-dur').
Shabbat	The Jewish day of rest and renewal which begins at sunset on Friday and ends at nightfall on Saturday. Jews of Eastern European origin use the term 'Shabbes', while non-Jews often use the term 'Sabbath'.
Sikhism	The religion which began in the Punjab region of north-west India with the teaching of Guru Nanak (1449–1539).
Simchat Torah	An annual Jewish festival during which Jews show their love for the Torah. It occurs at the time when the weekly cycle of reading passages of the Torah ends and a new one begins.
Singh	A Punjabi word meaning 'lion'. It is the name used by Sikh men.
Sukkot	The annual autumn Jewish festival during which Jews build temporary shelters (singular: *sukkah*) to relive and remember their ancient ancestors leaving Egypt during the Exodus.
Surah	One of the 114 chapters of the Qur'an. As well as having a number, each surah has a traditional title related to its content. Surah 112, for example, is also known as *Surah Yusuf* (Joseph).
Synagogue	A place of Jewish worship and education. The word literally means 'place of assembly'.
Torah	The Hebrew word means 'instruction' or 'teaching' and is usually used by Jews as a title for the first five books of the Bible.

USEFUL BOOKS AND RESOURCES

Religious artefacts

The use of religious artefacts can greatly enliven teaching and learning in religious education. Though teachers will often find their own sources of religious artefacts (for example, shops, religious centres, teachers' centres, religious adherents) there are also several companies which publish catalogues so that artefacts may be ordered by post. Two examples are:

▲ *Articles of Faith*, Resource House, Kay Street, Bury, Lancashire BL9 6BU

▲ *Religion in Evidence*, Unit 7, Monk Road Industrial Estate, Alfreton, Derbyshire DE55 7RL

The following religious artefacts are included in the activities in this book:

Buddhist
A picture or statuette of a seated Buddha

Christian
A statuette of Jesus
A Bible
Different versions of the Bible
A crucifix
A plain cross
A nativity set or South American retablo
Painted eggs
An Advent candle
A baptismal candle

Hindu
A rakhi
A diva
A murti (three-dimensional image of a deity) or picture

Jewish
Shabbat candle(s)
Challot (Shabbat loaves)
Challah cover
A miniature Torah scroll
A Seder plate
A children's hagadah
Matzah (unleavened bread)
A kiddush cup
A kappel

Muslim
A Qur'an stand
A qiblah compass
A prayer-mat

Sikh
Examples of the five K's

Sources of models

Card models of religious artefacts and buildings have sometimes been marketed. For example, Iqra Trust, a Muslim educational organisation, has produced card model kits of the Ka'bah and part of the Great Mosque in Makkah, the

RELIGIOUS
EDUCATION

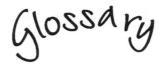
USEFUL BOOKS AND RESOURCES (continued)

Dome of the Rock in Jerusalem, London Central Mosque and a Qur'an stand. For further information, contact:
▲ *Iqra Trust*, 24 Culross Street, London W1Y 3HE

Poster and picture packs
A number of major publishers, such as The Pictorial Charts Educational Trust, produce posters of relevance to religious education. For further information, contact:
▲ *PCET*, 27 Kirchen Road, London W13 0UD
   The series of photographic packs produced by the Religious Education Centre in Birmingham is of particularly fine quality. The following packs are currently available:
▲ *Christians Photo Pack*;
▲ *Jews Photo Pack*;
▲ *Hindus Photo Pack*;
▲ *Muslims Photo Pack*;
▲ *Black Churches and Black Church Traditions Photo Pack*.
For further information, contact:
▲ *The Westhill RE Centre*, Westhill College, Selly Oak, Birmingham B29 6LL

Video programmes and packs
Many major publishers, such as the Religious and Moral Education Press (RMEP), include video material in their published list of resources. For further information, contact:
▲ *Religious and Moral Education Press*, St Mary's Work, St Mary's Plain, Norwich, Norfolk NR3 3BH
Some excellent video programmes are also available from organisations which have been established to provide educational resources about particular religious traditions. 'Buddhism for Key Stage 2', for example, is available from The Clear Vision Trust. For further information, contact:
▲ *The Clear Vision Trust*, 16–20 Turner Street, Manchester M4 1DZ

Subscription services for teachers of religious education
A number of organisations provide a regular supply of material and publications for teachers and others interested in religious education.
   The Christian Education Movement (CEM)/Professional Council of Religious Education (PCfRE) offers a number of subscription services. Its termly mailing can include a number of periodicals such as the magazine *RE Today* (with an emphasis on practical classroom ideas) and the journals *British Journal of Religious Education* (with an emphasis on academic research), *Resource* (which contains articles of general interest), and *Look Hear!* (a review of recently published material relevant to religious education). The popular 'Teaching RE' series of booklets, with titles such as *Christmas*, *The Church*, *Buddhism* and *Festival* include those aimed at Key Stage 1. For further information, contact:
▲ *CEM*, Royal Buildings, Victoria Street, Derby DE1 1GW

Books about religion or religious themes
A large number of high-quality books about religions and religious themes are available. The following are recommended to support the activities in this book:
Beggars, Beasts and Easter Fire: Book of Saints and Heroes by Carol Greene (Lion Publlishing, 1993).
The Birth of Jesus retold by W. Owen Cole and Judith Evans-Lowndes (Heinemann, 1995).
Creation Stories by Maurice Lynch. Available from British and Foreign Schools Society (BFSS), National RE Centre, Brunel University College, Borough Road, Isleworth, Middlesex TW7 5DU
Creation Stories by Jon Mayled (Wayland, 1987).
Easter by Gail Gibbons (Picture Knight, 1989).
The Easter Story by Brian Wildsmith (Oxford University Press, 1994).
The Story of Easter retold by W. Owen Cole and Judith Evans-Lowndes (Heinemann, 1995).
People Jesus Met retold by W. Owen Cole and Judith Evans-Lowndes (Heinemann, 1995).

Reference books for children and teachers
Of the many excellent books which are now available, the 'Religions of the World' series (published by Simon & Schuster Young Books) is distinguished by the rich combination of very clear text with large, colour photographs and illustrations. The following titles are available:
The Buddhist World by Anne Bancroft;
The Christian World by Alan Brown;
The Hindu World by Patricia Bahree;
The Jewish World by Douglas Charing;
The Muslim World by Richard Tames;
The New Religious World by Anne Bancroft;
The Sikh World by Daljit Singh and Angela Smith.

Background reading for teachers
Teachers will need to familiarise themselves with their locally agreed syllabus and any associated guidance material which has been produced. Other books of relevance to religious education are too numerous to mention. A list would include such books as:
Don't Just Do Something – Sit There: Developing Children's Spiritual Awareness by Mary Stone (RMEP, 1995).
Hindu Children in Britain by Robert Jackson and Eleanor Nesbitt (Trentham Books, 1992).
Religious Education and the Primary Curriculum: Teaching Strategies and Practical Activities by W. Owen Cole and Judith Evans-Lowndes (RMEP, 1994).
Teaching World Religions, edited by Clive Erricker (Heinemann Educational, 1993).
The Uses of Enchantment: The Meaning and Importance of Fairy Tales by Bruno Bettelheim (Penguin, 1991).

Photocopiables

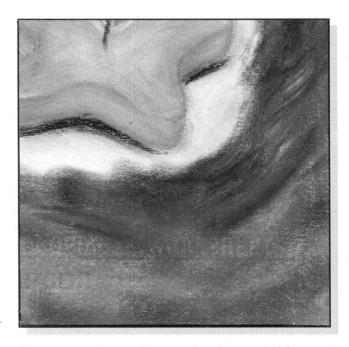

The pages in this section can be photocopied for use in the classroom or school which has purchased this book, and do not need to be declared in any return in respect of any photocopying licence.

They comprise a varied selection of both pupil and teacher resources, including pupil worksheets, resource material and record sheets to be completed by the teacher or children. Most of the photocopiable pages are related to individual activities in the book; the name of the activity is indicated at the top of the sheet, together with a page reference indicating where the lesson plan for that activity can be found.

Individual pages are discussed in detail within each lesson plan, accompanied by ideas for adaptation where appropriate – of course, each sheet can be adapted to suit your own needs and those of your class. Sheets can also be coloured, laminated, mounted on to card, enlarged and so on where appropriate.

Pupil worksheets and record sheets have spaces provided for children's names and for noting the date on which each sheet was used. This means that, if so required, they can be included easily within any pupil assessment portfolio.

Masks (1)

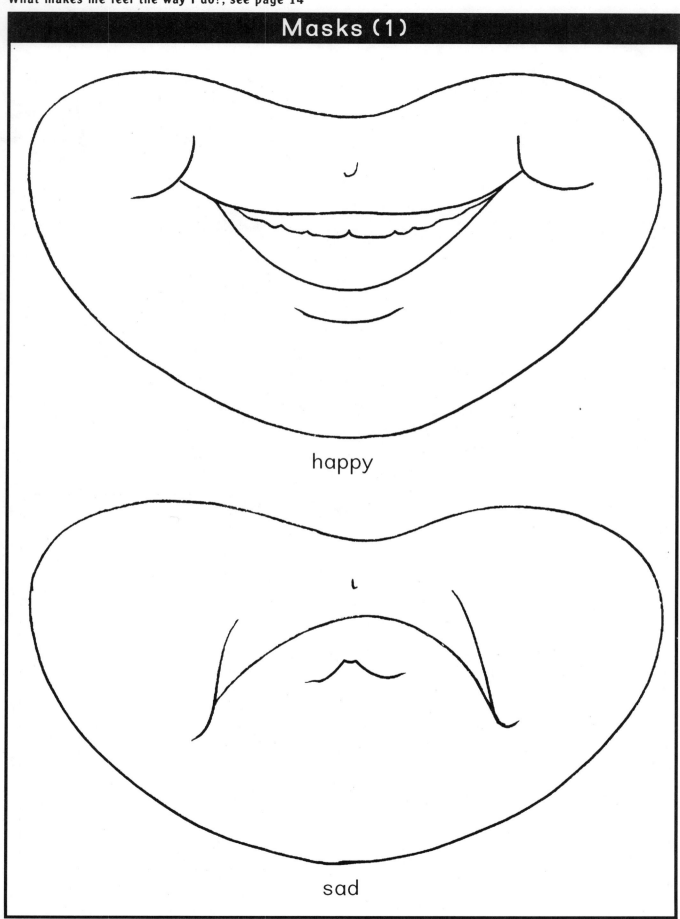

happy

sad

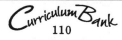

What makes me feel the way I do?, see page 14

Masks (2)

angry

I look like this when I feel

RELIGIOUS
EDUCATION

Which is my special room?, see page 16

Which is my special room?

Name _____

Date _____

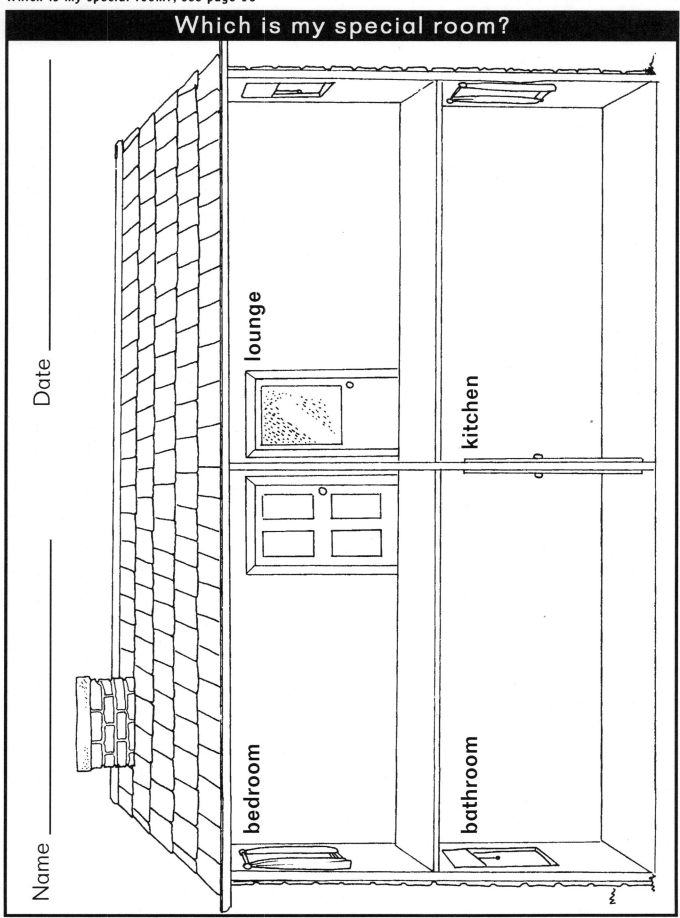

lounge

kitchen

bedroom

bathroom

RELIGIOUS
EDUCATION

How do I feel when I wear different clothes?

Name _____

Date _____

I feel smart when I wear these clothes

because _____

I feel uncomfortable when I wear these

clothes because _____

RELIGIOUS EDUCATION

Why do we help others?, see page 27

The monkey king

There was once a beautiful tree which grew by a river high up in the mountains. It had sweet-smelling blossom in the spring and, in the summer, delicious fruit.

A tribe of monkeys lived in the branches of the tree together with their king. The monkeys loved the tree. They slept in its shade and ate its fruit.

One summer day, a large fruit fell from the tree and landed in the moving water of the river. The river carried the fruit down the mountain into a large city where some fishermen caught it in their nets. The fishermen had never seen such a fruit before and took it straight to the king of the city. The king tasted the fruit, and because it tasted so good he wanted more. So, with his ministers, he followed the river up into the mountains until they came to the tree.

The king and his ministers were surprised to see so many monkeys living in the tree and decided that the monkeys must all be killed. But some of the monkeys heard their plans and told the monkey king.

The monkey king thought of a way to save his monkeys. He made a great jump to the other side of the river and tied a creeper around a tree. He planned to tie the other end to the fruit tree, so making a bridge for the monkeys to escape. But the creeper was too short. So the monkey king held the end of the creeper in his back legs and clung on to the fruit tree with his front paws. The monkeys ran across his back and escaped, but there were so many of them and they were so heavy that his back was broken.

The king from the city watched and, when he saw what the monkey king had done, ordered his men to bring the monkey king to him. The king from the city cared for the monkey king, though he knew he was dying. The king from the city never forgot what the monkey had done, and for the rest of his life ruled with care and kindness.

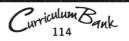

RELIGIOUS
EDUCATION

Photocopiables

Why do we need rules?

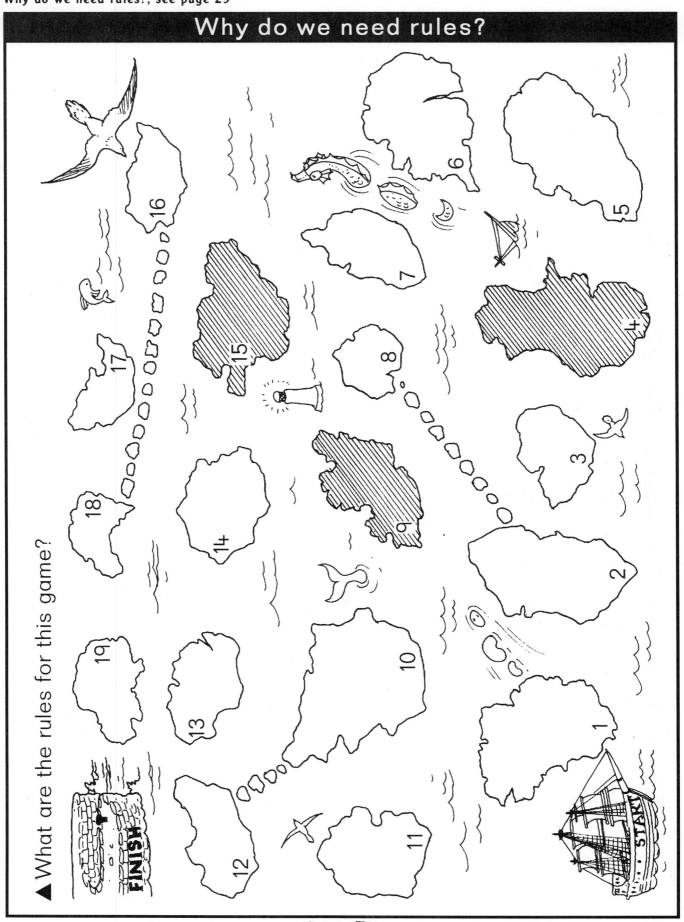

▲What are the rules for this game?

RELIGIOUS EDUCATION

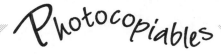

Why do we sometimes want to look like other people?, see page 32

The Sikh Baisakhi story

It was New Year's Day and Guru Gobind Singh had called his Sikh followers together. The Guru had put up a large tent on the top of a hill in a town called Anandpur and the Sikhs were gathering around it. A hush fell on the crowd as Guru Gobind Singh came out of the tent carrying a sword in his hand. Everyone listened as the Guru spoke: 'Who will give up his head for God and the Guru?'

No one moved, and the Guru asked his question again. The crowd began to whisper together. Some of them thought their Guru had gone mad. After a while, one man came forward. The Guru took him into the tent and the crowd heard

the sound of a sword swishing through the air. When the Guru came out of the tent he was alone and there was blood on his sword.

'Who will give up his head for God and the Guru?' Gobind Singh asked for the second time. Another Sikh stepped forward and was taken into the tent. Again there was the sound of a swishing sword and the Guru came out of the tent alone, his sword dripping with blood. This happened three more

times until five Sikhs had gone into the tent with their Guru. Many of the crowd were afraid of what would happen next and were amazed to see the five men walk out of the tent following Guru Gobind Singh. 'These five men showed great bravery and loyalty. I want all Sikhs to be brave like them,' Guru Gobind Singh told the crowd. 'From now on all Sikh men will be called Singh (which means lion) and all Sikh women will be called Kaur (which means princess). We will all wear special signs to show everyone we are proud to be Sikhs. We will never cut our hair, but to keep it tidy we will wear it tied up on our heads with a small comb and cover it with a turban. We will wear special short trousers and carry a sword to protect the weak. On our wrists we will wear a steel bangle because steel is strong like the Sikhs. We will live together as equals.'

Then the Guru stirred a bowl of sweetened water with his sword and gave a little to the five men to drink. Many other Sikhs drank the water and promised to wear the special signs. This was the beginning of the Khalsa, a new family of Sikhs.

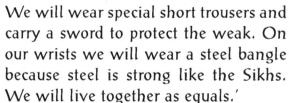

RELIGIOUS EDUCATION

The five K's of the Sikhs

Name _____ Date _____

▲ Join up each picture to the correct label.

 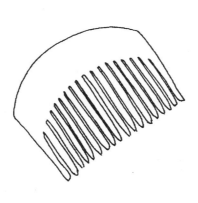 

| kachera | kesh | kirpan | kangha | kara |

Guru Gobind Singh wanted Sikhs to wear the five K's because...

RELIGIOUS EDUCATION

The parable of the Loving Father

Name _____   Date _____

1 Should the father have given the young son what he wanted?

2 Why didn't the son go home straight away when his money was all gone?

3 Why did the father go out to meet the young son?

4 Did the young son deserve his party?

5 Why didn't the older brother go to the party?

6 What was Jesus trying to teach when he told his story?

RELIGIOUS
EDUCATION

What are the 'ups' and 'downs' of family life?, see page 35

Joseph sold into slavery

Long ago, in a land we now call Israel, lived an old man named Jacob and his family. Jacob loved one of his sons, Joseph, more than the others, and to show this he gave him a special coat. When Joseph's brothers saw that their father loved Joseph more than any of them, they became jealous.

One day Joseph told his brothers about his dreams. One of the dreams had been about sheaves of corn in a field. Joseph told his brothers that his sheaf had stood up tall and their sheaves had bowed down to Joseph. The brothers were now not only jealous, they were angry with Joseph.

Joseph's brothers went away to look after the sheep and Jacob asked Joseph to go and see if they were well. When the brothers saw Joseph coming, they wanted to kill him. But Reuben, one of the brothers, said, 'We must not kill him. We can throw him into a pit and tell our father a wild animal has killed him.' So they took the special coat off Joseph and threw him into the pit.

After a while, the brothers saw some traders with their camels coming towards them and they decided to sell Joseph to be a slave. The traders paid the brothers 20 pieces of silver for Joseph and took him with them to Egypt. The brothers tore the special coat, dipped it in blood and took it home to show Jacob. Jacob was very sad because he thought a wild animal had killed Joseph.

Joseph sold into slavery

Name _____   Date _____

1 Jacob gave Joseph a

special _____

to show that he loved him.

▲ Draw Joseph's present from Jacob.

2 Joseph had dreams about

☐ sheaves of corn?

☐ sheep?

☐ wild animals?

☐ the sun, moon and stars?

3 Joseph's brothers wanted to _____ Joseph.

4 Joseph was put into

a _____.

▲ Draw Joseph's brothers throwing him in the pit.

5 Joseph was sold to a

☐ slave?

☐ trader?

☐ shepherd?

☐ soldier?

6 Jacob thought that a _____ had killed Joseph.

RELIGIOUS EDUCATION

What are the 'ups and 'downs' of family life?, see page 35

Joseph in Egypt

Name _____   Date _____

1 In Egypt, Joseph was sold to

☐ Pharaoh?   ☐ Potiphar?

☐ Jacob?   ☐ Potiphar's wife?

2 Potiphar's wife was _____ of Joseph.

3 Joseph was put in prison

with _____

and _____

▲ Draw a picture of Joseph in prison.

4 Joseph said that the

baker's dream meant

that _____

5 The person who had a

dream about cows was

☐ Joseph?   ☐ the baker?

☐ the butler?   ☐ Pharaoh?

6 Joseph said that there would be a famine for

_____ years.

7 Pharaoh gave Joseph his _____.

RELIGIOUS
EDUCATION

Joseph sold into slavery

Name _____   Date _____

1 Joseph was an important man in _____

2 Joseph kept _____ at home with him.

3 Joseph accused his brothers of being

☐ family?   ☐ slaves?

☐ spies?   ☐ brothers?

4 Joseph put food and _____ in his brothers' bags.

▲ Draw a picture of the brothers' bags being filled.

5 When the food had been eaten, Jacob told his sons to take Benjamin, money and _____ to Egypt.

6 What was put in Benjamin's bag with the food?

☐ money?   ☐ food?

☐ a silver cup?   ☐ presents?

7 The brothers offered to stay in _____ place.

8 Joseph told his brothers who he was because he knew

_____

RELIGIOUS
EDUCATION

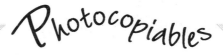
In what ways do we help and harm our world?, see page 41

The girl who saved the people

The sound of the prayer drum filled the air but still the rain did not fall. The plain had become dusty and dry, the crops had withered and died and now the people were dying too. The wise man prayed to the Great Spirit, 'What wrong have we done? Why does the rain not fall?' But still the rain did not come.

Then one evening the wise man came running down the hill from the place of the fire. He waved his arms and called for the people to listen. 'At last the Great Spirit has spoken. We have grown selfish. We have taken from the earth and never given anything back in return. We must offer the most precious thing in our camp, then the rain will come and life will return to the earth.'

The people gave thanks and tried to find the most precious thing in the camp. Some said it was the tepee which sheltered them from the winds and rain. Others said it was the blankets which kept them warm in winter. The young braves thought it was the bow and arrow that gave them food to eat and furs to wear. All night they talked but they could not agree.

Sitting at the edge of the camp fire was a young girl. The people called her 'The Girl Who Has No Name' because her family had all died when the crops had failed. She listened, holding her doll in her lap. The doll was the only thing she had left. Her grandfather had found a piece of wood in the forest and had carved it into the shape of a doll. Her grandmother had used berries from deep within the forest to make dyes to colour the wood and give the doll eyes and lips. Her brothers had used soft leather to make a jacket and leggings. Her father had found blue feathers from the jay bird and had made them into a deep-blue head-dress for the little doll.

The girl knew what was the most precious thing in the camp. She took her doll and, without saying a word, thrust it into the fire. She watched as the flames licked round it till it was only a black shape and finally it disappeared into ashes. When the ash had grown quite cold she stopped and gathered all of it in her hands. She turned and scattered the ash to the homes of the wind, to the North, the South, the East and West. Then she lay down and fell asleep.

The sun woke her early next morning. When she opened her eyes she could not believe what she saw. The hillside was covered with tiny blue flowers rippling in the wind. They looked like waves on a lake. The people came to her and danced around her and, as they danced, the rain began to fall.

That day the people changed her name. No longer was she 'The Girl Who Has No Name', for now they called her 'The Girl Who Saved the People'. They asked her to name the blue flowers. She called them 'forget-me-nots'.

RELIGIOUS
EDUCATION

Photocopiables

Why do some Christians say thank you at harvest time?, see page 42

Harvest time

Name _____   Date _____

Christians say thank you to God at harvest time.

▲ Draw four foods for which you would say thank you.

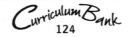

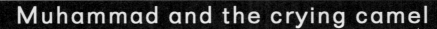

Why was Muhammad sad when he heard a camel cry?, see page 44

Muhammad and the crying camel

The sun had been shining for days. Everywhere was dry and dusty. Muhammad walked in the shade of the trees but he was still hot and thirsty.

Suddenly, he heard the sound of a camel crying. Muhammad followed the sound and saw a thin camel standing in the full heat of the sun with no food to eat or water to drink. Muhammad looked around for the camel's owner. He was laughing and drinking with his Muslim friends in a cool, shady spot nearby.

Muhammad walked over to the camel and began stroking its nose. After a while, the camel stopped crying but it still panted with thirst.

'Why is this camel tied in the full sun with nothing to eat or drink?' Muhammad shouted to the camel owner. 'Look how thin and unhappy this camel is. Allah has given the camel to help us in our work, but in return we must look after it and give it food to eat and water to drink.'

The owner of the camel saw how thin and unhappy his camel was and felt ashamed.

'I have done wrong,' he said. 'Muhammad has reminded me that the camel is one of God's creatures. I am sorry for what I have done.'

He ran to untie his camel and led it to the shade. He gave it cool water to drink and food to eat. From that day the camel owner cared for all his camels and showed them great kindness.

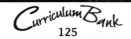

**RELIGIOUS
EDUCATION**

Creation

Name _____ Date _____

On the first day God created

_____

On the second day God created

_____

On the third day God created

_____

On the fourth day God created

_____

On the fifth day God created

_____

On the sixth day God created

_____

On the seventh day God _____

 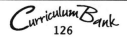
RELIGIOUS EDUCATION

Should Little Red Riding Hood have spoken to the wolf?, see page 50

Little Red Riding Hood (1)

▲ Cut out the pictures and stick them in the correct order.

RELIGIOUS
EDUCATION

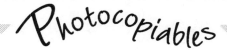

Should Little Red Riding Hood have spoken to the wolf?, see page 50

Little Red Riding Hood (2)

▲ Cut out the sentences and match them to the pictures.

Little Red Riding Hood's mummy said, 'Don't talk to strangers.'

Little Red Riding Hood knocked on the door.

Little Red Riding Hood said, 'What big teeth you have.'

Little Red Riding Hood met a wolf.

Little Red Riding Hood was sorry.

The wolf chased Little Red Riding Hood.

RELIGIOUS EDUCATION

Zacchaeus changes his life (1)

Zacchaeus climbs a tree.

Jesus goes to Zacchaeus' house.

Jesus sees Zacchaeus in the tree.

Zacchaeus gives money back to people.

Jesus walks into Jericho.

Zacchaeus feels happy.

A crowd wants to see Jesus.

Jesus speaks to Zacchaeus.

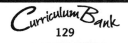
RELIGIOUS
EDUCATION

How did Jesus change the life of Zacchaeus?, see page 53

Zacchaeus changes his life (2)

Name _____   Date _____

▲ Fill in the missing words. (There are some words to choose from in the box.)

Zacchaeus climbs a _____.

Jesus goes to Zacchaeus' _____.

Jesus sees Zacchaeus in the tree.

Zacchaeus gives _____ back to people.

Jesus walks into _____.

Zacchaeus feels _____.

A _____ wants to see Jesus.

_____ speaks to Zacchaeus.

| Jericho | happy | crowd | tree |
| Jesus | money | house | |

▲ Now cut out the sentences and put them in order to make the story.

RELIGIOUS
EDUCATION

When do Jews dance in the synagogue? (1)

Name _____

Date _____

▲ Fill in the missing words. (There are some words to choose from in the box.)

The Torah s_____ are carried

around the s_____ on

S_____ Torah. Jews

celebrate by waving f_____.

They are very h_____.

		Simchat
	synagogue	
scrolls		
flags		
happy		

When do Jews dance in the synagogue? (2)

Name _____ Date _____

Jews show how much they love the Torah
scrolls on Simchat Torah by

seven	**times**	**ark**	**flags**	**dance**
apples	**synagogue**	**celebration**	**children**	

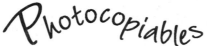

Why is the Qur'an a special book for Muslims?, see page 57

Muhammad receives a special message

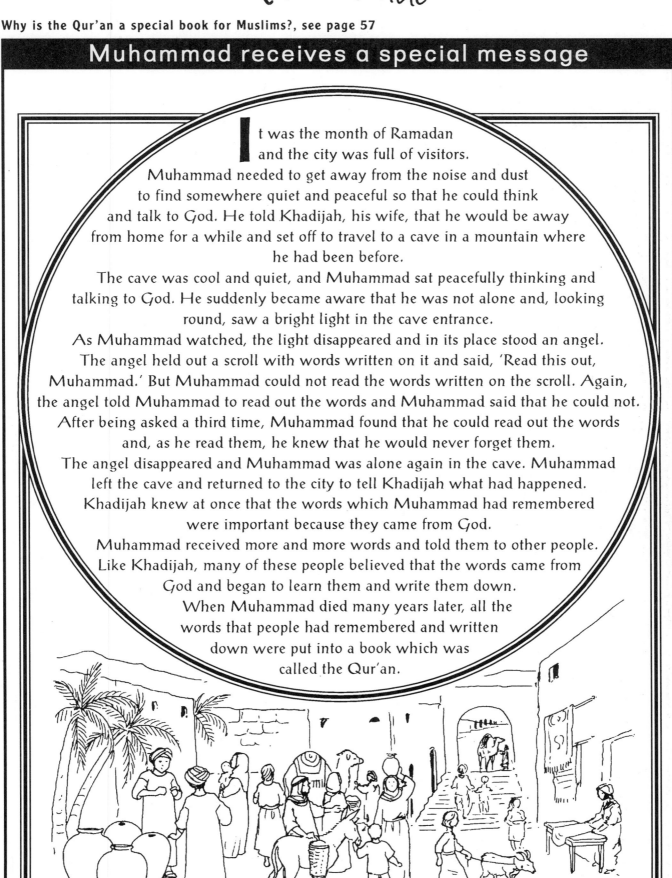

It was the month of Ramadan
and the city was full of visitors.
Muhammad needed to get away from the noise and dust
to find somewhere quiet and peaceful so that he could think
and talk to God. He told Khadijah, his wife, that he would be away
from home for a while and set off to travel to a cave in a mountain where
he had been before.
The cave was cool and quiet, and Muhammad sat peacefully thinking and
talking to God. He suddenly became aware that he was not alone and, looking
round, saw a bright light in the cave entrance.
As Muhammad watched, the light disappeared and in its place stood an angel.
The angel held out a scroll with words written on it and said, 'Read this out,
Muhammad.' But Muhammad could not read the words written on the scroll. Again,
the angel told Muhammad to read out the words and Muhammad said that he could not.
After being asked a third time, Muhammad found that he could read out the words
and, as he read them, he knew that he would never forget them.
The angel disappeared and Muhammad was alone again in the cave. Muhammad
left the cave and returned to the city to tell Khadijah what had happened.
Khadijah knew at once that the words which Muhammad had remembered
were important because they came from God.
Muhammad received more and more words and told them to other people.
Like Khadijah, many of these people believed that the words came from
God and began to learn them and write them down.
When Muhammad died many years later, all the
words that people had remembered and written
down were put into a book which was
called the Qur'an.

**RELIGIOUS
EDUCATION**

Why did Joan of Arc lead an army?, see page 58

The story of Joan of Arc

Many years ago, in a village in France, a baby girl was born called Jeanne d'Arc. She grew up in the village and, although she didn't learn to read or write, she helped her father look after his sheep and helped her mother in the house. Jeanne knew many people who had gone to fight in a war with England. Many of them had been hurt or killed.

When Jeanne was 13, she began to hear voices speaking to her in her head, but no one else heard them. After a while, Jeanne began to see visions of the people who were speaking to her. Jeanne said that they were all people who loved God. Sometimes the voices told her that she must go to church. At other times, the voices told her that she must help France fight the war against the English. Every time Jeanne heard the voices, she would say that she was only a poor village girl and she couldn't possibly do as she was being asked. But the voices didn't stop, and when they said that God was telling her to help France she decided that she must try.

Jeanne travelled to the nearest town where French soldiers were staying. She asked to see the person in charge of the army. When Jeanne told him that God wanted her to help him fight, he just laughed at her and sent her away. But Jeanne did not give up and eventually she was taken to see Prince Charles, the son of the French king. The prince listened to Jeanne and believed what she told him about hearing voices. He gave her an army of soldiers to lead, a black horse to ride, a suit of white armour to wear and a flag with the names 'Jesus' and 'Mary' on it. He also gave her a sword, but Jeanne said that she would never use it.

Jeanne led her army to the town of Orléans, which had been captured by the English, listening to the voices which spoke to her all the way. In less than two weeks Orléans was free and Jeanne led her army to the city of Rheims, where Prince Charles was crowned king of France. Jeanne told the king that she had done what God had wanted her to do.

Jeanne didn't hear the voices again but carried on leading her army. After one battle, she was caught by her English enemies and put in prison. Her guards told her that she would be set free if she said that the voices she heard had not come from God. Jeanne kept on saying that the voices had come from God so she was taken to the market place in the town of Rouen, tied to a post and burned to death.

The story of Jeanne's bravery has been told by French and English people ever since. The English call her 'Joan of Arc'. Many Christians believe she was a saint.

RELIGIOUS EDUCATION

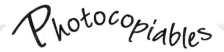
Why did Noah build the ark?, see page 61

Noah builds an ark

God looked at the world that he had made and didn't like what he saw any more. People were spoiling it. It wasn't good any more. God became angry and decided to start again with a new world, but as he looked he saw one or two things that he liked and were worth keeping.

'Noah,' God said.

'Yes, God,' Noah answered. 'I'm listening.'

'I can see that you are a good man and I want you to help me. You must build an ark big enough to keep two of every animal and your own family safe.'

Noah began work straight away. As the ark became bigger, more and more people came to see what he was building. When Noah told them that it was going to be a huge boat, they asked him where he was going to sail it. Noah lived a long way from the sea! The people began to  laugh at Noah. They called him names and said he was mad, but still Noah carried on building the ark. It was hot work. The sun shone on Noah every day. Noah wondered when the rain-clouds would arrive and how much time he had left.

The ark was nearly finished. It was time to get everything on board: first his wife, then his three sons and their wives and, last of all, the animals and birds. Noah had collected two of every sort of animal and bird. It was very noisy on the ark but Noah had made a place for everything. He took one last look at the sky as he closed the door.

The clouds were beginning to gather. It wasn't long before the first spots of rain fell. The people outside the ark stopped laughing and went home. It rained and it rained. The streams grew into rivers and the rivers into seas, until the whole land was covered with water. The ark was now afloat. The rain kept falling and soon the flood was so deep that it even covered the tops of the mountains.

At last the rain stopped falling and Noah began to wonder if they would ever see dry land again. Then he had an idea. If he sent out a bird and it did not come back, he would know that it had found land to live on. So he fetched a white dove and set it free. But the dove flew round and round and then returned to the ark. A week later, Noah set the dove free again. This time it flew out of sight and then, some time later, flew back with an olive branch in its beak. Noah grew hopeful. Another week passed and Noah threw the same dove into the sky. It flew off and did not return.

One night, when people were not expecting it, a big shudder went through the ark, from end to end. The ark had grounded on a high piece of land. The flood was going down. By next morning the ground was dry again. Noah opened the doors and the animals rushed out to find new homes for themselves. The birds flew high into the sky looking for places to build their nests. Noah, his sons and their wives made homes for themselves and began to farm God's new world.

**RELIGIOUS
EDUCATION**

Invitation to Teddy's birthday

Come to Teddy's birthday party

on ....

at ....

time ....

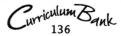

RELIGIOUS EDUCATION

Why do we have eggs at Easter?, see page 67

Why do we have eggs at Easter?

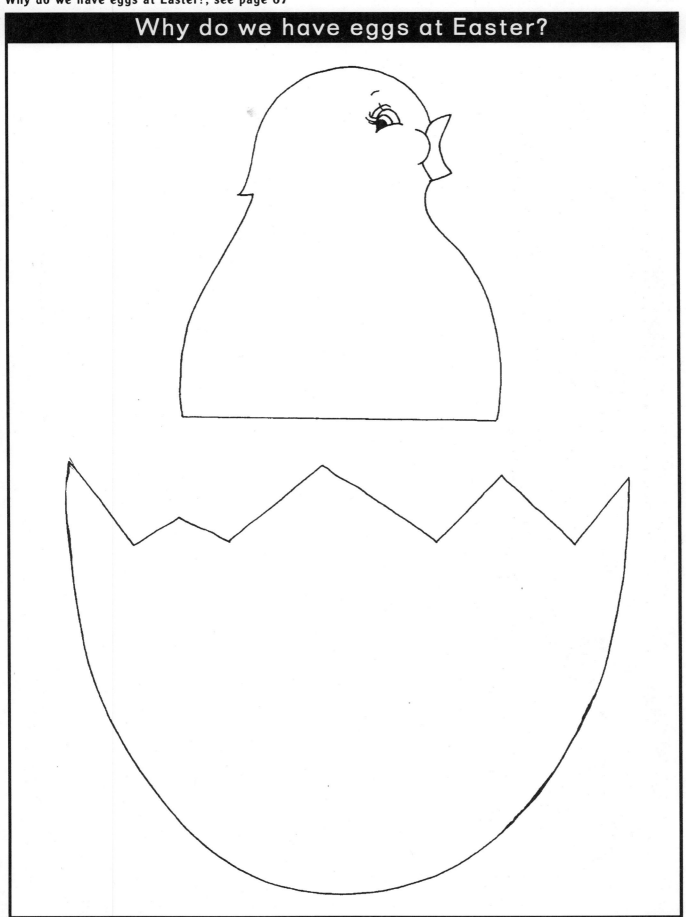

RELIGIOUS EDUCATION

How do we know that Christmas is coming?, see page 68

Christmas is coming

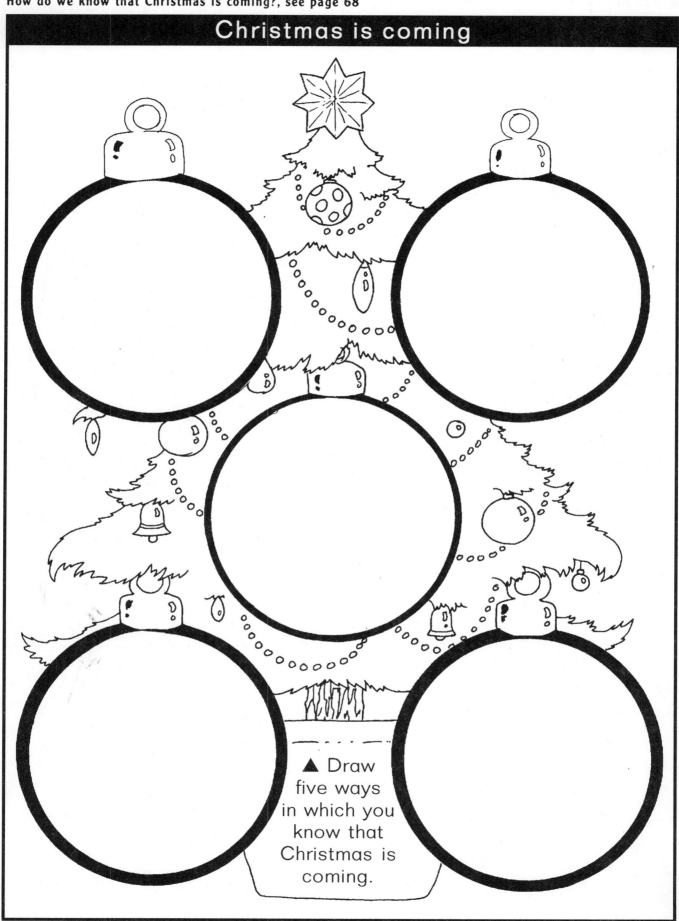

▲ Draw five ways in which you know that Christmas is coming.

RELIGIOUS EDUCATION

Why is Divali a special time for Hindus?, see page 71

The story of Rama and Sita

Many years ago, in a city in India called Ayodhya, Prince Rama lived with his beautiful wife Sita and his stepbrother Lakshman.

The king sent Rama away from the palace to live in the forest for 14 years. Lakshman and Sita decided to go with Rama. The people of Ayodhya loved Rama and were sad to see him leave the city.

Rama, Sita and Lakshman were very happy living in the forest. They ate the fruits and berries and made friends with the birds and animals.

The wicked king of Lanka, whose name was Ravana, watched Sita and wanted her to be his own wife. He waited until Rama and Lakshman had left Sita alone in their hut in the forest and, disguised as a beggar, he went to Sita to ask for food. When Sita opened the door, Ravana kidnapped her and carried her off in his magic flying chariot to the island of Lanka. As they flew through the skies Sita shouted for help, but the only living thing to hear her was a bird. The bird tried to help, but Ravana shot him with his arrow.

When Rama and Lakshman found that Sita was missing, they went in search of her. They found the injured bird, who told them that Ravana had taken Sita to Lanka. The only way Rama could rescue Sita was to fight the wicked Ravana.

Rama and Lakshman travelled to Lanka. On their journey they met Hanuman, the monkey king, who promised to help them. When they got to the sea, Hanuman ordered his monkeys to make a bridge so that Rama and Lakshman could cross to the island. A great battle was fought until Rama killed Ravana and rescued Sita.

By now, the 14 years were over and Rama, Sita and Lakshman could return to Ayodhya. The people came out to welcome them, and to show their joy lit small lamps called divas. The twinkling lights led Rama, Sita and Lakshman back to the palace. Rama became king and ruled the people well and with kindness.

**RELIGIOUS
EDUCATION**

Why is Divali a special time for Hindus?, see page 71

The story of Rama and Sita

▲ Cut out these pictures and put them in order to make the story.

▲ Write what you think the people are saying in the speech bubbles that your teacher has given to you.

RELIGIOUS EDUCATION

Why is Divali a special time for Hindus?, see page 71

How to make barfi

Coconut barfi is a tasty fudge-like sweet which is often eaten at Divali time.

Ingredients
1 cup of sugar
½ cup of water
2 cups of full-cream milk-powder
4 tablespoons of desiccated coconut
(chopped nuts and cherries for decoration)

Method

1 *Put a cup of sugar into a saucepan with half a cup of water.*

2 *Boil the water and the sugar until the mixture begins to thicken, then put two cups of milk powder into the pan.*

3 *Stir the mixture of sugar, water and milk well until it takes on a soft fudge-like consistency, adding more water or milk powder as appropriate. Add the coconut.*

4 *Pour the mixture into a dish.*

5 *Decorate the mixture with the chopped nuts and cherries.*

6 *The barfi is ready to eat when it is firm. Cut into squares and serve.*

RELIGIOUS EDUCATION

Why is Ramadan a special month for Muslims?, see page 76

Important times in the year

▲ Think about each month and try to think of something special that happens in it. Put a tick next to the month which is most important to you.

spring	January ☐
	February ☐
	March ☐
summer	April ☐
	May ☐
	June ☐
autumn	July ☐
	August ☐
	September ☐
winter	October ☐
	November ☐
	December ☐

RELIGIOUS EDUCATION

Why is Ramadan a special month for Muslims?, see page 76

A special month for Muslims

Name _____   Date _____

▲ Begin by reading this information.

Ramadan is an important month for Muslims. They get up very early, while it is still dark, and eat a big breakfast. They do not eat or drink again until it is dark in the evening. Choosing not to eat at normal mealtimes because of their religion is called fasting. When it becomes dark, many Muslims eat dates and drink milk before they eat their evening meal.

This is because Muhammad ate dates and drank milk and Muslims want to be like Muhammad.

During Ramadan, Muslims spend a lot of time reading the Qur'an, their holy book, and thinking about Allah (God). They try to be very kind to others and to think about people in the world who do not have enough to eat.

▲ Now answer each of the following questions.

1 What is the name of the important month for Muslims?	
2 When do Muslims eat during this month?	
3 What does fasting mean?	
4 Why do some Muslims eat dates and drink milk before their evening meal?	
5 What do Muslims spend a lot of time doing during this month?	

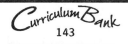
RELIGIOUS
EDUCATION

The Christmas story

▲ Cut out these sentences and put them in order to make the story.

Baby Jesus is born in a stable.

The wise men give their gifts.

There is no room in the inn.

Angel Gabriel brings Mary a message.

The shepherds are told that Jesus has been born.

A bright star leads the wise men to Jesus.

Mary and Joseph go to Bethlehem.

The shepherds visit baby Jesus.

RELIGIOUS
EDUCATION

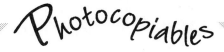

How do Sikhs celebrate Divali?, see page 83

Guru Har Gobind and his cloak (1)

Guru Har Gobind and the emperor were friends, but one of the emperor's officials, whose name was Chandu, didn't like Har Gobind. One day, the emperor became ill and sent for his wise men to see if they could make him better. Chandu saw his chance to get rid of Har Gobind for good. Chandu fetched the wise men, but before he took them in to see the emperor he spoke quietly with them. He offered them a huge reward if they told the emperor to send Guru Har Gobind away to prison. The wise men were greedy and agreed to do what Chandu wanted.

When the wise men went in to see the emperor and were asked what the emperor should do to get rid of the illness, they replied, 'Oh emperor! You must send that holy man, Guru Har Gobind, to prison. Only then will you become well again.'

The emperor was very sad at the thought of sending his friend to prison, but he wanted to be well again. He told himself that he would have Guru Har Gobind released from prison as soon as he was better.

Guru Har Gobind was taken to the prison in Fort Gwalior. It was a miserable place, dark and damp, and the prisoners were very sad. Guru Har Gobind was put in a prison cell with 52 Indian princes, who were being held prisoner for something they hadn't done. They were hungry and dirty and the Guru felt sorry for them. He managed to persuade the guards to give them clean clothes and more food. He told them jokes and stories and they became more cheerful.

RELIGIOUS EDUCATION

How do Sikhs celebrate Divali?, see page 83

Guru Har Gobind and his cloak (2)

After two years, when the emperor was well again, he gave an order that Guru Har Gobind should be released. Although Guru Har Gobind wanted to leave the prison, he didn't want his 52 friends to stay there. So he sent a message to the emperor saying that he wouldn't leave unless the 52 princes were freed as well.

The emperor wanted to see Guru Har Gobind again but he didn't think that he could release all 52 Indian princes together. He sent a message back to Guru Har Gobind saying that as many princes as could hold on to the Guru's cloak could be released. The emperor knew that the doorway of Fort Gwalior was very narrow and only one or two of the prisoners would manage to squeeze through it with Guru Har Gobind.

The Guru sent for a special cloak with 52 tassels of different lengths sewn on to it. He had a plan which meant that none of the princes would be left behind. On the day of his release, he put on his special cloak and each of the prisoner princes held on to one of the tassels. The Guru walked through the doorway and each of the princes followed behind holding on to a different tassel.

The Guru and the princes walked free from the prison at the time when Hindus were celebrating the Divali festival. Ever since this time, Sikhs have also celebrated Divali and remembered their own story.

RELIGIOUS EDUCATION

How do Sikhs celebrate Divali?

No. 101

The Amritsar *Times*

30p

Guru tricks Emperor

52 princes walk free

When do Jews eat in a special place?

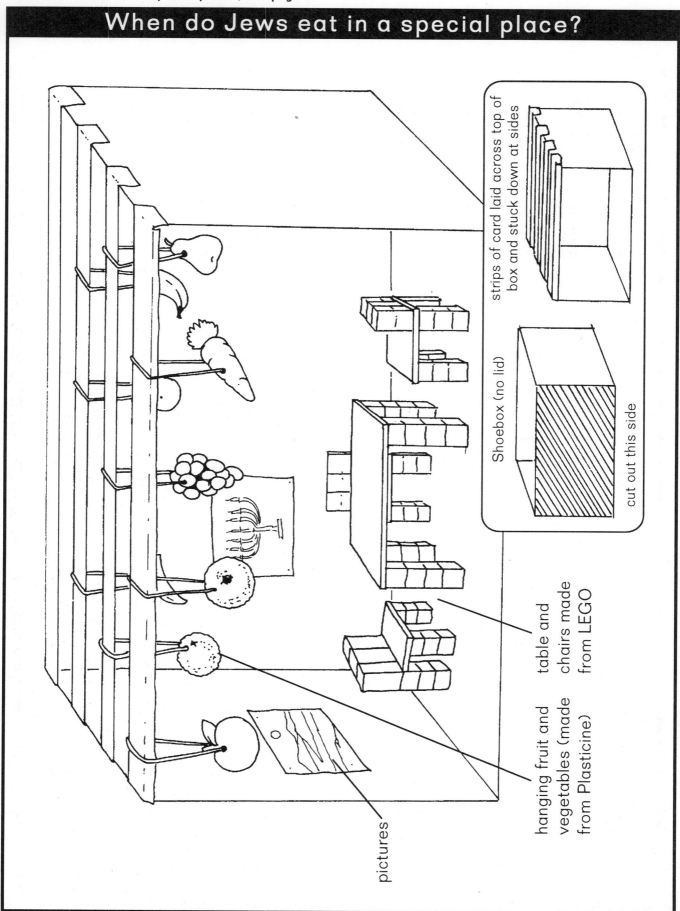

strips of card laid across top of box and stuck down at sides

Shoebox (no lid)

cut out this side

table and chairs made from LEGO

hanging fruit and vegetables (made from Plasticine)

pictures

Why do some Christians go to Lourdes?, see page 92

The story of Bernadette

Bernadette pulled her woollen shawl more tightly round her shoulders. She wished her friends would hurry back. It was getting cold. They were collecting firewood but Bernadette couldn't help them. She knew that if she went in the long grass to pick up sticks, her feet would get wet and she would be ill again. While she waited, she looked around and noticed a small cave in the hillside. As she looked at the cave, a strange light seemed to glow inside it. Bernadette rubbed her eyes and looked again, but the light was still there. It was growing brighter all the time and, as Bernadette watched, she saw a lady appear out of the light. Bernadette felt frightened at first, but when she looked at the lady's face she felt peaceful and happy. The lady was wearing a white dress with a blue sash, and in her hand she held a rosary. Bernadette knew at once that this was a vision of Mary. She sank to her knees, not caring about the wet grass any more, took her rosary out of her pocket and said a prayer as she moved the beads through her fingers.

'Bernadette, get up! What are you doing kneeling in the wet grass?' Bernadette staggered to her feet and, turning round, saw her friends, their arms full of firewood. 'Can't you see her?' Bernadette asked, but the vision had disappeared. Bernadette told her friends what had happened but they didn't believe her. They thought that she had been day-dreaming again.

When her mother saw Bernadette's wet skirt, she was very angry and told Bernadette that she was not to go back to the cave. But Bernadette did go back. She went back to the cave every day, and each time she saw the vision of Mary. On one of her visits, the lady pointed to the earth and told Bernadette to drink. Bernadette used her fingers to dig, and after a while the soil felt damp. As she dug, the hole began to fill with water from an underground spring. Bernadette drank the water, which was cold and clear.

Bernadette told the people in her village about what she had seen. Some of them teased her and called her names, but others visited the cave themselves to see if Mary would appear to them. No one else saw the vision of Mary, but many people drank the water from the spring and some of them who had been ill said that the water had made them better. More and more people came to drink from the spring. People who felt ill, people who felt sad, people who were lonely, came to drink the water and went away feeling better.

After a while, a big church was built near the cave and pools were made to hold the spring water. People came from all over the world to visit the spot where Bernadette had seen the vision of Mary. Today, thousands of people make a pilgrimage and bathe in the water. Many of them come in wheelchairs, some have to be carried on stretchers but there are always people ready to help them. Some of the people who make the pilgrimage say that they have been cured by visiting this special place and drinking the water.

Many Christians call Bernadette a saint, and in their homes have pictures of Lourdes, the village in France where Bernadette saw the vision.

A prayer-mat

Name _____   Date _____

Many Muslims pray f_____ time every day. When they pray, they sometimes use a p_____-m_____. This shows that praying is a s_____ thing to do. It often has pictures of a m_____ and the K_____ in M_____ on it. The pictures r_____ Muslims of these special places.

remind	mosque	special	five
Makkah	Ka'bah	prayer-mat	

▲ Draw a picture of a Muslim prayer-mat.

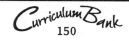
RELIGIOUS
EDUCATION

Why do most Hindus have a shrine in their homes?, see page 95

My special cupboard

Name _____   Date _____

If I had a cupboard for important things in my room at home, I would put in it

_____

_____

_____

_____

_____

RELIGIOUS EDUCATION

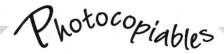
What do Jews have on their table at the Shabbat meal?, see page 99

The story of Kiddush Cup

Kiddush Cup thought that she was very beautiful. She stood on the top shelf all week looking down on the family, waiting for Friday afternoon when she would be taken down and polished. She loved the feel of the soft cloth which soon made her sparkle. She felt proud, standing on the crisp white tablecloth with her friends Shabbat Candles, Challah Cover and Sharp Knife. She enjoyed seeing the family dressed in their best clothes and the boys and men wearing their best kappels on their heads. But there was one part of Shabbat that Kiddush Cup didn't like. She hated the moment when the sweet, red wine was poured into her. It took away her sparkle and left her feeling wet and sticky.

Every Shabbat, Kiddush Cup grumbled about being filled with wine. Her friends – Shabbat Candles, Challah Cover and Sharp Knife – told her that she was very lucky to have such an important place in the Shabbat meal. But still she grumbled and told them that they were the lucky ones.

One Friday morning, Kappel could bear it no longer. He asked Prayer Book, who was very old and wise, how he could stop Kiddush Cup grumbling.

Prayer Book opened his covers and out popped Aleph. First, Aleph put the Shabbat Candles inside Kiddush Cup. Kiddush Cup thought the flickering lights made her shine, but after a while she began to feel very warm, and then hot and then very hot. She did not like being Shabbat Candles. Next, Aleph covered Kiddush Cup with Challah Cover. It was dark under Challah Cover and the crumbs from the matzah made her sneeze. Kiddush Cup did not like being Challah Cover. When Aleph lifted Sharp Knife towards Kiddush Cup and she saw the sharp teeth, Kiddush Cup shivered. She did not like being Sharp Knife. Finally, Kappel asked Kiddush Cup if she would like to be him, sitting high up on the top of Father's head. Kiddush Cup thought for a moment. If she were high, no one would see her. No, Kiddush Cup did not want to be Kappel.

That evening, when Kiddush Cup was taken from the top shelf, polished and put on the Shabbat table, she stood very still and quiet. As the wine bottle was opened, her friends looked at each other and waited for the grumbles to begin. To their surprise, Kiddush Cup smiled as the sweet, red wine was poured into her. She had learned that she wanted to be Kiddush Cup and no one else on Shabbat.

RELIGIOUS EDUCATION

What do Jews have on their table at the Shabbat meal?, see page 99

The Shabbat meal

Name _____   Date _____

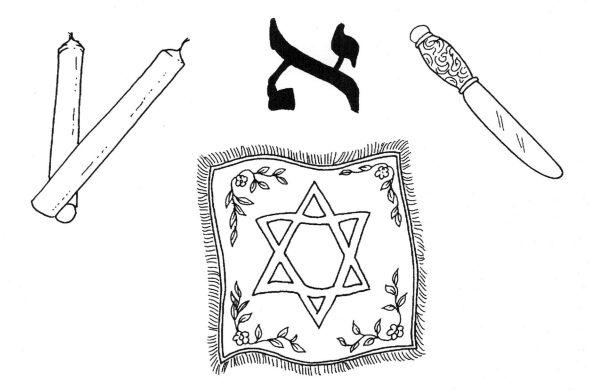

knife   challah cover   kiddush cup   challah   candles

RELIGIOUS EDUCATION

What do things make us remember?, see page 100

What do things make us remember?

Name _____   Date _____

▲ What did these things remind Miss Nancy Alison Delacourt Cooper of?

medal

shell

egg

puppet on a string

football

▲ What reminds you of something?

Draw the object or write about it.

RELIGIOUS
EDUCATION

Why do Christians pray?, see page 102

A Christian prayer

Name _____   Date _____

> Our Father who lives in Heaven,
> You are great and holy.
> We long for the time when everyone lives as
> you would like them to live.
> Please give us all that we need to live.
> And forgive us all those things that we have
> done wrong
> In the same way that we forgive other people
> who do bad things against us.
> Please keep us safe and away from things
> that could hurt us.
> All really good and wonderful things are yours,
> For all time.
> Amen

▲ Three of the following situations can be found in the prayer above. Circle each one as you find it.
Which situation is missing?

> 1 Saying thank you.
> 2 Asking.
> 3 Saying sorry.
> 4 Saying how good someone is.
>
> Number _____ is missing.

RELIGIOUS EDUCATION

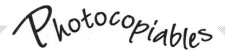
Why do Sikhs tell the story of Guru Nanak bathing in the river?, see page 103

A story about Guru Nanak

Nanak went down to the river as usual. Every morning he bathed in the water to make himself clean before he prayed to God. But this morning Nanak didn't come home. His friends and family went to the river to look for him, but all they found was a pile of clothes. They searched up and down the river bank expecting to find a drowned body. 'Where has Nanak gone!' they cried. Every day for three days people went to search for him. 'He must have drowned,' they said, 'and his body swept away down river.'

After three days, Nanak returned. His family and friends were very pleased to see him. 'Where have you been!' they asked. 'What happened to you!' All Nanak would say was that he had been to God's house and that he had been speaking with God. He looked so calm and peaceful. He was different to the Nanak who had gone away. Many people came to listen to Nanak as he talked about his conversation with God. 'God loves you,' Nanak said, 'and you must love God.'

The people who listened to Nanak began to call him Guru because he was someone who taught them about God. He often made up songs about what God had said and sang them as he taught. Guru Nanak spent the rest of his life travelling and teaching people about God. The people who listened to him became known as Sikhs. Sikhs still sing Guru Nanak's songs today.

RELIGIOUS EDUCATION

Why do Sikhs tell the story of Guru Nanak bathing in the river?, see page 103

The story of Guru Nanak

Name _____   Date _____

Nanak went into the _____. He did not

come out for _____ days. Everyone

thought that he had _____. When he

came back he said that he had been

_____ with God. God had told him to

_____ the people. Nanak made up

_____ about God. People who followed

him were called _____.

talking	three	Sikhs	teach
songs	drowned	river	

A message in this story is:

**RELIGIOUS
EDUCATION**

INFORMATION TECHNOLOGY WITHIN RELIGIOUS EDUCATION

Main IT Focus
The information technology activities outlined in this book can be used to develop and assess children's IT capability as outlined in the National Curriculum. The main emphasis for the development of IT capability within these activities is on communicating information.

Word processing
Many of the activities and extension ideas in this book which incorporate some form of writing activity can be used to develop children's IT capability through the use of a word processor. However, children do not have to undertake every suggested writing task using the computer. They could be organised into different writing tasks over a term or longer, some using more conventional written methods and others the computer. This would also provide an opportunity for teachers to provide activities at varying levels of IT capability and to discuss with children the relative merits of the use of IT for different purposes.

However, it is important that children do have an opportunity to originate their work at the computer. It is often appropriate for children to make their first draft at the keyboard, save it, print it out and then redraft it away from the keyboard, thus giving other children the opportunity to use the computer. They can then return later, retrieve their work, make any changes they have decided upon and format the final copy for printing.

Young children will take a long time to enter text at the keyboard, so it is important to ensure that the writing tasks are kept short. If parents or other adults are available, they can often be used for support, provided they have the relevant skills.

During Key Stage 1, children will be developing their confidence and competence to use the standard computer keyboard. They should be taught a range of basic keyboard and word-processing skills. These should include:
▲ an understanding of the layout of the keyboard and where the letter and number keys are found;
▲ how to find capital letters and those characters located above the number keys using the shift key;
▲ how to use the delete key to erase words and letters;
▲ how to use the cursor/arrow keys or mouse to position the cursor at the desired position;
▲ the use of more than a single finger/hand when typing, particularly as they become more proficient and know where letters are located;
▲ how to use the space bar, using their thumbs to press the space bar;
▲ an understanding of how the word processor 'wraps' the text around the end of the line so that there is no need to press return at the end of each line;
▲ how to join text using the delete key, and separate text or create new lines using the return key;
▲ how to move the cursor to a mistake and correct it, rather than deleting all the text back to the mistake, making the correction and then retyping the deleted text;
▲ how to print out completed work, initially with teacher support but eventually on their own.

Children will also need to save their work if they are unable to finish it in one session. They should be taught how to do this on to the hard or floppy disk so that eventually they can do it without teacher assistance. They will then need to be shown how to locate and retrieve their work at a later date.

For many of the writing tasks, children can use the standard page format that is presented to them when the software is started. However, for more complex tasks the teacher may wish to set up the page layout before the children start, and save it, for example, as a birthday card, Christmas card or invitation layout. Children can then start with this basic layout and then alter it if they wish.

CD-ROMs
Many of the activities in this book could be extended through the use of CD-ROMs for children to research other information about the area being studied.

The most useful types of CD-ROM for this work are those which provide an encyclopaedia type of environment, either as an encyclopaedia or as a resource on a single theme. These CD-ROMs will contain text and pictures, with some of the more recent ones including music, sound effects and speech. Children can access the information in a number of ways. They may be able to make a simple search for the topic they are interested in, by typing in appropriate words, for example 'Seder'. This will then take them to the relevant part of the CD-ROM. When they read the page they may also find that some words are highlighted in a different colour. By clicking on these words they will be taken to another section of the encyclopaedia which has further, or linked, information. Moving from one part to another via these 'hot links' is called browsing. (It is advisable for the teacher to spend some time with the software before embarking on a project.)

A good starting point for children is for the teacher to set some questions to be answered using the CD-ROM. This ensures that the information is available for the children. Once this has been found the children can explore other parts of the CD-ROM for extra information or set some questions for other children to research.

Ensure that the children know how to access the CD-ROM. Demonstrate the various ways in which searches can be made, and how to move back to the starting point and backwards through pages that the children have already explored.

IT links

The grids on this page relate the activities in this book to specific areas of IT and to relevant software resources. Types of software rather than names of specific programs have been listed to enable teachers to use the ideas regardless of the computers to which they have access. The software featured should be available from most good educational software retailers. Teachers may still want to include specific software which runs on their computers and which addresses the content and understanding of the religious education being taught. Activities are referenced by page number rather than by name. (Bold page numbers indicate activities which have expanded IT content.)

AREA OF IT	SOFTWARE	ACTIVITIES (PAGE NOS.)						
		CHAP 1	CHAP 2	CHAP 3	CHAP 4	CHAP 5	CHAP 6	CHAP 7
Communicating Information	Word Processor	15, 16, 19, **20**, 21	**29**, 33	42, 45, 46	50, 53, 58, 60	**65**, 70, 82	**87**, 88, 92, 95	100, 103
Communicating Information	DTP			45		**65**, 78, 80, 82, 83	88	103
Communicating Information	Concept Keyboard				**50**, 53	70		
Communicating Information	Drawing package	15	32	45	51	65, 71, 74		
Communicating Information	Art package	15, 19	32	**38**, 39, 42, 45, 46	51, 53	65, 71, 74	94	**101**
Communicating Information	Framework	16				68, 76	88	
Communicating Information	Multimedia			40, 46	51	**78**		
Information			26, 32	40, 46		71, 74, 75	88, 90, 92	99

SOFTWARE TYPE	BBC/MASTER	RISCOS	NIMBUS/186	WINDOWS	MACINTOSH
Word processor	Stylus Folio Prompt/Writer	Phases Pendown Desk Top Folio	All Write Write On	My Word Kid Works 2 Creative Writer	Kid Works 2 EasyWorks Creative Writer
DTP	Front Page Extra	Desk Top Folio 1st Page Pendown DTP	Front Page Extra NewSPAper	Creative Writer NewSPAper	Creative Writer
Framework		My World 2		My World 2	Kid Pix 2
Art package		1st Paint Kid Pix Splash		Colour Magic Kid Pix 2	
Drawing package	Picture Builder	Draw Picture IT	Picture Builder		
Authoring		Hyperstudio Rainbow		Hyperstudio MM Box	Hyperstudio

RELIGIOUS EDUCATION

	ENGLISH	MATHS	SCIENCE	HISTORY	GEOGRAPHY	D&T	ART	MUSIC	PE
LIVING WITH OURSELVES	Using role-play to express feelings. Discussing artefacts. Listening to stories. Writing stories and poems. Discussing the concept of death.		Sorting pictures of clothing according to use and properties. Thinking about the concept of growth and change.	Reflecting on personal experiences of change.		Designing and making a special area in the classroom.	Drawing special objects.		
LIVING WITH OTHERS	Talking about artefacts. Listening and responding to stories from a range of cultures. Using role-play.	Inventing appropriate rules for a game.				Designing and making a friendship band. Designing a school uniform.		Responding to recorded music.	
LIVING IN THE WORLD	Listening and responding to stories from a range of cultures. Writing poems.		Observing the process of change in growing things. Thinking about the conditions that animals require to stay healthy. Talking about pollution.		Reflecting on how people care for and harm the world. Thinking where foods originate. Expressing views about good and bad features of the school environment.	Using construction equipment to make models.	Making a Mod-Roc snowman. Painting pictures of a special animal. Designing and making posters. Drawing pictures to express feelings.	Listening to sounds from the natural world. Responding to a video of *The Snowman*.	Creating a dance sequence.
FOLLOWING GUIDANCE	Discussing the importance of books. Using role-play. Listening and responding to stories. Discussing artefacts.								
ENCOUNTERING SPECIAL TIMES	Discussing artefacts. Listening and responding to stories. Writing dialogue. Writing poems about feelings.	Designing symmetrical patterns.	Observing the changes in materials when making party food.	Learning about ways in which the passage of time can be marked.	Learning about the months of the year. Understanding how they can be divided into seasons.	Making a pop-up Easter card.	Making party items and clay pots. Designing and making patterns. Making observational drawings and items for a festival.		
ENCOUNTERING SPECIAL PLACES	Listening and responding to stories. Writing letters. Discussing special places. Talking about artefacts.				Learning about the concept of a journey.	Designing and making a Jewish sukkah.	Painting pictures of a special place. Taking brass rubbings. Making observational drawings.	Listening to organ music. Responding to peaceful music.	
EXPRESSING WHAT IS IMPORTANT	Listening to stories. Discussing artefacts. Thinking about the role of story. Writing stories.			Reflecting on the importance of objects as reminders of the past.			Using colour to express feelings.	Listening to calm music.	

RELIGIOUS
EDUCATION